Everyday Mathematics®

Journal 2

The University of Chicago
School Mathematics Project

EVERYDAY LEARNING™

Chicago, Illinois

Authors
Max Bell
Robert Balfanz
William Carroll
Robert Hartfield
James McBride
Peter Saecker

Teachers in Residence
Amy Dillard
Kathleen Pitvorec
Denise Porter

**Everyday Learning
Development Staff**
Editorial: John Bretzlauf,
Rosi Marshall, Steve Mico,
Michael Murphy, Ann Reid
Production/Design: Héctor Cuadra,
Jess Schaal, Norma Underwood

Additional Credits
Curtis Design
Chris Sheban (*cover*)

Revision Content Reviewer
Sheryl O'Connor

Field-Test Teachers
Ann Brown
Terry DeJong
Craig Dezell
John Dini
Donna Goffron
Steve Heckley
Karen Hedberg
Marilyn Pavlak
John Sabol
Rose Ann Simpson
Debbi Suhajda
Jackie Winston

Contributors
David Barley
Diana Barrie (*selected art*)
Sarah Busse
James Flanders
Craig Hilsenbeck
Sharon Levy
Jianhua Li
Sharon McHugh
Janet M. Meyers
William Pattison
Kelly Porto
Shelia Sconiers
Laura Sunseri
Kim Van Haitsma
Mary Wilson
Nancy Wilson
Kenneth Wong
Michelle Wong
Carl Zmola
Theresa Zmola (*original design*)

Acknowledgments

Page 236 Illustration: From *Comparisons* by The Diagram Group. Copyright © 1980 by The Diagram Group. Reprinted by permission.

Page 237 Map: From *Scott, Foresman Social Studies: Communities Near and Far* by James B. Kracht and Leslie Wheeler. Copyright © 1991, 1988, Scott, Foresman and Company, Glenview, Illinois. Reprinted by permission of Scott Foresman/Addison-Wesley.

Page 248 Photograph: Courtesy of the National Archaeological Museum, Athens, Greece.

Page 250 Ilustration: From *The Illustrated Encyclopedia of the Butterfly World* by Paul Smart. Copyright © Salamander Books Limited, 1975. Reprinted by permission of Salamander Books; Illustrations (snowflake, shell): From *The Geometry of Art and Life* by Matila Ghyka. New York: Dover Publications, 1977. Reprinted by permission.

Page 366 Illustrations: From *The Measure of Man and Woman.* Copyright © 1993 by Henry Dreyfus Associates, published by The Whitney Library of Design, an imprint of Watson-Guptill Publications.

Page 387 Poem: From *Math Talk—Mathematical Ideas in Poems for Two Voices* by Theoni Pappas. Copyright © 1991. Reprinted by permission of Wide World Publishing/Tetra, San Carlos, California.

Pages 399–401 Text: Reprinted with permission from the *Arithmetic Teacher.* Copyright © March 1988 by the National Council of Teachers of Mathematics. All rights reserved.

This material is based upon work supported by the National Science Foundation under Grant No. ESI-9252984. Any opinions, findings, and conclusions or recommendations expressed in this material are those of the authors and do not necessarily reflect the views of the National Science Foundation.

ISBN 1-57039-514-4

3 4 5 6 7 8 9 BP 02 01 00 99

Contents

Unit 8: Number Systems & Algebra Concepts

Unit 9: More about Variables, Formulas, & Graphs

Unit 10: Geometry Topics

Activity Sheets

Per-Unit Rates

Fill in the missing numbers in the rate tables. Then record the per-unit rates.

1. There are 8 pints in a gallon.

pints	8	16		64	1	2	4
gallons	1		5				

per-gallon rate: _____ pints per gallon   per-pint rate: _____ gallon per pint

2. A recipe for a 2-pound loaf of bread calls for 4 cups of flour.

cups		4	6	5	1	3	$\frac{1}{2}$
pounds	1	2					

per-pound rate: _____ cups per pound   per-cup rate: _____ pound per cup

3. A computer printer makes 6 copies every 2 minutes.

copies		6	9		1	2	4
minutes	1	2		5			

per-minute rate: _____ copies per minute   per-copy rate: _____ minute per copy

4. The **furlong** is a unit of distance. This unit is now most commonly used in horse racing. There are 40 furlongs in 5 miles.

miles	1	2	5	10			
furlongs			40		1	4	

per-mile rate: _____ furlongs per mile   per-furlong rate: _____ mile per furlong

5. Ten gallons of gasoline weigh about 70 pounds.

pounds				70	1	2	5
gallons	1	2	5	10			

per-gallon rate: _____ pounds per gallon   per-pound rate: _____ gallon per pound

Per-Unit Rates (cont.)

6. Three inches of rain fell between 7 A.M. and 3 P.M.

inches			3	6		1	2
hours	1	2			32		

per-hour rate: _____ inch per hour   per-inch rate: _____ hours per inch

7. You are studying "wobbles" and "globs." The per-wobble rate is

25 globs/wobble. What is the per-glob rate? _____ wobble per glob

8. Look at your answers for Problems 1–7. If you know one per-unit rate, how

can you find the other per-unit rate? _____

_____

Conversion facts, such as 1 gallon = 8 pints, can be expressed as per-unit
rates. For example, in Problem 1 the per-gallon rate for the conversion fact
1 gallon = 8 pints is "8 pints per gallon," and the per-pint rate is "$\frac{1}{8}$ gallon per
pint." Write the two per-unit rates for each conversion fact below.

9. 1 gallon = 16 cups

per-gallon rate: _____ cups per gallon   per-cup rate: _____ gallon per cup

10. 36 inches = 1 yard

per-yard rate: _____ inches per yard   per-inch rate: _____ yard per inch

11. 1 meter = 100 centimeters

per-meter rate: _____ per _____

per-centimeter rate: _____ per _____

12. There are about 28 grams in every ounce.

per-ounce rate: _____ per _____

per-gram rate: _____ per _____

13. 39 inches is about 1 meter.

per-meter rate: _____ per _____

per-inch rate: _____ per _____

Use with Lesson 55.

Math Boxes 55

1. Complete.

  a. $\frac{2}{5}$ of 90 = _____

  b. $\frac{3}{8}$ of 64 = _____

  c. $\frac{2}{3}$ of 72 = _____

  d. $\frac{4}{7}$ of 49 = _____

  e. $\frac{8}{10}$ of 300 = _____

2. Rename each fraction as a mixed number or whole number.

  a. $\frac{43}{4}$ = _____

  b. _____ = $\frac{122}{5}$

  c. $\frac{56}{8}$ = _____

  d. $\frac{79}{9}$ = _____

  e. _____ = $\frac{63}{3}$

3. The table at the right shows the area in square miles of some of the largest lakes and inland seas in the world.

  a. Which lake has an area about $\frac{1}{10}$ the area of the Caspian Sea? _____

  b. Which lake has an area a little less than 4 times the area of Lake Eyre? _____

  c. Which lake has an area about $\frac{1}{5}$ the area of the Aral Sea? _____

  d. Which lake has an area about $\frac{9}{10}$ the area of the Aral Sea? _____

Body of Water (Continent)	Area (mi²)
Caspian Sea (Asia)	143,244
Lake Victoria (Africa)	26,828
Aral Sea (Asia)	24,904
Lake Michigan (N. America)	22,300
Lake Tanganyika (Africa)	12,700
Lake Erie (N. America)	9910
Lake Maracaibo (S. America)	5217
Lake Eyre (Australia)	3600

4. Solve.   Solution

  a. $\frac{q}{7} = 56$ _____

  b. $\frac{18}{27} = \frac{f}{18}$ _____

  c. $\frac{81}{n} = \frac{36}{4}$ _____

  d. $7 = \frac{x}{77}$ _____

  e. $\frac{48}{12} = \frac{96}{k}$ _____

5. Rename each mixed number as a fraction.

  a. _____ = $5\frac{3}{5}$

  b. _____ = $9\frac{1}{4}$

  c. $8\frac{5}{6}$ = _____

  d. $14\frac{2}{3}$ = _____

  e. _____ = $10\frac{19}{20}$

Rate Problems

Complete the rate diagram to help you solve each problem. Fill in the missing numbers in the answer. The first one has been done for you.

1. A copier makes 90 copies per minute. How many copies will it make in 30 minutes?

30 minutes	*	90 copies	per minute	=	2700 copies

   Answer: The copier will make ___2700___ copies in ___30___ minutes.

2. Angela earns $6 per hour baby-sitting. How long must she work to earn $72?

	*		per	=	

   Answer: Angela must work _____ hours to earn _____.

3. If carpet costs $22.95 per square yard, how much will 12 square yards of carpet cost?

	*		per	=	

   Answer: _____ square yards of carpet will cost _____.

4. A TV station runs 12 minutes of commercials per hour. How many minutes of commercials will it run during 7 half-hour programs?

	*		per	=	

   Answer: The station will run _____ minutes of commercials during

   _____ half-hour shows.

5. There are 80 calories in 1 serving of soup. How many servings of soup contain 120 calories?

	*		per	=	

   Answer: There are _____ calories in _____ servings of soup.

            Use with Lesson 56.

Rate Problems (cont.)

6. There are 9 calories per gram of fat. How many grams of fat are there in 33 calories?

	*		per _____	=	

   Answer: There are _____ of fat in _____ calories.

7. A car averages 24 miles for each gallon of gasoline. How far will it go on 5.4 gallons?

	*		per _____	=	

   Answer: The car will go _____ miles on _____ gallons of gasoline.

8. Arun read the first 48 pages of a mystery novel in 3 hours. At this rate, how long would it take him to read 80 pages? (*Hint:* What is the per-hour rate?)

	*		per _____	=	

   Answer: It would take Arun _____ hours to read _____ pages.

9. All-Bright chewing gum is sold in packages of 8 sticks per package. A package costs $0.85. How much will 56 sticks of gum cost? _____

   Explain how you found your answer. _____

   _____

   _____

   _____

   _____

10. How many teaspoons are there in 1 cup? _____

    Explain how you found your answer. _____

    _____

    _____

    _____

    _____

Math Boxes 56

1. Write the percent equivalent for each of the "easy" fractions below.

    a. $\frac{4}{5}$ = _____

    b. $\frac{5}{8}$ = _____

    c. $\frac{2}{6}$ = _____

    d. $\frac{8}{10}$ = _____

    e. $\frac{9}{12}$ = _____ | 47 |

2. Insert parentheses to make each sentence true. | 158 |

    a. 42 / 12 / 2 = 7

    b. 18 + 5 * 2 = 46

    c. 125 − 25 * 5 = 0

    d. 12 * 6 − 22 / 5 = 10

    e. 15 * 20 − 16 / 2 = 30

3. The area A of a circle can be found by the formula $A = \pi * r^2$.

    a. Find the area if r = 3.7 centimeters.

    _____

    b. Find the area if r = 9 inches.

    _____ | 118 |

4. Multiply mentally.

    a. 5 * 8050 = _____

    b. 50 * 63 = _____

    c. 500 * 120 = _____

    d. 500 * 146 = _____

    e. 25 * 35 * 4 = _____

5. Write each number in scientific notation.

    a. There are about 12,000,000,000 chickens in the world,

    or _____ chickens.

    b. A trained tracking dog can follow the sweat scent left by a foot when only

    0.00000000004 gram of sweat, or _____ gram, is present.

    c. There are 60,000,000,000,000 cells, or _____ cells, in the body.

    d. When a toilet is flushed, between 5,000,000,000 and 10,000,000,000 water droplets, or between _____

    and _____ water droplets, are released into the air.

    e. The smallest dust particles are about 0.01 centimeter,

    or _____ centimeter, in width.

Sources: *The Top Ten of Everything, 1996; The Sizesaurus.* | 7 | 8 |

Use with Lesson 56.

Math Message: Reviewing Rates

Jessy swam 5 lengths of the pool in 2 minutes.

|140|

1. Complete the rate table and find the per-minute rate.

lengths		5		10		1
minutes	1	2	3		6	

per-minute rate: _____ lengths per minute

per-length rate: _____ minute per length

2. At this rate, how many lengths would Jessy swim in 15 minutes?

_____	*	_____ per _____	=	_____

Answer: Jessy would swim _____ lengths in _____ minutes.

Calculating Per-Unit Rates

One way to find a per-unit rate is to divide one of the quantities in a rate pair by the other.

Example: Six cartons of juice cost $3.

cartons	?	6	1
dollars	1	3	?

Number of cartons you can buy for $1 (the per-dollar rate):
  (6/3) cartons per dollar = 2 cartons per dollar

Cost of 1 carton (the per-carton rate):
  (3/6) dollar per carton = $0.50 per carton

Use division to find the two per-unit rates. Then solve the problem. Make a rate diagram on a separate sheet of paper if you need help organizing the information.

1. Belle bought 8 yards of ribbon for $5. How many yards could she buy for $6?

yards	?	8	1
dollars	1	5	?

per-dollar rate: _____ yards per dollar   per-yard rate: $ _____ per yard

Answer: Belle could buy _____ yards of ribbon for $ _____ .

Calculating Per-Unit Rates (cont.)

2. Before going to France, Maurice exchanged
$25 for 125 French francs. At that exchange
rate, how many French francs would he get
for $80?

dollars	?	25	1
francs	1	125	?

per-franc rate: $ _____ per franc   per-dollar rate: _____ francs per dollar

Maurice would get _____ French francs for $_____.

3. One gloomy fall day, 4 inches of rain fell in
6 hours. At this rate, how many inches of
rain had fallen after 4 hours?

inches	?	4	1
hours	1	6	?

per-hour rate: _____ inch per hour   per-inch rate: _____ hours per inch

_____ inches of rain had fallen in _____ hours.

4. Ben's apartment building has 9 flights of
stairs. To climb to the top floor, he must
go up 144 steps. How many steps would
he need to climb to get to the fifth floor?

steps	?	144	1
flights	1	9	?

per-flight rate: _____ steps per flight   per-step rate: _____ flight per step

Ben would have to climb _____ steps to get to the _____ floor.

5. The Moon circles Earth 12 times every
327.6 days. How many revolutions does the
Moon make around Earth in 1 year
(365 days)?

days	?	327.6	1
revolutions	1	12	?

per-revolution rate: _____ days per revolution

per-day rate: _____ revolution per day

The Moon circles Earth _____ times in 1 year.

6. At sea level, sound travels 0.62 mile in
3 seconds. What is the speed of sound
in miles per hour?

miles	?	0.62	1
seconds	1	3	?

per-second rate: _____ mile per second

per-mile rate: _____ seconds per mile

Sound travels at the rate of _____ miles per hour.

Rate Problems

213

1. Last year, 55 students sold $1210 worth of candy for their band's fund-raiser.

    a. On average, how many dollars'
       worth of candy did each student sell? _____

    b. This year, 67 students will be selling candy.
       If they sell at the same rate as last year,
       how much money can they expect to raise? _____

2. According to the 1990 U.S. Census, Wichita, Kansas, has a population
    of 304,017. The area of the city is 101 square miles.

    a. What is the average number of people per square mile? _____

    b. What is the average number of square miles per person? _____

3. Art worked at the checkout counter from 5:30 P.M. to
    11 P.M. He earned $36. How much did he earn per hour? _____

4. A 12-ounce can of juice sells for $1.57. A 16-ounce can
    of the same juice sells for $2.07. Which is the better buy? _____
    (*Hint:* Calculate the **unit cost**—the cost per ounce.)

    Explain your answer. _____

    _____

    _____

5. The CN Tower in Toronto, Canada, is the world's tallest freestanding structure.
    According to the 1993 *Guinness Book of Records,* in 1989, Brendan Keenoy
    ran to the top of the tower in a record-breaking time.

    Facts: The tower has 1760 steps.
           There is a rise of 7.65 inches per step.
           Brendan ran at a rate of 3.73 steps per second.

    a. What is the height of the CN Tower

       in inches? _____   in feet? _____

    b. How many seconds did it take Brendan to run to the top of the tower?

       _____ seconds (rounded to the nearest second) That's how

       many minutes and seconds? _____ minutes _____ seconds
       (*Hint:* Use the [INT÷] key on your calculator.)

Rate Problems (cont.)

6. **a.** Find the average speed (in meters per second) for each running event.

Winning Times for Women's Running Events, 1996 Olympic Games

Event	Time (minutes & seconds)	Time (seconds)	Average Speed (meters per second)
100 meters	0 min 10.94 sec	10.94 sec	m/sec
200 meters	0 min 22.12 sec	22.12 sec	m/sec
400 meters	0 min 48.25 sec	48.25 sec	m/sec
800 meters	1 min 57.73 sec		m/sec
1500 meters	4 min 0.83 sec		m/sec

b. Why do you think the average speed is different for each event?

_____

_____

7. The picture at the right shows a stack of 50 pennies, drawn to actual size.

   a. Carefully measure the height of the stack. Use your measurement to calculate about how many pennies there would be in a stack 1 centimeter high.

   about _____ pennies

   b. About how many pennies would there be in a 50-foot stack of pennies? (1 inch is about 2.5 centimeters.)

   about _____ pennies

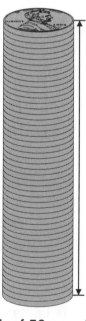

stack of 50 pennies (actual size)

8. To determine the temperature in degrees Fahrenheit, you can count the number of times a cricket chirps in 14 seconds and add 40.

   a. What is the temperature if a cricket chirps 3 times per second? _____ °F

   b. At a temperature of 61°F, how many times does a cricket chirp per second? _____

Source: *The Handy Science Answer Book.*

Use with Lesson 57.

Rate Problems (cont.)

9. The recipe at the right lists the ingredients used to make 1 pound of peanut butter fudge but not how much of each ingredient is needed. Use the following clues to calculate the amount of each ingredient needed to make 1 pound of peanut butter fudge and record each amount in the recipe.

   Clues
   - Use 20 cups of sugar to make 10 pounds of fudge.

   - You need $3\frac{3}{4}$ cups of milk to make 5 pounds of fudge.

   - You need 15 cups of peanut butter to make 48 pounds of fudge.

   - An 8-pound batch of fudge uses 1 cup of corn syrup.

   - Use 6 teaspoons of vanilla for each 4 pounds of fudge.

   - Use $\frac{1}{2}$ teaspoon of salt for each 4 pounds of fudge.

Peanut Butter Fudge (makes one pound)
_____ cups of sugar
_____ cup of milk
_____ tablespoons of peanut butter
_____ tablespoons of corn syrup
_____ teaspoons of vanilla
_____ teaspoon of salt

10. Suppose you wanted to make an 80-pound batch of fudge. Record how much of each ingredient you would need.

Recipe for 80 Pounds of Peanut Butter Fudge	
_____ cups of sugar	_____ tablespoons of corn syrup
_____ cups of milk	_____ teaspoons of vanilla
_____ tablespoons of peanut butter	_____ teaspoons of salt

More on Measuring Food

Some foods have their own special units of measure. Have you ever heard of a *hand* of bananas (a small bunch)?

Some other special units are a *cran* of fresh herring (45 gallons), a *firkin* of butter (56 pounds), a *frail* of raisins (50 pounds), and a *clove* of cheese (8 or 10 pounds).

Source: *Numbers.*

Math Boxes 57

1. Rename each fraction as a mixed number.

   a. $\frac{7}{4} = $ _____

   b. $\frac{9}{2} = $ _____

   c. $\frac{14}{5} = $ _____

   d. $\frac{28}{6} = $ _____

   e. $\frac{31}{4} = $ _____ | 24 |

2. Complete the following.

   a. 15 mm = _____ cm

   b. 25 cm = _____ m

   c. 143 mm = _____ cm

   d. 2.06 m = _____ cm

   e. _____ mm = 1.43 m | 109 |

3. Two of the lines shown are parallel. Without using a protractor, find the degree measure of each numbered angle. Write each measure on the drawing.

| 71 | 72 |

4. Evaluate the following algebraic expressions for $b = \frac{1}{6}$.

   a. $5\frac{2}{3} + b = $ _____

   b. $5 - b = $ _____

   c. $8 * b = $ _____

   d. $b - 2 = $ _____

| 156 |

5. The spreadsheet below shows the number of hours three students slept on two different nights. | 174 |

	A	B	C	D
1	Student	Monday	Tuesday	Average
2	Elaine	7.5	9	
3	Frank	6	10.5	
4	David	8	8.5	

   a. Calculate the average number of hours of sleep for each student. Write these averages on the spreadsheet.

   b. Using cell names, write a formula for calculating David's average number of hours of sleep. _____

Math Boxes 58

1. Rename each mixed number as a fraction.   [23]

     a. $1\frac{4}{5} =$ _____

     b. $6\frac{5}{7} =$ _____

     c. $4\frac{3}{5} =$ _____

     d. $10\frac{5}{12} =$ _____

     e. $8\frac{4}{7} =$ _____

2. Build a numeral. Write   [41]

8 in the tenths place;
0 in the hundreds and ones places;
5 in the thousands place;
7 in the ten-thousands place;
9 in the hundredths place;
6 in the hundred-thousands place;
2 in the tens place.

Answer:

___ ___ ___ , ___ ___ ___ . ___ ___

3. Complete.

     a. _____ tsp = 3 c

     b. 12 oz = _____ tbs

     c. 2 c = _____ tbs

     d. _____ tbs = 1 qt

     e. $5\frac{1}{2}$ gal = _____ pt

4. Multiply mentally.

     a. $30 * 1.5 =$ _____

     b. $7.3 * 20 =$ _____

     c. $0.37 * 100 =$ _____

     d. $1.68 * 10 =$ _____

     e. $50 * 0.6 =$ _____   [52]

5. Complete the table.

Words	Exponential Notation	Base	Exponent	Calculator Key Sequence	Standard Notation
nine to the third power				$9\ [y^x]\ 3\ [=]$	
two to the twelfth power					
				$10\ [y^x]\ 7\ [+\!=]\ [=]$	
		5	−6		

[6]

How Many Calories Do You Use per Day?

1. The following table shows the number of calories per minute and per hour used by the average sixth grader for various activities. Complete the table. Round your answers.

Calorie Use by Average 6th Graders		
Activity	calories/minute	calories/hour
Sleeping	0.7	40
Studying, writing, sitting	1.2	70
Eating, talking, sitting in class	1.2	70
Standing	1.3	80
Dressing & undressing		90
Walking (slow, at 2 mph)	2.2	130
Walking (brisk, at 3.5 mph)	3.0	180
Housework, gardening	2.0	
Vacuuming	2.7	160
Raking leaves	3.7	220
Shoveling snow	5.0	300
Bicycling (6 mph)		170
Bicycling (13 mph)	4.5	
Bicycling (20 mph)	8.3	500
Running (5 mph)	6.0	360
Running (7.5 mph)		560
Swimming (20 yards/minute)	3.3	200
Swimming (40 yards/minute)	5.8	350
Basketball & soccer (vigorous)	9.7	580
Volleyball	4.0	240
Aerobic dance (vigorous)	6.0	360
Square dancing	4.0	240

Use with Lesson 58.

How Many Calories Do You Use per Day? (cont.)

2. Think of all the things you do during a typical 24-hour school day.

    a. List your activities in the table below.

    b. Record your estimate of the time you spend on each activity. Be sure that the times add up to 24 hours.

    c. For each activity, record the number of calories per hour or per minute. Then calculate the number of calories you use for the activity.

Example: Suppose you spend 8 hours and 15 minutes sleeping.
Choose the per-hour rate: Sleeping uses 40 calories per hour.
Multiply: 8.25 hours * 40 calories per hour = 330 calories.

My Activities during a Typical 24-Hour School Day			
Activity	**Time Spent in Activity**	**Calorie Rate (cal/hr or cal/min)**	**Calories Used for Activity**

3. When you have completed the table, find the total number of calories you use in a typical 24-hour day.

    In a typical 24-hour school day, I use about _____ calories.

Calorie Use for a Triathlon

A **triathlon** is a contest in which athletes compete in swimming, cycling, and running races. In a "short course" triathlon, athletes go the distances in the table.

Event	Miles
Swimming	1
Cycling	25
Running	6.2

Alan is a fit sixth grader who plans to compete in the short-course triathlon. He estimates his rate of speed for each event to be as follows:

Swimming   40 yards per minute
Cycling   20 miles per hour
Running   7.5 miles per hour

Refer to the information above and the table on page 218 to answer these questions.

1. **a.** About how long will it take Alan to swim the mile? _____

   b. About how many calories will he use? _____

2. **a.** About how long will it take Alan to cycle the 25 miles?

   _____

   b. About how many calories will he use? _____

3. **a.** About how long will it take Alan to run the 6.2 miles? _____

   _____

   b. About how many calories will he use? _____

4. About how many calories will Alan use to complete the triathlon?

   _____

Healthy Hearts

Some scientists theorize that most mammals live for about 800 million heartbeats. Since a mouse's heart beats at a rate of about 650 times per minute, it would live about $\frac{1}{10}$ as long as a giraffe, which has a heart rate of about 60 beats per minute.

Humans are a notable exception to this rule. Humans live about three times as long as they should according to the 800-million-heartbeats-per-lifetime rule.

Source: *Numbers*.

Use with Lesson 58.

Nutrition Labels for Foods

Study the food label for a container of low-fat yogurt.

- There are 240 calories per serving. There are 3 grams of fat per serving.

- There are 44 grams of carbohydrate per serving. The label does not say how many calories come from carbohydrate. But the label does give the information you need to calculate the number of calories from carbohydrate. One gram of carbohydrate generates 4 calories of energy. So 44 grams generates 44 grams * 4 calories per gram, or 176 calories.

- There are 9 grams of protein per serving. One gram of protein generates 4 calories. So 9 grams generates 9 grams * 4 calories per gram, or 36 calories.

Nutrition Facts
Serving Size 1 container (227 g)

Amount per Serving	
Calories 240 Calories from Fat 27	
	% Daily Value
Total Fat 3 g	**5%**
Saturated Fat 1.5 g	**8%**
Cholesterol 15 mg	**5%**
Sodium 150 mg	**6%**
Potassium 450 mg	**13%**
Total Carbohydrate 44 g	**15%**
Dietary Fiber 1 g	**4%**
Sugars 43 g	
Protein 9 g	

Vitamin A 2%   •   Vitamin C 10%
Calcium 35%   •   Iron 0%
Calories per gram:
Fat 9   •   Carbohydrate 4   •   Protein 4

For each food label below, record the number of calories from fat.
Also calculate the number of calories from carbohydrate and from protein.

Nutrition Facts
Serving Size 1 slice (23 g)
Servings per Container 20

Amount per Serving	
Calories 65 Calories from Fat 9	
	% Daily Value
Total Fat 1 g	**2%**
Total Carbohydrate 12 g	**4%**
Protein 2 g	

White Bread

Nutrition Facts
Serving Size 1 link (45 g)
Servings per Container 10

Amount per Serving	
Calories 150 Calories from Fat 120	
	% Daily Value
Total Fat 13 g	**20%**
Total Carbohydrate 1 g	**<1%**
Protein 7 g	

Hot Dog

1. Calories

   from fat _____

   from carbohydrate _____

   from protein _____

   Total calories _____

2. Calories

   from fat _____

   from carbohydrate _____

   from protein _____

   Total calories _____

Plan Your Own Lunch

1. Choose 5 items you would like to have for lunch from the following menu. Choose your favorite foods—pay no attention to calories. Make a check mark next to each item.

Food	Total Calories	Calories from Fat	Calories from Carbohydrate	Calories from Protein
Ham sandwich	265	110	110	45
Turkey sandwich	325	70	155	100
Hamburger	330	135	120	75
Cheeseburger	400	200	110	90
Double burger, cheese, sauce	500	225	175	100
Grilled cheese sandwich	380	220	100	60
Peanut butter & jelly sandwich	380	160	170	50
Chicken nuggets (6)	250	125	65	60
Bagel	165	20	120	25
Bagel with cream cheese	265	105	125	35
Hard-boiled egg	80	55	0	25
French fries (small bag)	250	120	115	15
Apple	100	10	90	0
Carrot	30	0	25	5
Orange	75	0	70	5
Cake (slice)	235	65	160	10
Cashew nuts (1 ounce)	165	115	30	20
Doughnut	205	100	75	25
Blueberry muffin	110	30	70	10
Apple pie (slice)	250	125	115	10
Frozen yogurt cone	100	10	75	15
Orange juice (8 oz)	80	0	75	5
2% milk (8 oz)	145	45	60	40
Skim milk (8 oz)	85	0	50	35
Soft drink (8 oz)	140	0	140	0
Diet soft drink (8 oz)	0	0	0	0

Plan Your Own Lunch (cont.)

2. Record the 5 items you chose in the table below. Fill in the rest of the table and find the total number of calories for each column.

Food	Total Calories	Calories from Fat	Calories from Carbohydrate	Calories from Protein
Total				

What percent of the total number of calories in your lunch comes from fat? _____

From carbohydrate? _____ From protein? _____

3. Nutritionists recommend that, at most, 30% of the total number of calories comes from fat, about 12% of the calories from protein, and at least 58% of the calories from carbohydrate. Does the lunch you chose meet these recommendations? _____

4. Plan another lunch. This time, try to limit the percent of calories from fat to 30% or less, from protein to between 10% and 15%, and from carbohydrate to between 55% and 60%.

Food	Total Calories	Calories from Fat	Calories from Carbohydrate	Calories from Protein
Total				

What percent of the total number of calories in your lunch comes from fat? _____

From carbohydrate? _____ From protein? _____

Math Boxes 59

1. Rewrite each fraction as a percent.

a. $\frac{10}{50}$ = _____

b. $\frac{6}{9}$ = _____

c. $\frac{15}{18}$ = _____

d. $\frac{14}{16}$ = _____

e. $\frac{10}{15}$ = _____

2. Insert parentheses to make each sentence true.

a. $18 + 2 / 5 + 5 = 9$

b. $72 / 8 + 4 / 6 = 1$

c. $72 / 8 + 4 / 6 = 9\frac{2}{3}$

d. $95 - 10 / 3 + 2 = 93$

e. $74 * \frac{1}{2} + \frac{1}{2} + 1 = 148$

3. The perimeter p of a rectangle can be found by the formula $p = 2 * (b + h)$.

a. Find the perimeter if $b = 9$ inches and $h = 6$ inches. _____

b. Find the perimeter if $b = 3\frac{1}{4}$ inches and $h = 5\frac{3}{8}$ inches. _____

4. Multiply mentally.

a. $5 * 460 =$ _____

b. $50 * 48 =$ _____

c. $500 * 64 =$ _____

d. $500 * 63 =$ _____

e. $25 * 23 * 4 =$ _____

5. Write each number in scientific notation.

a. A modern personal computer can perform 10,000,000 mathematical operations, or _____ operations, in one second.

b. A fiber-optic wire carries 1,700,000,000 bits per second, or _____ bits per second. This is equivalent to 25,000 people, or _____ people, speaking over a wire roughly the width of a human hair.

c. An ant weighs about 0.00001 kilogram, or _____ kilogram.

d. The approximate weight of the ocean is 1,320,000,000,000,000,000,000 kilograms, or _____ kilograms.

e. One grass pollen weighs approximately 0.0000000047 gram, or _____ gram.

Sources: *The World Almanac for Kids, 1996; The Sizesaurus.*

Part-to-Whole and Part-to-Part Ratios

Solve the following problems. You may use a deck of cards to help you.

1. You have 24 cards. One out of 4 cards is faceup, and the rest are facedown.

   How many cards are faceup? _____   Facedown? _____

2. You have 30 cards. Six out of 9 cards are faceup, and the rest are facedown.

   How many cards are faceup? _____   Facedown? _____

3. You have 16 cards. Twenty-five percent of the cards are faceup, and the rest are facedown.

   How many cards are faceup? _____   Facedown? _____

4. You have 18 face-up cards. The ratio of face-up cards to face-down cards is 1 to 2.

   How many cards are faceup? _____   Facedown? _____

5. You have 20 cards. The ratio of face-up cards to face-down cards is 1.5 to 1.

   How many cards are faceup? _____   Facedown? _____

6. You have 5 face-up cards and no face-down cards. You add some face-down cards so that 1 in 3 cards is faceup. How many cards are there now?

   _____

7. You have 5 face-up cards and 15 face-down cards. You add some face-up cards so that 2 out of 5 cards are faceup. How many cards are there now?

   _____

8. You have 8 face-up cards and 12 face-down cards. You add some face-up cards so that $\frac{2}{3}$ of the cards are faceup.

   How many cards are faceup? _____   Facedown? _____

Challenge

9. The ratio of face-up cards to face-down cards is 0.3 to 1. Fewer than 10 cards are faceup. At least 21 cards are facedown.

   How many cards are faceup? _____   Facedown? _____

"Times as Many" Problems

1. Madison, Wisconsin, has a population of 190,000. Milwaukee, Wisconsin, has a population of 630,000.

   a. The ratio of the population of
   Milwaukee to the population of Madison is about _____ to 1.

   b. The population of Milwaukee is about _____ times as much as the
   population of Madison.

   c. About what fraction of the population of Milwaukee
   is the population of Madison?   _____

2. The Concorde SST airplane has a maximum seating capacity of 110 people.
   The Boeing 747 has a maximum seating capacity of 498 people.

   a. The ratio of the maximum seating capacity of
   the Boeing 747 to that of the Concorde SST is about _____ to 1.

   b. The Boeing 747 can seat about _____ as many people as the
   Concorde SST. (Round the answer to the nearest tenth.)

3. The men's world record for the high jump is 8 feet $\frac{1}{2}$ inch; the women's world
   record is 6 feet $10\frac{1}{4}$ inches.

   a. Convert each record from a measurement in feet and inches to a
   measurement in inches, written as a decimal.

   8 feet $\frac{1}{2}$ inch = ____.____ inches   6 feet $10\frac{1}{4}$ inches = ____.____ inches

   b. The men's record jump is about _____ times as high as the
   women's record jump. (Round your answer to the nearest hundredth.)

4. The table at the right shows the average
   number of wet days in selected cities for
   the month of October.

   a. How many more wet days does
   Moscow have than Beijing?   _____

   b. How many times as many wet days
   does Moscow have as Beijing?   _____

   c. How many fewer wet days does
   Beijing have than Sydney?   _____

City	Wet Days
Beijing, China	3
Boston, U.S.	9
Frankfurt, Germany	14
Mexico City, Mexico	13
Moscow, Russia	15
Sydney, Australia	12

Use with Lesson 60.

Math Boxes 60

1. Rename each fraction as a mixed number.

a. $\frac{8}{5}$ = _____

b. $\frac{33}{9}$ = _____

c. $\frac{42}{8}$ = _____

d. $\frac{37}{3}$ = _____

e. $\frac{46}{9}$ = _____

2. Complete the following.

a. _____ m = 368 mm

b. _____ cm = 0.245 m

c. 32 mm = _____ m

d. 45.2 cm = _____ mm

e. 0.25 mm = _____ cm

3. Two of the lines shown are parallel. Without using a protractor, find the degree measure of each numbered angle. Write each measure on the drawing.

4. Evaluate the following algebraic expressions for $k = \frac{3}{5}$.

a. $k + 2\frac{3}{10}$ = _____

b. $7 - k$ = _____

c. $k * 4$ = _____

d. $k - 1$ = _____

5. The spreadsheet below shows students' times, in seconds, for two different runs.

	A	B	C	D
1	Student	Run 1	Run 2	Average
2	Jake	23	21	
3	Steve	20	19	
4	Allison	21.5	21	

a. Calculate the average time for each student. Write these average times on the spreadsheet.

b. Using cell names, write a formula for calculating Jake's average time.

Math Message: Ratio Number Stories

Work with a partner. Solve the number stories.

1. It rained 2 out of 5 days in the month of April.
   On how many days did it rain that month? _____

2. If a spinner lands on blue 4 times for every
   6 times it lands on green, how many times
   does it land on green if it lands on blue 12 times? _____

3. For every 4 times John was at bat, he got 1 hit.
   If he got 7 hits, how many times did he bat? _____

4. Russ saves $3 for every $7 he spends. One month
   he spent $35. How much money did he save? _____

5. A choir has 50 members. Twenty members
   are sopranos. How many sopranos are
   there for every 5 members of the choir? _____

6. There are 20 students in Mrs. Kahlid's 6th grade
   class. Two out of 8 students have no brothers
   or sisters. How many students have no siblings? _____

7. Shirley misspelled 2 words in her composition for every
   98 words she spelled correctly. If she misspelled 6 words

   how many words did she spell correctly? _____

   what percent of the words did she misspell? _____

   how many words long was her composition? _____

8. Rema eats 2 eggs twice a week. How many eggs will
   she eat in the month of February of a non–leap year? _____

   How many weeks will it take her to eat 32 eggs? _____

9. If the ratio of time you sleep to the time you are awake
   is 1 to 2, how many hours are you awake in one day? _____

10. At Kozminski School, the ratio of weeks of school
    to weeks of vacation is 9 to 4. How many weeks
    of vacation do students at the school get in one year? _____

Use with Lesson 61.

Ratio Number Stories

You can solve ratio number stories by first writing a number model for the story.

Example:

Sidney missed 2 out of 9 problems on the math test. There were 36 problems on the test. How many problems did he miss?

Step 1: Write a number model.

(missed) $\dfrac{2}{9} = \dfrac{x}{36}$ (total)

Step 2: Find the missing number.

Think: "9 times what number equals 36?" $9 * \mathbf{4} = 36$

Multiply the numerator, 2, by this number: $2 * \mathbf{4} = 8$

$$\dfrac{2 * 4}{9 * 4} = \dfrac{8}{36}$$

Step 3: Answer: Sidney missed 8 out of 36 problems.

Write a number model for each problem. Then solve the problem.

1. Of the 42 animals in the Children's Zoo, 3 out of 7 are mammals. How many mammals are there in the Children's Zoo?

   Number model: _____   Answer: _____

2. Last week, Charles spent 2 hours doing homework for every 3 hours he watched TV. If he spent 6 hours doing homework, how many hours did he spend watching TV?

   Number model: _____   Answer: _____

3. Five out of 8 students in Lane School play a musical instrument. 140 students play an instrument. How many students attend Lane School?

   Number model: _____   Answer: _____

4. The class library has 3 fiction books for every 4 nonfiction books. If the library has a total of 63 books, how many fiction books does it have?

   Number model: _____   Answer: _____

Ratio Number Stories (cont.)

5. Mr. Dexter sells subscriptions to a magazine for $18 each. For each subscription he sells, he earns $8. One week, he earned $200. How many subscriptions did he sell?

Number model: _____   Answer: _____

6. There are 48 students in the 6th grade at Robert's school. Three out of 8 sixth graders read two books last month. One out of 3 students read just one book. The rest of the students read no books at all.

How many books in all did the 6th graders read last month? _____

Explain what you did to find the answer. _____

_____

_____

7. Find the missing number.

a. $\frac{1}{3} = \frac{x}{39}$

    Solution: _____

b. $\frac{3}{4} = \frac{24}{y}$

    Solution: _____

c. $\frac{7}{8} = \frac{f}{56}$

    Solution: _____

d. $\frac{1}{5} = \frac{13}{n}$

    Solution: _____

e. $\frac{5}{6} = \frac{m}{42}$

    Solution: _____

f. $\frac{9}{25} = \frac{g}{100}$

    Solution: _____

Challenge

8. A recipe for salad dressing calls for 3 tablespoons of oil for every tablespoon of vinegar. How many tablespoons of oil would you need to make 1 cup of salad dressing? Answer: _____

Tell what you did to solve the problem. _____

_____

_____

_____

230

Math Boxes 61

---

1. Rename each mixed number as a fraction.

 a. $12\frac{1}{8} =$ _____

 b. $1\frac{7}{10} =$ _____

 c. $2\frac{3}{4} =$ _____

 d. $2\frac{6}{11} =$ _____

 e. $5\frac{1}{3} =$ _____

2. Build a numeral. Write

 6 in the hundredths place;
 5 in the tens place;
 4 in the ten-thousands place;
 9 in the hundreds place;
 1 in the ones place;
 0s where you need them.

 Answer:

 ___ ___ , ___ ___ ___ . ___ ___

---

3. Complete.

 a. 24 oz = _____ pt

 b. _____ c = 8 gal

 c. _____ pt = 20 qt

 d. _____ gal = 4 c

 e. 7 c = _____ oz

4. Multiply mentally.

 a. $10 * 1.7 =$ _____

 b. $20 * 1.6 =$ _____

 c. $2.5 * 40 =$ _____

 d. $10 * 0.38 =$ _____

 e. $100 * 0.92 =$ _____

---

5. Complete the table.

Words	Exponential Notation	Base	Exponent	Repeated Factors	Standard Notation
		10	12		
				$8 * 8 * 8 * 8 * 8$	
	10^{-5}				
				$0.1 * 0.1 * 0.1$	

The Fat Content of Foods

1. Use the information about calories on each food label below and on the next page.

   a. Write the ratio of calories that come from fat to the total number of calories as a fraction.

   b. Then **estimate** the percent of calories that come from fat. Do not use your calculator.

   c. Finally, use your calculator to find the percent of calories that come from fat. (Round to the nearest whole percent.)

Food Label	Food	Calories from Fat / Total Calories	Estimated Fat Percent	Calculated Fat Percent
Nutrition Facts Serving Size 1 slice (28 g) Servings per Container 12 **Amount per Serving** **Calories** 90 Calories from Fat 80	bologna	$\frac{80}{90}$	about 85%	89%
Nutrition Facts Serving Size 2 waffles (72 g) Servings per Container 4 **Amount per Serving** **Calories** 190 Calories from Fat 50	waffle			
Nutrition Facts Serving Size 2 tablespoons (32 g) Servings per Container 15 **Amount per Serving** **Calories** 190 Calories from Fat 140	peanut butter			
Nutrition Facts Serving Size 1 slice (19 g) Servings per Container 24 **Amount per Serving** **Calories** 70 Calories from Fat 50	American cheese			
Nutrition Facts Serving Size 1 egg (50 g) Servings per Container 12 **Amount per Serving** **Calories** 70 Calories from Fat 40	egg			

Continued on the next page.

Use with Lesson 62.

The Fat Content of Foods (cont.)

Food Label	Food	Calories from Fat / Total Calories	Estimated Fat Percent	Calculated Fat Percent
Nutrition Facts Serving Size 1/4 cup (60 mL) Servings per Container 6 — **Amount per Serving** — **Calories** 110 Calories from Fat 0	orange juice			
Nutrition Facts Serving Size 1/2 cup (125 g) Servings per Container About 3 1/2 — **Amount per Serving** — **Calories** 90 Calories from Fat 5	corn			
Nutrition Facts Serving Size 1 package (255 g) Servings per Container 1 — **Amount per Serving** — **Calories** 280 Calories from Fat 90	macaroni & cheese			
Nutrition Facts Serving Size 1/2 cup (106 g) Servings per Container 4 — **Amount per Serving** — **Calories** 270 Calories from Fat 160	ice cream			

2. Compare whole milk to skim (nonfat) milk.

	Total Calories	Calories from Fat	Calories from Carbohydrate	Calories from Protein
1 cup whole milk	160	75	50	35
1 cup skim milk	85	trace	50	35

For whole milk, what percent of the total calories comes from

fat? _____ %   carbohydrate? _____ %   protein? _____ %

For skim milk, what percent of the total calories comes from

fat? _____ %   carbohydrate? _____ %   protein? _____ %

3. Find the missing percents.

   a. 25% + 30% + _____ % = 100%   **b.** 82% + _____ % + 9% = 100%

Math Boxes 62

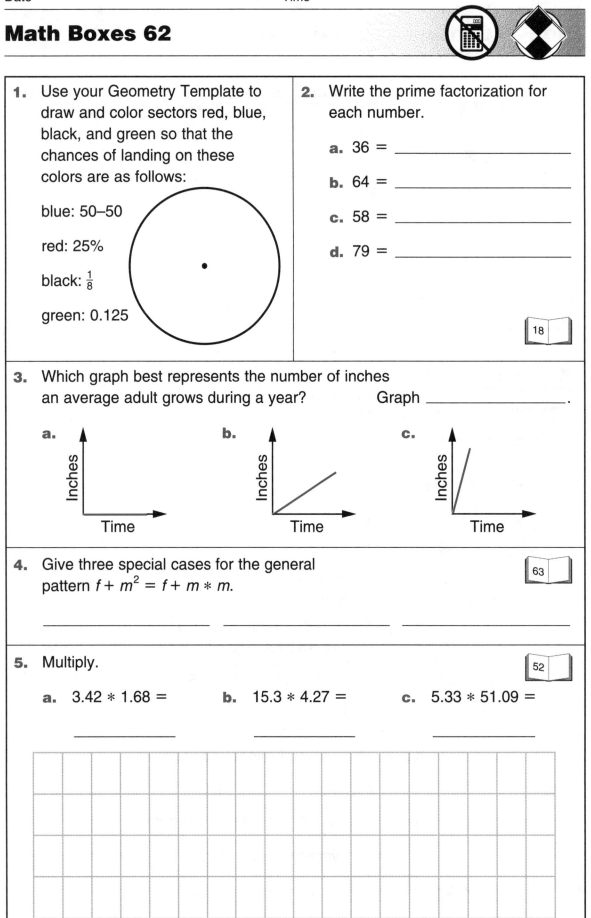

1. Use your Geometry Template to draw and color sectors red, blue, black, and green so that the chances of landing on these colors are as follows:

blue: 50–50

red: 25%

black: $\frac{1}{8}$

green: 0.125

2. Write the prime factorization for each number.

a. 36 = _____

b. 64 = _____

c. 58 = _____

d. 79 = _____

18

3. Which graph best represents the number of inches an average adult grows during a year?   Graph _____.

a.

Inches | Time

b.

Inches | Time

c.

Inches | Time

4. Give three special cases for the general pattern $f + m^2 = f + m * m$.

63

_____ _____ _____

5. Multiply.

52

a. $3.42 * 1.68 =$ **b.** $15.3 * 4.27 =$ **c.** $5.33 * 51.09 =$

_____ _____ _____

Enlargements

1. A copy machine was used to make a 2X enlargement of part of the Geometry Template. Use your ruler to measure the line segments shown in the figures at the bottom of the page to the nearest $\frac{1}{16}$ inch. Then fill in the table below.

Line Segment	Length of Original	Length of Enlargement	Ratio of Enlargement to Original
Diameter of circle			
Longer axis of ellipse			
Shorter axis of ellipse			
Longer side of kite			
Shorter side of kite			
Longer diagonal of kite			
Shorter diagonal of kite			

2. Are the figures in the enlargement similar to the original figures? _____

3. What does a 3.5X enlargement mean? _____

_____

_____

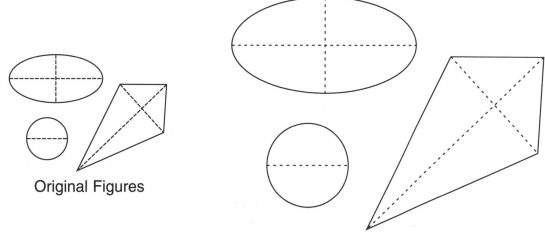

Original Figures

Enlargements

Reductions: Scale Models

1. The dimensions given in the drawing are for a scale model of the Volkswagen Beetle. The scale model is an exact replica of the actual car. Every length measured on the scale model is $\frac{1}{30}$ of the same length on the actual car.

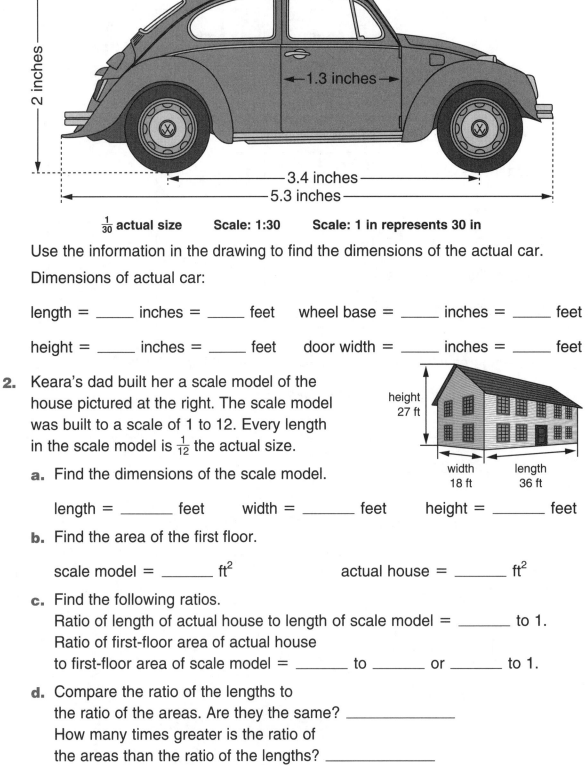

$\frac{1}{30}$ actual size   Scale: 1:30   Scale: 1 in represents 30 in

Use the information in the drawing to find the dimensions of the actual car.

Dimensions of actual car:

length = _____ inches = _____ feet   wheel base = _____ inches = _____ feet

height = _____ inches = _____ feet   door width = _____ inches = _____ feet

2. Keara's dad built her a scale model of the house pictured at the right. The scale model was built to a scale of 1 to 12. Every length in the scale model is $\frac{1}{12}$ the actual size.

   height 27 ft

   width 18 ft   length 36 ft

   a. Find the dimensions of the scale model.

   length = _____ feet   width = _____ feet   height = _____ feet

   b. Find the area of the first floor.

   scale model = _____ ft^2 actual house = _____ ft^2

   c. Find the following ratios.
   Ratio of length of actual house to length of scale model = _____ to 1.
   Ratio of first-floor area of actual house
   to first-floor area of scale model = _____ to _____ or _____ to 1.

   d. Compare the ratio of the lengths to
   the ratio of the areas. Are they the same? _____
   How many times greater is the ratio of
   the areas than the ratio of the lengths? _____

Map Scale

This map shows the downtown area of the city of Chicago. The shaded area shows the part of Chicago that was destroyed in the Chicago fire of 1871.

The map was drawn to a scale of 1:50,000. This means that each 1-inch length on the map represents 50,000 inches (about $\frac{3}{4}$ mile) of actual distance.

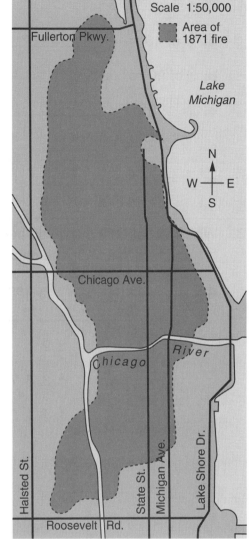

1. Measure the distance on the map between Fullerton Parkway and Roosevelt Road, to the nearest $\frac{1}{4}$ inch. This is the approximate north-south length of the part that burned.

   burn length on map = _____ inches

2. Measure the width of the part that burned, along Chicago Avenue, to the nearest $\frac{1}{4}$ inch. This is the approximate east-west length of the part that burned.

   burn width on map = _____ inches

3. Use the map scale to find the actual length and width of the part of Chicago that burned.

   actual burn length = _____ inches

   actual burn width = _____ inches

4. Convert the answers in Problem 3 from inches to miles, to the nearest tenth of a mile.

   actual burn length = _____ miles

   actual burn width = _____ miles

5. Estimate the area of the part of Chicago that burned, to the nearest square mile.

   area of part that burned: about _____ square miles

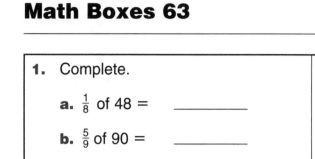

Math Boxes 63

1. Complete.

a. $\frac{1}{8}$ of 48 = _____

b. $\frac{5}{9}$ of 90 = _____

c. $\frac{2}{17}$ of 51 = _____

d. $\frac{3}{19}$ of 95 = _____

e. $\frac{8}{10}$ of 800 = _____ 134

2. Solve.   Solution

a. $24 * f = 12$ _____

b. $\frac{y}{15} = 3$ _____

c. $n - 136 = 65$ _____

d. $\frac{36}{q} = 3$ _____

158

3. Which set of data displayed below has the following landmarks: maximum 27, mode 21, median 19, and minimum 8? Circle the letter of the best choice.

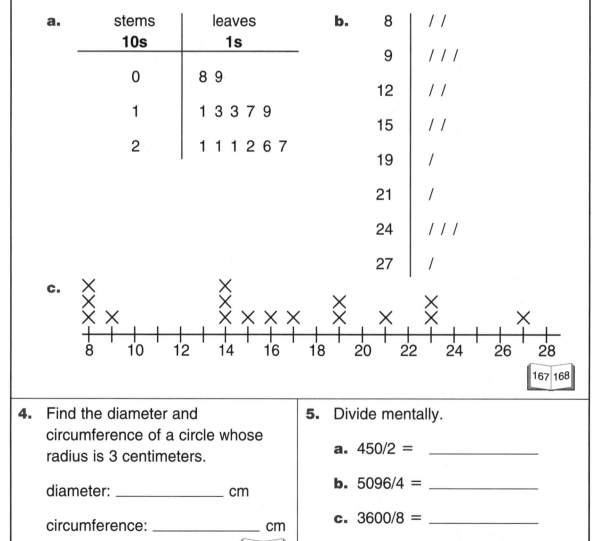

a.
stems 10s	leaves 1s
0	8 9
1	1 3 3 7 9
2	1 1 1 2 6 7

b.
8	/ /
9	/ / /
12	/ /
15	/ /
19	/
21	/
24	/ / /
27	/

c.

167 168

4. Find the diameter and circumference of a circle whose radius is 3 centimeters.

diameter: _____ cm

circumference: _____ cm

118

5. Divide mentally.

a. 450/2 = _____

b. 5096/4 = _____

c. 3600/8 = _____

d. 5000/8 = _____

Similar Polygons

1. Use pattern-block trapezoids to construct a trapezoid whose sides are twice the size of the corresponding sides of the single pattern-block trapezoid. Then use your Geometry Template to record what you did.

2. Draw a trapezoid whose sides are 3 times the size of a pattern-block trapezoid. You may use any drawing or measuring tools—for example, a compass, a ruler, a protractor, the trapezoid on your Geometry Template, or a trapezoid pattern block.

    What tools did you use? _____

3. Try to cover the trapezoid you drew in Problem 2 with pattern-block trapezoids. Then use your Geometry Template to record the way you covered the trapezoid.

Similar Polygons (cont.)

4. Measure line segments *AB, CD,* and *EF* with a
centimeter ruler. Draw a line segment *GH* so that
the ratio of the lengths of *AB* to *CD* is equal to the
ratio of the lengths of *EF* to *GH*.

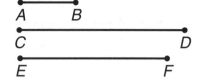

5. Pentagons *PAINT* and
MODEL are similar
polygons. Find the
missing lengths of sides.

a. Length of side *MO* =

_____ units.

b. Length of side *EL* =

_____ units.

c. Length of side *DE* = _____ units.

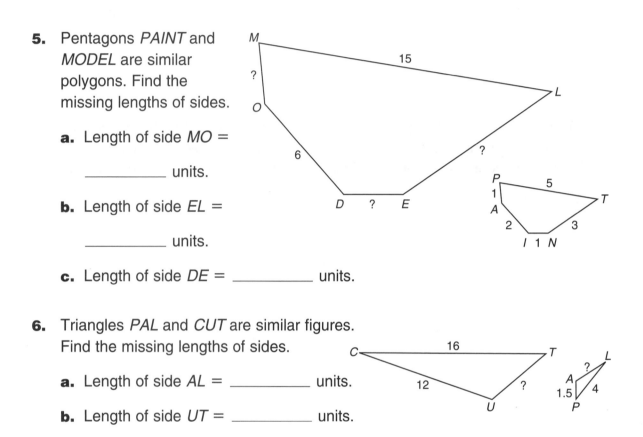

6. Triangles *PAL* and *CUT* are similar figures.
Find the missing lengths of sides.

a. Length of side *AL* = _____ units.

b. Length of side *UT* = _____ units.

7. Alexi is looking at a map of her town. The scale given on the map is
1 inch = $\frac{1}{2}$ mile. Alexi measures the distance from her home to school on
the map—it's $3\frac{3}{4}$ inches. What is the actual distance from home to school?

_____ miles

8. For a school fair to be held in the cafeteria, Nina wants to construct a scale
model of the 984-foot-tall Eiffel Tower. She wants to use a scale of 1 to 6—
every length of the scale model will be $\frac{1}{6}$ of the actual size of the Eiffel Tower.
Does this scale seem reasonable? If yes, explain why. If no, suggest a more
reasonable scale.

_____

_____

Math Boxes 64

1. The following table shows the results of rolling a six-sided die 50 times.

Number showing	1	2	3	4	5	6
Number of times	10	5	11	12	4	8

Tell whether each sentence below is true or false.

a. On the next roll of the die, a 5 is more likely
to come up than a 1.   _____

b. There is a 50–50 chance of rolling a prime number.   _____

c. There is a 50–50 chance of rolling a composite number.   _____

18

2. Write the following in standard
notation.

a. _____ $= 3.67 * 10^4$

b. $45.2 * 10^{-4} =$ _____

c. $2.01 * 10^{-2} =$ _____

d. _____ $= 0.0443 * 10^6$

7 | 8

3. a. Divide: 5893/15 → _____

b. Write a number story for the
division problem in Part a.

_____

_____

_____

_____

15

4. Write each number in standard
notation.

a. 1.8 million = _____

b. 0.6 billion = _____

c. 7.8 billion = _____

d. 3.7 trillion = _____

e. 0.6 trillion = _____

5

5. Three special cases of a pattern are
given below. Using one variable,
write a mathematical sentence to
describe the general pattern.

a. $(6 + 5) * 3 = (15 - 4) * 3$

b. $(6 + 5) * 2 = (15 - 4) * 2$

c. $(6 + 5) * 12 = (15 - 4) * 12$

General pattern:

_____

Math Boxes 65

---

1. a. Use your Geometry Template to draw and color sectors red and blue so that the chances of landing on these colors are as follows:

red: 1 out of 4

blue: $\frac{3}{8}$

b. On this spinner, what is the chance of *not* landing on red or blue?

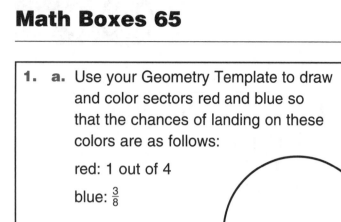

_____

2. Write the prime factorization for each number.

a. 27 = _____

b. 45 = _____

c. 62 = _____

d. 57 = _____

---

3. Which graph best represents the number of phone calls an average person makes during a day? Graph _____

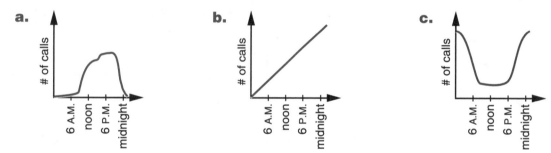

---

4. Give three special cases for the general pattern below.
$(b * h) + 4 = 4 + (h * b)$

_____   _____   _____

---

5. Multiply.

a. $64.8 * 12.9 =$ _____

b. $22.04 * 48.7 =$ _____

c. $31.65 * 29.12 =$ _____

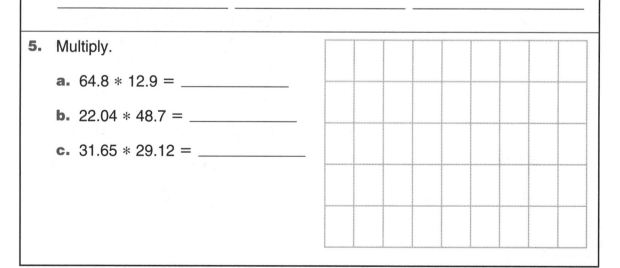

Use with Lesson 65.

Renaming Ratios

For the rectangles in this lesson, use length as the measure of the longer sides and width as the measure of the shorter sides.

Refer to the data you collected on Study Link 61 to complete the sentences. Use your calculator when renaming ratios. Round your answers to the nearest tenth.

1. The ratio of left-handed to right-handed people in my household is about _____ to 1.

2. The ratio of the length of the American flag I found to its width is about _____ to 1.

3. The ratio of the length of the screen of my TV set to its width is about _____ to 1.

4.   a. The ratio of the length of a small book to its width is about _____ to 1.

     b. The ratio of the length of a medium book to its width is about _____ to 1.

     c. The ratio of the length of a large book to its width is about _____ to 1.

     d. What is the shape of a book whose ratio of length to width is 1 to 1? _____

5.   a. The ratio of the length of a postcard to its width is about _____ to 1.

     b. The ratio of the length of an index card to its width is about _____ to 1.

     c. The ratio of the length of a regular-size envelope to its width is about _____ to 1.

     d. The ratio of the length of a business envelope to its width is about _____ to 1.

     e. The ratio of the length of a sheet of notebook paper to its width is about _____ to 1.

     f. Which of the items in Parts a–e above is the narrowest? _____

6. The ratio of the length of rectangle:

     a. A to its width is about _____ to 1.   b. B to its width is about _____ to 1.

     c. C to its width is about _____ to 1.   d. D to its width is about _____ to 1.

     e. Which of the four rectangles was the most popular? _____

7. The ratio of the rise to the run of my stairs is about _____ to 1.

Comparing Ratios

Share the data you recorded on page 243 with the other members of your group. Use these data to answer the following questions.

1. Which group member has the largest ratio of left-handed people to right-handed people at home? _____

   What is this ratio? _____

2. By law, the length of an official United States flag must be 1.9 times its width.

   a. Did the flag you measured meet this standard? _____

   b. What percent of the flags measured by your group meet this standard?

   _____

   c. Why do you think such a law exists? _____

   _____

   d. One of the largest United States flags was displayed at the J.L. Hudson store in Detroit, Michigan. The flag was 235 feet by 104 feet. Does this flag meet the legal requirements? _____

   e. How can you tell? _____

   _____

   _____

3. a. For most television sets, the ratio of the length to the width of the screen is about 4 to 3. Is this true of the television sets in your group? _____

   b. Why do you think it is important to have similar ratios of length to width for TV screens? _____

   _____

   _____

4. Compare the ratios for small, medium, and large books measured by your group. Which size books tends to have the largest ratio of length to width? _____

   Which size tends to have the smallest ratio? _____

Comparing Ratios (cont.)

5. It is often claimed that the "nicest looking" rectangular shapes have a special ratio of length to width. Such rectangles are called **Golden Rectangles.** In a Golden Rectangle, the ratio of length to width is about 8 to 5.

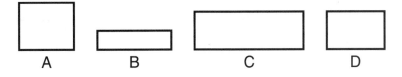

A   B   C   D

a. Which of the four rectangles—A, B, C, or D—is closest to having the shape of a Golden Rectangle? _____

b. Did most people in your family choose the Golden Rectangle? _____

c. Draw a Golden Rectangle whose shorter sides are 2 centimeters long.

d. Are any of the items in Problem 5 on page 243 Golden Rectangles? _____

If so, which are they? _____

6. Most stairs in homes have a rise of about 7 inches and a run of about $10\frac{1}{2}$ inches. Therefore, the rise is about $\frac{2}{3}$ of the run.

a. Is this true of your stairs? _____

b. Which stairs would be steeper, stairs with a rise-to-run ratio of

2:3 or 3:2? _____

c. Which member of your group has the steepest stairs?

_____

What is the ratio of rise to run?

_____

d. On the grid at the right, draw stairs whose rise is $\frac{2}{5}$ of the run.

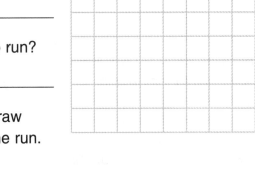

Constructing a Golden Rectangle

1. Draw a square *ABCD*.

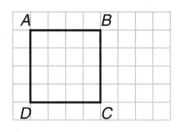

2. Draw $\overline{EF}$ to divide the square in half.

3. Draw the diagonal $\overline{FB}$. Extend $\overline{DC}$.

4. Use your compass to draw an arc from point *F* through point *B* that intersects $\overline{DC}$ at point *G*. (Place the compass point on *F* and the pencil point on *B*. Draw the arc.)

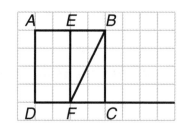

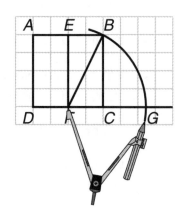

5. Extend $\overline{AB}$. Draw a line segment that is perpendicular to $\overline{DG}$ at point *G* and that intersects the extension of $\overline{AB}$ at point *H*.

Rectangle *AHGD* is a Golden Rectangle.

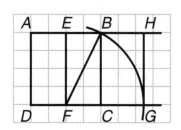

Constructing a Golden Rectangle (cont.)

6. Construct a Golden Rectangle. Use $\overline{AD}$ below as one of the **shorter** sides of the rectangle.

7. Measure the sides of your rectangle, to the nearest tenth of a centimeter.

length = _____ . _____ cm   width = _____ . _____ cm

8. Find the ratio of the length to the width of the rectangle.

ratio of length to width = _____ to 1

A Classical Face

The Golden Ratio can be found in many of the sculptures that were made during the classical period of Greek art (about 480–350 B.C.). The picture at the right is a good example of a "classically Greek" face. It shows a sculpture of the head of the Greek goddess Hera, who, according to Greek mythology, was queen of the Olympian gods and the wife of the Greek god Zeus. Found in a temple in Argos, a city of which Hera was a patron, the sculpture was probably completed about 420 B.C. The sculpture is currently owned by the National Archaeological Museum in Athens, Greece.

By measuring various parts of the face, you will find many Golden Ratios in the sculpture.

1. Measure each of the following parts of the face pictured on the next page. Measure *carefully,* to the **nearest tenth of a centimeter.**

    a. total width of head (including hair) = _____14.8_____ cm

    b. top of hair to pupils = _____ cm

    c. top of eye to bottom of chin = _____ cm

    d. top of hair to bottom of chin = _____ cm

    e. distance from ear to ear = _____ cm

    f. peak of hairline to bottom of chin = _____ cm

    g. from outside of one eye to outside of other eye = _____ cm

    h. pupil to chin = _____ cm

    i. from inside of one eye to inside of other eye = _____ cm

A Classical Face (cont.)

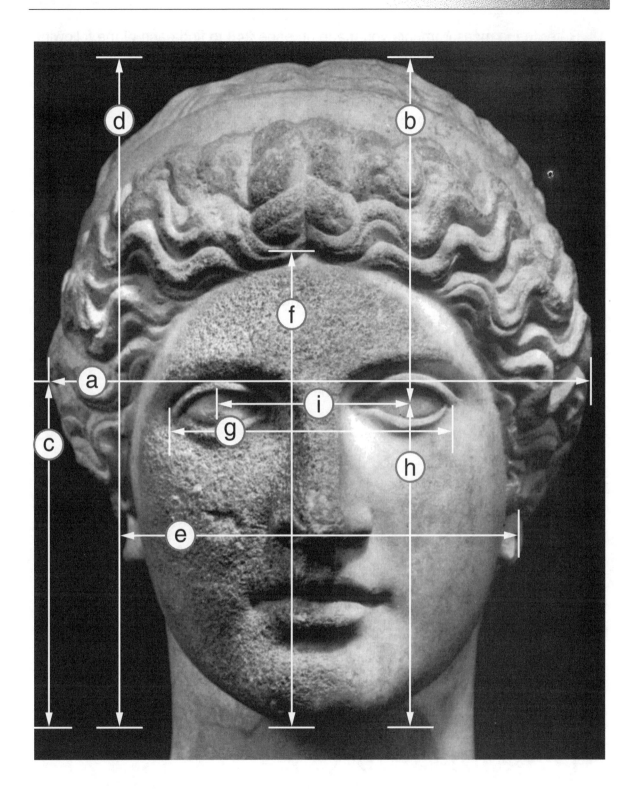

A Classical Face (cont.)

2. Refer to the measurements you made on page 248 to find each of the following ratios to the nearest tenth. Use your calculator.

    a. (total width of head) to (top of hair to pupils)

    ___14.9___ to ___9.2___ = ___1.6___ to 1

    b. (total width of head) to (top of eye to bottom of chin)

    _____ to _____ = _____ to 1

    c. (top of hair to bottom of chin) to (distance from ear to ear)

    _____ to _____ = _____ to 1

    d. (peak of hairline to bottom of chin) to (from outside of one eye to outside of other)

    _____ to _____ = _____ to 1

    e. (pupil to chin) to (from inside of one eye to inside of other eye)

    _____ to _____ = _____ to 1

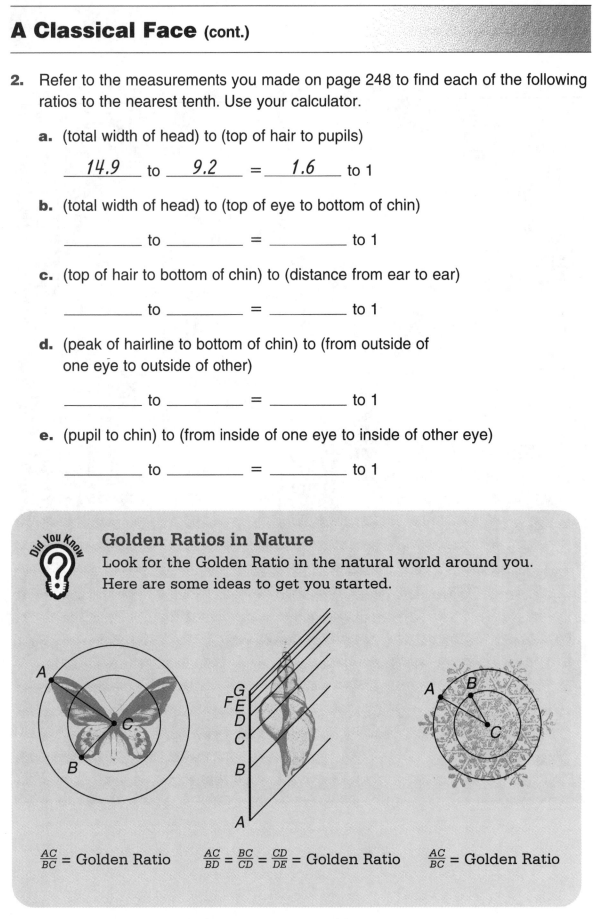

Did You Know

Golden Ratios in Nature

Look for the Golden Ratio in the natural world around you. Here are some ideas to get you started.

$\frac{AC}{BC}$ = Golden Ratio $\frac{AC}{BD} = \frac{BC}{CD} = \frac{CD}{DE}$ = Golden Ratio $\frac{AC}{BC}$ = Golden Ratio

Date   Time

A Classical Face (cont.)

a

b

c

a

e

d

f

g

h

i

Use with Lesson 66.

251

Are There Golden Ratios in Your Face?

Work with a partner to try to find Golden Ratios in your face. Be careful when measuring near your partner's eyes. For several of the measurements, it will be helpful to close your eyes while your partner does the measuring.

1. Have your partner measure each of the following parts of your face, to the **nearest centimeter.**

    a. total width of head (including hair) = _____ cm

    b. top of hair to pupils = _____ cm

    c. top of eye to bottom of chin = _____ cm

    d. top of hair to bottom of chin = _____ cm

    e. distance from ear to ear = _____ cm

    f. peak of hairline to bottom of chin = _____ cm

    g. from outside of one eye to outside of other eye = _____ cm

    h. pupil to chin = _____ cm

    i. from inside of one eye to inside of other eye = _____ cm

2. On page 248, you measured each part of the picture of Hera's face to the nearest **tenth of a centimeter.** When you measured your partner's face, you measured each part to the nearest **centimeter.** Why does it not make sense to measure your partner's face to the nearest tenth of a centimeter?

Are There Golden Ratios in Your Face? (cont.)

3. Refer to the measurements you made on page 252 to find each of the following ratios to the **nearest tenth.** Use your calculator.

   a. (total width of head) to (top of hair to pupils)

   _____ to _____ = _____ to 1

   b. (total width of head) to (top of eye to bottom of chin)

   _____ to _____ = _____ to 1

   c. (top of hair to bottom of chin) to (distance from ear to ear)

   _____ to _____ = _____ to 1

   d. (peak of hairline to bottom of chin) to (from outside of one eye to outside of other eye)

   _____ to _____ = _____ to 1

   e. (pupil to chin) to (from inside of one eye to inside of other eye)

   _____ to _____ = _____ to 1

4. Is your face like the face in the sculpture? Why or why not?

   _____

   _____

   _____

   _____

   _____

   _____

   _____

   _____

   _____

   _____

Math Boxes 66

1. Complete.

a. $\frac{1}{2}$ of 2 = _____

b. $\frac{1}{4}$ of 2 = _____

c. $\frac{1}{2}$ of 4 = _____

d. $\frac{1}{4}$ of $\frac{1}{2}$ = _____

e. $\frac{1}{2}$ of $\frac{1}{2}$ = _____

2. Solve.   Solution

a. $7 * d = 77$ _____

b. $\frac{t}{9} = 6$ _____

c. $s - 68 = 143$ _____

d. $\frac{125}{x} = 25$ _____

3. Which set of data displayed below has the following landmarks: maximum 40, mode 35, median 20, and minimum 0? Circle the letter of the best choice.

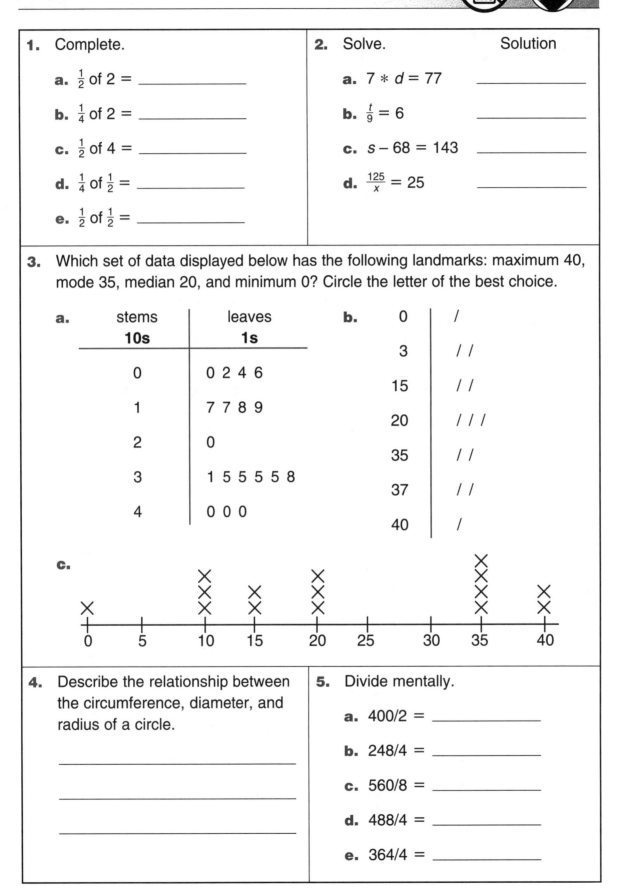

a.
stems 10s	leaves 1s
0	0 2 4 6
1	7 7 8 9
2	0
3	1 5 5 5 5 8
4	0 0 0

b.
0	/
3	/ /
15	/ /
20	/ / /
35	/ /
37	/ /
40	/

c.

4. Describe the relationship between the circumference, diameter, and radius of a circle.

_____

_____

_____

5. Divide mentally.

a. 400/2 = _____

b. 248/4 = _____

c. 560/8 = _____

d. 488/4 = _____

e. 364/4 = _____

Use with Lesson 66.

Math Message: Time to Reflect

1. How would you define the word **ratio** to a new student in your class? Write what you might say. Draw pictures if that helps you explain.

_____

_____

_____

_____

_____

_____

_____

_____

2. What was something that you enjoyed doing in this unit? Why did you enjoy it?

_____

_____

_____

_____

_____

_____

_____

_____

Math Boxes 67

1. You roll two 6-sided dice. Give the probability of rolling the following totals.

   a. 2 _____   **b.** 12 _____

   c. 11 _____   **d.** 7 _____

   e. 0 _____   **f.** 3 or 4 _____

   g. an even number _____

2. Write the following in standard notation.

   a. $5.4 * 10^3 =$ _____

   b. $18 * 10^{-2} =$ _____

   c. $0.078 * 10^5 =$ _____

   d. _____ $= 44.35 * 10^{-3}$

3.   **a.** Divide: 5224/87 → _____

   b. Write a number story for the division problem in Part a.

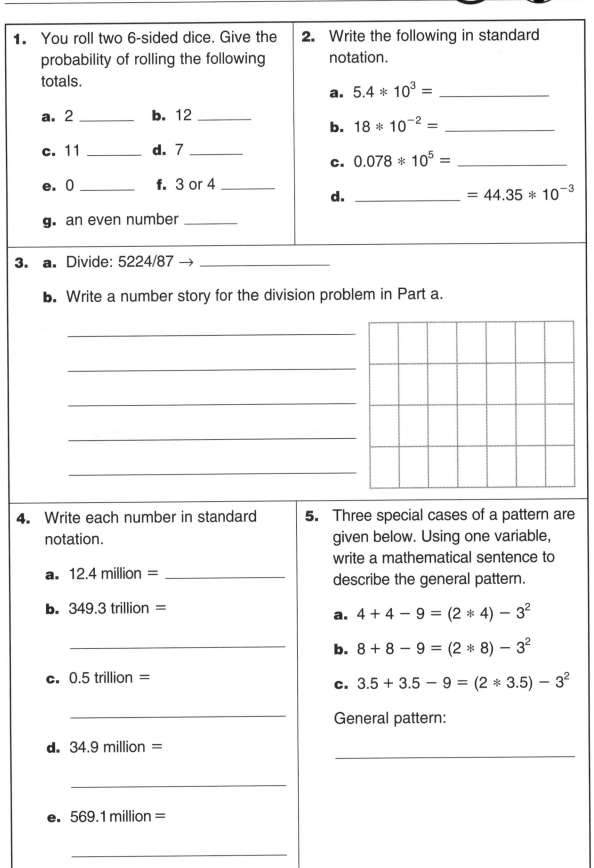

4. Write each number in standard notation.

   a. 12.4 million = _____

   b. 349.3 trillion = _____

   c. 0.5 trillion = _____

   d. 34.9 million = _____

   e. 569.1 million = _____

5. Three special cases of a pattern are given below. Using one variable, write a mathematical sentence to describe the general pattern.

   a. $4 + 4 - 9 = (2 * 4) - 3^2$

   b. $8 + 8 - 9 = (2 * 8) - 3^2$

   c. $3.5 + 3.5 - 9 = (2 * 3.5) - 3^2$

   General pattern:

   _____

Use with Lesson 67.

Math Message: Fraction Multiplication

1. Use this number line to help you answer the problems in Columns 1 and 2 below. Remember that in *Fifth Grade Everyday Mathematics,* you learned that "of" indicates multiplication.

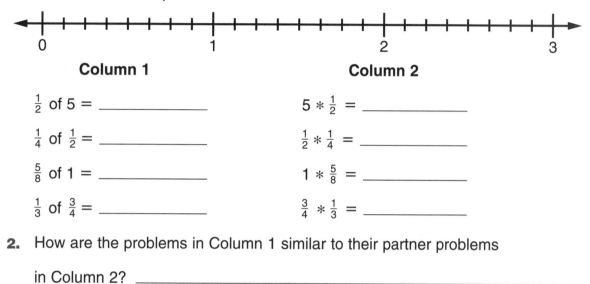

Column 1   **Column 2**

$\frac{1}{2}$ of 5 = _____ $5 * \frac{1}{2}$ = _____

$\frac{1}{4}$ of $\frac{1}{2}$ = _____ $\frac{1}{2} * \frac{1}{4}$ = _____

$\frac{5}{8}$ of 1 = _____ $1 * \frac{5}{8}$ = _____

$\frac{1}{3}$ of $\frac{3}{4}$ = _____ $\frac{3}{4} * \frac{1}{3}$ = _____

2. How are the problems in Column 1 similar to their partner problems

in Column 2? _____

_____

3. Circle the general pattern(s) below that are true for the partner problems in Columns 1 and 2.

$a + b = b + a$ $a * b = b * a$ a of $b = b * a$ $a \div b = b \div a$

A Fraction Multiplication Algorithm

1. Six special cases of a pattern are given below. Write the answer in simplest form for each special case. The first one has been done for you.

$\frac{1}{5} * \frac{2}{3} = \frac{1 * 2}{5 * 3} = \underline{\frac{2}{15}}$ $\frac{3}{4} * \frac{1}{2} = \frac{3 * 1}{4 * 2} = \underline{\hspace{2cm}}$

$\frac{2}{1} * \frac{2}{4} = \frac{2 * 2}{1 * 4} = \underline{\hspace{2cm}}$ $\frac{2}{4} * \frac{3}{5} = \frac{2 * 3}{4 * 5} = \underline{\hspace{2cm}}$

$\frac{4}{6} * \frac{1}{2} = \frac{4 * 1}{6 * 2} = \underline{\hspace{2cm}}$ $\frac{3}{7} * \frac{1}{3} = \frac{3 * 1}{7 * 3} = \underline{\hspace{2cm}}$

Describe the general pattern in words. (*Hint:* Look at the numerators and

denominators of the factors and products.) _____

_____

_____

A Fraction Multiplication Algorithm (cont.)

2. Try to write the general pattern for Problem 1 using variables.
(*Hint:* You will need to use four variables.)

_____

3. Use the general pattern above to solve the following multiplication problems. The first one has been done for you.

a. $\frac{3}{8} * \frac{2}{3} = \frac{3*2}{8*3} = \frac{6}{24}$　　　　**b.** $\frac{1}{3} * \frac{2}{3} =$ _____

c. $\frac{4}{5} * \frac{2}{8} =$ _____　　　　**d.** $\frac{3}{12} * \frac{2}{4} =$ _____

e. $\frac{3}{4} * \frac{5}{6} =$ _____　　　　**f.** $\frac{7}{9} * \frac{3}{8} =$ _____

g. $\frac{2}{5} * \frac{7}{8} =$ _____　　　　**h.** $\frac{5}{10} * \frac{4}{7} =$ _____

4. Write the following whole numbers as fractions. The first one has been done for you.

a. $6 = \frac{6}{1}$　　**b.** $3 =$ _____　　**c.** $5 =$ _____　　**d.** $7 =$ _____

5. Rewrite the following problems as fraction multiplication problems and solve them. The first one has been done for you.

a. $4 * \frac{2}{3} = \frac{4}{1} * \frac{2}{3} = \frac{8}{3}$　　**b.** $6 * \frac{3}{5} =$ _____ $=$ _____

c. $7 * \frac{5}{6} =$ _____ $=$ _____　　**d.** $3 * \frac{3}{4} =$ _____ $=$ _____

Challenge

6. Write a general pattern with variables for the special cases in Problem 5.
(*Hint:* You will need to use three variables.)

_____

7. Mark took a timed multiplication test and finished $\frac{3}{4}$ of the problems. He correctly answered $\frac{1}{2}$ of the problems he finished. What fraction of the problems on the test did Mark do correctly? _____

Math Boxes 68

1. Complete.

   a. 1/8 of 2 = _____

   b. 3/4 of 80 = _____

   c. 4/7 of 77 = _____

   d. 1/2 of 1/8 = _____

   e. 5/12 of 60 = _____

2. Write a mixed number for each fraction.

   a. $\frac{320}{25}$ = _____

   b. $\frac{43}{7}$ = _____

   c. $\frac{101}{5}$ = _____

   d. $\frac{75}{6}$ = _____

   e. $\frac{147}{4}$ = _____

3. **a.** Use your Geometry Template to draw sectors of this spinner and color them red, blue, and green so that the chances of landing on these colors are as follows: red, 3/10   blue, 0.33   green, 20%

   b. On this spinner, what is the chance of *not* landing on red, blue, or green?

   _____

4. Write a percent for each fraction.

   a. $\frac{4}{5}$ = _____

   b. $\frac{8}{12}$ = _____

   c. $\frac{7}{8}$ = _____

   d. $\frac{3}{4}$ = _____

   e. $\frac{2}{3}$ = _____

5. You draw one card at random from a regular deck of 52 playing cards (no jokers). What is the chance of drawing

   a. a 4? _____

   b. a card with a prime number? _____

   c. a face card (jack, queen, or king)? _____

   d. an even-numbered black card? _____

6. Rename each mixed number as a fraction.

   a. $3\frac{7}{8}$ = _____

   b. _____ = $5\frac{8}{9}$

   c. _____ = $8\frac{5}{6}$

   d. _____ = $6\frac{9}{7}$

   e. $14\frac{2}{3}$ = _____

Math Message: Mixed Numbers to Fractions

1. Write the following mixed numbers as fractions.

23

    a. $3\frac{1}{4}$ = _____   **b.** $2\frac{3}{8}$ = _____

    c. $5\frac{7}{8}$ = _____   **d.** $3\frac{6}{5}$ = _____

    e. $4\frac{3}{10}$ = _____   **f.** $2\frac{16}{3}$ = _____

2. Add.

    a. $\frac{5}{6} + 2$ = _____   **b.** $\frac{3}{8} + 4$ = _____   **c.** $6 + \frac{2}{3}$ = _____

3. Multiply. Be prepared to explain how you found your answer.

    $3\frac{3}{8} * 1\frac{2}{5}$ = _____

Multiplying Mixed Numbers

Below are examples of two algorithms for multiplying mixed numbers.

37

Adding Partial Products

Example 1: $3\frac{3}{4}$

$$* \ 2\frac{2}{3}$$

$2 * 3 \ = \ \overline{6} \ = \ 6$

$2 * \frac{3}{4} \ = \ \frac{6}{4} \ = \ 1\frac{1}{2}$

$\frac{2}{3} * 3 \ = \ \frac{6}{3} \ = \ 2$

$\frac{2}{3} * \frac{3}{4} \ = \ + \frac{6}{12} \ = \ \frac{1}{2}$

$$9\frac{2}{2} \text{ or } 10$$

Example 2: $2\frac{3}{8}$

$$* \ \frac{2}{5}$$

$\frac{2}{5} * 2 \ = \ \frac{4}{5}$

$\frac{2}{5} * \frac{3}{8} \ = \ + \frac{6}{40}$

$$\frac{38}{40}$$

Converting Mixed Numbers to Fractions

Example 1: $2\frac{2}{3} * 3\frac{3}{4} = \frac{8}{3} * \frac{15}{4}$

$$= \frac{8 * 15}{3 * 4}$$

$$= \frac{120}{12}$$

$$= 10$$

Example 2: $\frac{2}{5} * 2\frac{3}{8} = \frac{2}{5} * \frac{19}{8}$

$$= \frac{2 * 19}{5 * 8}$$

$$= \frac{38}{40}$$

Use with Lesson 69.

Multiplying Mixed Numbers (cont.)

1. Multiply. Use one of the algorithms from the preceding page or one of your own.

    a. $2\frac{3}{8} * \frac{1}{5} =$ _____

    b. $3\frac{2}{5} * 2\frac{2}{3} =$ _____

    c. $5\frac{3}{4} * 2\frac{5}{9} =$ _____

    d. _____ $= 4\frac{6}{7} * \frac{3}{7}$

    e. $4 * 6\frac{7}{10} =$ _____

    f. $3\frac{11}{12} * 2\frac{1}{2} =$ _____

    g. _____ $= 5\frac{7}{8} * 2\frac{1}{8}$

    h. $4\frac{1}{6} * 3\frac{9}{4} =$ _____

2. Lydia is putting photographs in an album. She does not like to leave more than $\frac{1}{3}$ of a page uncovered.

    a. At the right are the dimensions of an album page and four photographs. If Lydia puts these four photographs on one page, what area of the page will be left uncovered?

    _____ square inches

	Height	Width
Album page	$6\frac{3}{4}"$	$9"$
Photograph 1	$4\frac{1}{8}"$	$2\frac{1}{2}"$
Photograph 2	$3\frac{5}{8}"$	$4"$
Photograph 3	$2\frac{1}{8}"$	$2\frac{3}{4}"$
Photograph 4	$2\frac{1}{8}"$	$2\frac{1}{8}"$

    b. Is this more or less than $\frac{1}{3}$ of the total area of the page?

    _____

Math Boxes 69

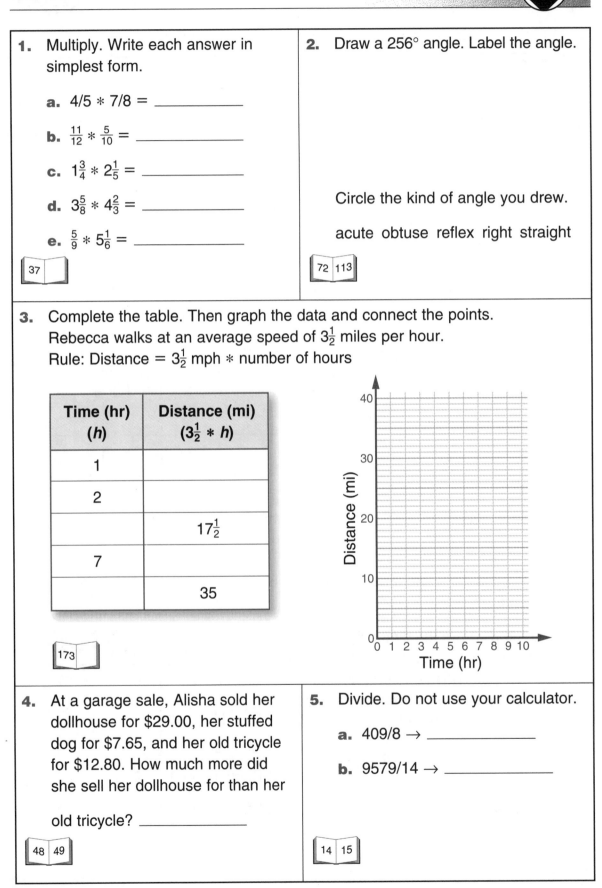

1. Multiply. Write each answer in simplest form.

a. 4/5 * 7/8 = _____

b. $\frac{11}{12} * \frac{5}{10}$ = _____

c. $1\frac{3}{4} * 2\frac{1}{5}$ = _____

d. $3\frac{5}{8} * 4\frac{2}{3}$ = _____

e. $\frac{5}{9} * 5\frac{1}{6}$ = _____

37

2. Draw a 256° angle. Label the angle.

Circle the kind of angle you drew.

acute   obtuse   reflex   right   straight

72 113

3. Complete the table. Then graph the data and connect the points.
Rebecca walks at an average speed of $3\frac{1}{2}$ miles per hour.
Rule: Distance = $3\frac{1}{2}$ mph * number of hours

Time (hr) (h)	Distance (mi) ($3\frac{1}{2}$ * h)
1	
2	
	$17\frac{1}{2}$
7	
	35

173

4. At a garage sale, Alisha sold her dollhouse for $29.00, her stuffed dog for $7.65, and her old tricycle for $12.80. How much more did she sell her dollhouse for than her old tricycle? _____

48 49

5. Divide. Do not use your calculator.

a. 409/8 → _____

b. 9579/14 → _____

14 15

Use with Lesson 69.

Math Message: Random Numbers on a Calculator

Press the following sequence of keys
on your calculator: [1] [2nd] [RAND] [4] [=]

> Note: [RAND] is the 2nd
> function of the [=] key.

What does the display show? _____

When you press the above sequence of keys, one of the numbers 1, 2, 3, or 4
appears. Since each of the four numbers has the same chance of appearing,
we say that the numbers found in this way are **random numbers.**

If you were to press this sequence many times, about what percent of the time

would you expect the number 1 to appear? about _____ percent of the time

Using a Calculator to Generate Random Numbers

Work with a partner. Use a calculator to **generate random numbers** from
1 to 4, as described above. Each number generated is called an **outcome.**

- While one partner generates the random numbers, the other partner tallies the
  outcomes on a piece of paper. Generate exactly 25 random numbers.

- Record the results in the table below. In the "My Partnership" column, write the
  number of times 1, 2, 3, and 4 appeared.

- In the "Other Partnership" column, record the results of the other partnership in
  your group.

- For each outcome, add the two results and write the sum in the "Both
  Partnerships" column.

- Convert each result under "Both Partnerships" to a percent and write it in the
  "% of Total" column. (For example, 10 out of 50 would be 20%.)

Outcome	My Partnership	Other Partnership	Both Partnerships	% of Total
1			out of 50	
2			out of 50	
3			out of 50	
4			out of 50	
Total	25	25	50 out of 50	100%

Use with Lesson 70.

Math Boxes 70

1. You can calculate about how long it will take an object to reach the bottom of a well by using the following formula

$$t = \frac{1}{4} * \sqrt{d}$$

where d is the distance in feet the object falls and t is the time in seconds it takes to reach the bottom. This formula does not take air resistance into account, so it is more accurate for heavier objects.

About how long would it take a bowling ball to hit the bottom of a well 100 feet deep? _____

159 160

2. **a.** Name a number that is a multiple of 4, 6, and 8. _____

b. Name a number that is a multiple of 3, 12, and 15. _____

c. Name a number that is a multiple of 6, 8, and 9. _____

30

3. Add or subtract.

a. $2\frac{2}{5} - \frac{8}{10} =$ _____

b. $\frac{16}{8} - 1\frac{1}{9} =$ _____

c. $\frac{14}{16} + 2\frac{1}{2} =$ _____

d. $1\frac{7}{8} + \frac{24}{16} =$ _____

33
34 35

4. Tell what additional information you need to solve the following problem: Melissa took 3 friends to lunch. She had $20 to spend on lunch. All 4 people ordered spaghetti. How much change did Melissa receive from her $20?

_____

_____

_____

_____

_____

5. Write each number in number-and-word notation.

a. 58,400,000,000,000

_____

b. 200,000

_____

c. 16,900,000,000

_____

d. 4,800,000

_____

e. 3,856,000,000

5   _____

Use with Lesson 70.

Math Boxes 71

1. Add or subtract.

    a. $25 - (-14) =$ _____

    b. $-18 - 5 =$ _____

    c. $-74 + (-8) =$ _____

    d. $46 + (-38) =$ _____

    e. $-87 + 42 =$ _____

57 58

2. I am a 3-dimensional geometric shape. I have 5 faces. One face is a rectangle. The other faces are triangles.

I am called a

_____.

77

3. Add or subtract.

    a. $\frac{7}{10} + 8\frac{1}{3} =$ _____

    b. $5\frac{4}{5} - 2\frac{7}{8} =$ _____

    c. $\frac{15}{4} + \frac{9}{7} =$ _____

    d. $\frac{23}{10} - 1\frac{1}{15} =$ _____

34 35

4. Write each number using digits. Then round each number to the nearest tenth.

    a. twenty-five thousand, four hundred ten and eight hundredths

       number: _____

       rounded: _____

    b. fifty-nine and six hundred seventy-two thousandths

       number: _____

       rounded: _____

5 131

5. Give three special cases for the general pattern $\frac{0}{k} = k - k$.

_____

_____

_____

6. The distance from New York to San Francisco is about 2930 miles. A bus made this trip in 6 days. On average, about how many miles did the bus travel each day?

_____

140

Using Random Numbers

Imagine that two equally matched teams play a game that cannot end in a tie—one team must win. The teams play the game many times.

Because the teams have an equal chance of winning, you could get about the same results by randomly generating the numbers 1 and 2 on a calculator to determine the winner of each game. If the number 1 is displayed, Team 1 wins. If the number 2 is displayed, Team 2 wins. Used in this way, the calculator **simulates** the outcome of the game. In a **simulation,** an object or event is represented by something else.

Suppose that Team 1 and Team 2 play a tournament. The first team to win three games wins the tournament. (This is similar to divisional playoffs in Major League baseball.) The winning team might win the first three games played; or three of the first four games; or three of five games.

Use your calculator to simulate such a tournament, as follows:

Game 1   Key sequence: [1] [2nd] [RAND] [2] [=]. If the number 1 appears, Team 1 wins the game. If the number 2 appears, Team 2 wins the game.

Games 2 and 3   Repeat the instructions for Game 1.

Games 4 and 5   Play only if necessary. Repeat the instructions for Game 1.

Sample results:

- The numbers generated are 1-1-1. Team 1 wins the tournament.
- The numbers generated are 1-1-2-1. Team 1 wins the tournament.
- The numbers generated are 2-1-1-2-2. Team 2 wins the tournament.

Number of Games in Tournament	Winner	Tally	Tally Total
3	Team 1		
	Team 2		
4	Team 1		
	Team 2		
5	Team 1		
	Team 2		
Total			25

Use with Lesson 71.

Using Random Numbers (cont.)

1. Make a tally mark in the table on the preceding page to show which team won the first tournament and in how many games. Play exactly 24 more tournaments. Make a tally mark to record the results for each tournament.

2. Use the tally table on the preceding page.

   a. Estimate the chance that a tournament takes exactly 3 games. _____%

   b. Estimate the chance that a tournament takes exactly 4 games. _____%

   c. Estimate the chance that a tournament takes exactly 5 games. _____%

   d. Estimate the chance that a tournament takes fewer than 5 games. _____%

Discuss the following situations with a partner. Record your ideas.

3. Suppose there is a list of jobs that need to be done for your class (for example, distributing supplies, collecting books, taking messages to the office). How could you use random numbers to assign the jobs to members of your class "at random," without any pattern or favoritism?

   _____

   _____

   _____

   _____

   _____

4. Scientists sometimes use random numbers to be sure that their research is "fair." Suppose you needed 6-digit random numbers for your research. How could you generate them with your calculator?

   _____

   _____

   _____

   _____

   _____

Math Message: Mazes

The diagram at the right shows a maze.
A person walking through the maze does
not know in advance how many paths
there are or how they divide.

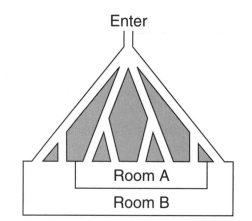

Enter

Room A

Room B

Pretend that you are walking through
the maze. When the path divides, you
select your next path at random. That
is, the paths all have the same chance
of being selected. You may not retrace
your steps.

Depending on which paths you follow,
you will end up either in Room A or
in Room B.

1. In which room are you more likely to end up—Room A or Room B? _____

2. Suppose that 80 people take turns walking through the maze.

    a. About how many people would you expect to end up in Room A? _____

    b. About how many people would you expect to end up in Room B? _____

Tree Diagrams

Your teacher will show you how to complete the following **tree diagram.**
Or you can find out for yourself on pages 178 and 179 of the *Student
Reference Book.*

178 179

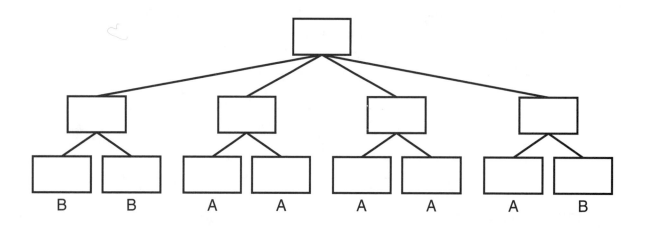

B   B   A   A   A   A   A   B

Use with Lesson 72.

Maze Problems

1. Use the tree diagram below to help you solve the following problem.

   Suppose that 60 people walk through the maze below.

   a. About how many people would you expect to end up in Room A? _____

   b. About how many people would you expect to end up in Room B? _____

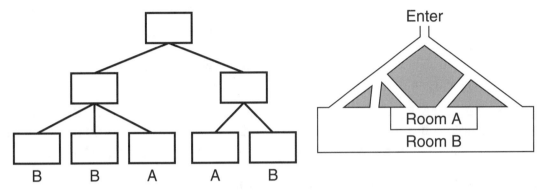

2. Make your own tree diagram to help you solve the following problem.

   Suppose that 120 people walk through the maze below.

   a. About how many people would you expect to end up in Room A? _____

   b. About how many people would you expect to end up in Room B? _____

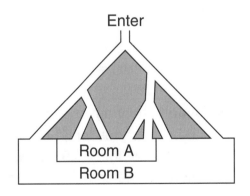

Math Boxes 72

1. Multiply. Write each answer in simplest form.

a. $\frac{3}{8} * 6 =$ _____

b. $2\frac{1}{7} * \frac{4}{5} =$ _____

c. $\frac{8}{9} * 3\frac{5}{6} =$ _____

d. $\frac{7}{8} * \frac{9}{5} =$ _____

e. $6\frac{2}{3} * 3\frac{3}{4} =$ _____

2. Draw a 72° angle. Label the angle.

Circle the kind of angle you drew.

acute   obtuse   reflex   right   straight

3. Complete the table. Then graph the data and connect the points. Heather earns $0.35 for each paper flower she makes for the school fun fair.

Rule: Earnings = $0.35 * number of flowers

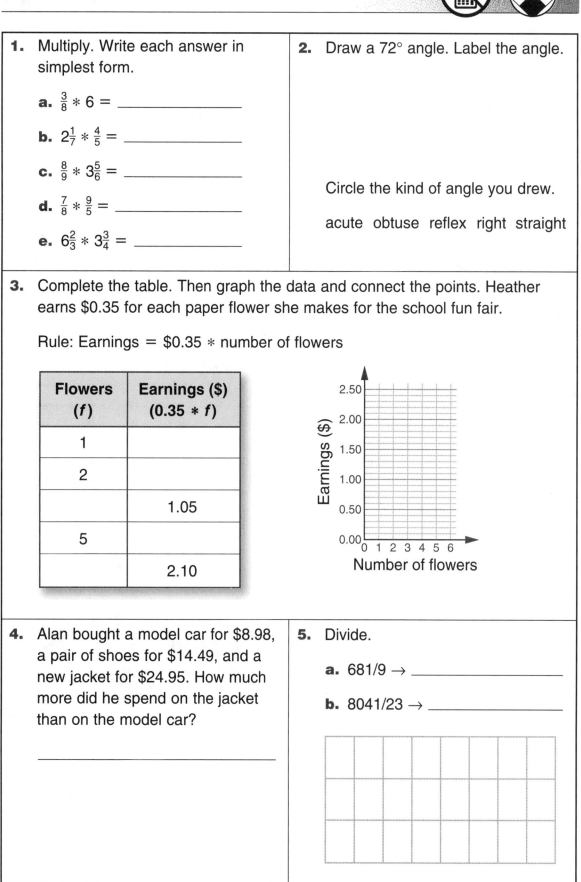

Flowers (f)	Earnings ($) (0.35 * f)
1	
2	
	1.05
5	
	2.10

4. Alan bought a model car for $8.98, a pair of shoes for $14.49, and a new jacket for $24.95. How much more did he spend on the jacket than on the model car?

_____

5. Divide.

a. 681/9 → _____

b. 8041/23 → _____

Use with Lesson 72.

Math Message: Probability

When you roll a fair, 6-sided die, each of the numbers from 1 to 6 has an equal chance of coming up. This does not mean that if you roll the die six times, each of the numbers 1 to 6 will come up exactly once. A 2 might come up three times, and a 6 might not come up at all. But if you roll the die 100 times, each number is *more likely* to come up about $\frac{1}{6}$ of the time. And if you roll it 1000 times, each number is even more likely to come up about $\frac{1}{6}$ of the time. We say that the **probability** of rolling a 1 (or a 2, 3, 4, 5, or 6) is $\frac{1}{6}$.

The spinner at the right is divided into 5 equal parts. Two of the parts are gray. If you spin it often enough, the spinner is likely to land on gray about $\frac{2}{5}$ of the time. The probability of landing on gray is $\frac{2}{5}$, or 40%.

Here are pictures of 6 spinners. Each statement below describes one of the spinners. Next to each statement, write the letter of the spinner it describes. A spinner may be matched with more than one statement.

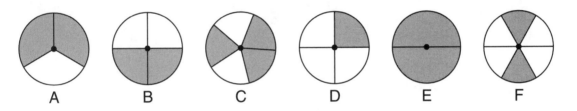

A   B   C   D   E   F

Example: The spinner will land on gray about 2 out of 3 times. _____ *A* _____

1. There is about a $\frac{1}{4}$ chance that the spinner will land on gray. _____

2. The spinner will land on gray 100% of the time. _____

3. There is about a 50–50 chance that the spinner will land on white. _____

4. The spinner will never land on white. _____

5. The probability of the spinner landing on gray is $\frac{3}{5}$. _____

6. The spinner will land on white about twice as often as on gray. _____

7. The spinner will land on white a little less than half of the time. _____

8. The probability of the spinner landing on white is 75%. _____

Probability Tree Diagrams

Complete the tree diagram for each maze.

Write a fraction next to each branch to show the probability of selecting that branch. Then calculate the probability of selecting each possible branch. Record your answers in the blank spaces at the bottom of the tree diagram.

1. What is the probability of entering Room A? _____

Of entering Room B? _____

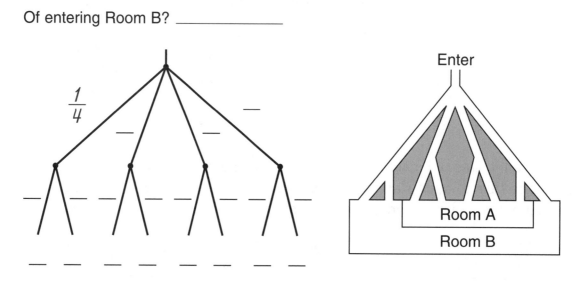

2. What is the probability of entering Room A? _____

Of entering Room B? _____

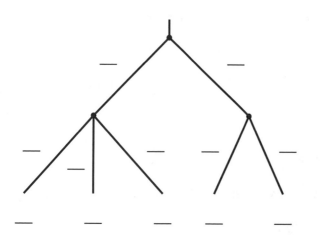

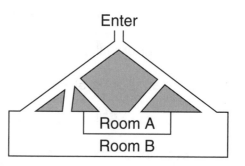

Probability Tree Diagrams (cont.)

3. Josh has 3 clean shirts (red, blue, and green) and 2 clean pairs of pants (tan and black). He randomly selects one shirt. Then he randomly selects a pair of pants.

a. Complete the tree diagram. Write a fraction next to each branch to show the probability of selecting that branch.

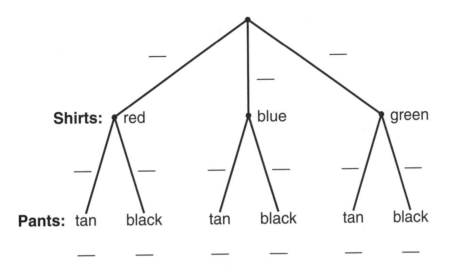

b. List all possible shirt-pants combinations. One has been done for you.

red-tan, _____

_____

_____

c. How many different shirt-pants combinations are there? _____

d. Do all the shirt-pants combinations have the same chance of being

selected? _____

e. What is the probability that Josh will select

the blue shirt? _____   the blue shirt and the tan pants? _____

the tan pants? _____   a shirt that is not red? _____

the black pants and a shirt that is not red? _____

Probability Tree Diagrams (cont.)

4. Mr. Gulliver travels to and from work by train. Trains to work leave at 6, 7, 8, 9, and 10 A.M. Trains from work leave at 3, 4, and 5 P.M. Suppose that Mr. Gulliver randomly selects a morning train and then randomly selects an evening train.

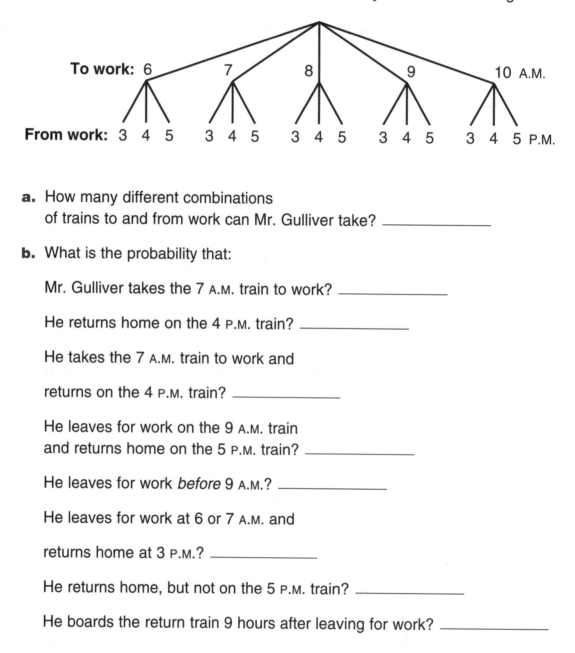

To work: 6   7   8   9   10 A.M.

From work: 3 4 5   3 4 5   3 4 5   3 4 5   3 4 5 P.M.

  a. How many different combinations
     of trains to and from work can Mr. Gulliver take? _____

  b. What is the probability that:

     Mr. Gulliver takes the 7 A.M. train to work? _____

     He returns home on the 4 P.M. train? _____

     He takes the 7 A.M. train to work and

     returns on the 4 P.M. train? _____

     He leaves for work on the 9 A.M. train
     and returns home on the 5 P.M. train? _____

     He leaves for work *before* 9 A.M.? _____

     He leaves for work at 6 or 7 A.M. and

     returns home at 3 P.M.? _____

     He returns home, but not on the 5 P.M. train? _____

     He boards the return train 9 hours after leaving for work? _____

Date _____   Time _____

Math Boxes 73

1. Suppose *N* is a 2-digit whole number that ends in 5, such as 15. It's easy to calculate the square of *N* by using the formula

$$N^2 = (t * (t + 1) * 100) + 25$$

where *t* is the tens digit of the number you are squaring. Use this formula to find the following. (*Hint:* In Part a, *t* = 3.)

a. $35^2 =$ _____   **b.** $75^2 =$ _____   **c.** $95^2 =$ _____

2. **a.** Name a number that is a multiple of 3, 4, and 8. _____

b. Name a number that is a multiple of 2, 5, and 6. _____

c. Name a number that is a multiple of 3, 4, and 5. _____

3. Add or subtract.

a. $3\frac{8}{9} + 1\frac{3}{12} =$ _____

b. $\frac{18}{6} - 1\frac{2}{3} =$ _____

c. $\frac{9}{5} + 4\frac{3}{10} =$ _____

d. $4\frac{5}{8} - 2\frac{7}{12} =$ _____

4. Tell what additional information you need in order to solve the following problem: Sam has 2 baseball cards that are worth $20 each and 3 baseball cards that are worth $7 each. The rest of his cards are worth $1 each. How much is his collection worth in all?

_____

_____

_____

_____

_____

_____

5. Write each number in number-and-word notation.

a. 56,000,000

_____

b. 101,900,000

_____

c. 900,000

_____

d. 70,800,000,000,000

_____

e. 796,300,000,000

_____

Use with Lesson 73.

275

A Coin-Flipping Experiment

1. Suppose you flip a coin 3 times. What is the probability that the coin will land

   a. heads up 3 times? _____

   b. heads up 2 times and tails up 1 time? _____

   c. heads up 1 time and tails up 2 times? _____

   d. tails up 3 times? _____

   e. on the same side of the coin all 3 times (that is, all heads **or** all tails)?

   _____

   Make a tree diagram to help you solve the problem.

2. If you did 3 flips of the coin 100 times, about how many times would you expect

   the coin to land with the same side up on all 3 flips? _____

   What percent of the time is that? _____

276

A Coin-Flipping Experiment (cont.)

3. Flip your coin 3 times. Record the results with a check mark (✔) in the table below, in the "Trial 1" row. Do four more trials, flipping the coin 3 times on each trial. Record the results in the table.

	2 heads, 1 tail	1 head, 2 tails	3 heads	3 tails
Trial 1				
Trial 2				
Trial 3				
Trial 4				
Trial 5				

4. Use the results for your whole class to answer the following questions.

    a. How many times did the coin land with the same side up on all 3 flips? _____

    b. What was the total number of trials (5 times the number of students in the class)? _____

    c. What percent of the time did the coin land with the same side up on all 3 flips? _____

5. Look up your answer to Problem 2 on page 276. Did the class results come close to what you expected? _____

    (The more times you flip the coin, the closer the results should be to what you expected.)

6. Martha flipped a coin 10 times. Each time, the coin landed heads up. She said: "The next time I flip the coin, it must land tails up."

    Is she right? _____ Explain your answer. _____

_____

_____

_____

Math Boxes 74

1. Add or subtract.

   a. $32 + (-52) =$ _____

   b. $16 - 29 =$ _____

   c. $48 - (-63) =$ _____

   d. $-56 + 94 =$ _____

   e. $-28 - (-43) =$ _____

2. I am a 3-dimensional geometric shape. I have 5 faces. Two faces are triangles. The other faces are rectangles.

I am called a

_____.

3. Add or subtract.

   a. $3\frac{2}{3} + 1\frac{4}{5} =$ _____

   b. $8\frac{1}{7} - 3\frac{3}{4} =$ _____

   c. $6\frac{1}{8} - 4\frac{5}{6} =$ _____

   d. $\frac{8}{5} + 3\frac{1}{9} =$ _____

4. Write each number using digits. Then round each number to the nearest ten thousand.

   a. four million, three hundred seventy-two thousand, nine hundred five

    number: _____

    rounded: _____

   b. thirteen million, sixty-eight thousand, four hundred twenty-three

    number: _____

    rounded: _____

5. Give three special cases for the general pattern $\frac{a}{a} = 2 - \frac{a}{a}$.

_____

_____

_____

6. The distance from Chicago to Los Angeles is about 2060 miles. A family drove this distance in 4 days. On average, about how many miles did the family travel each day?

_____

Math Message: Venn Diagrams

A **Venn diagram** is a picture in which circles show relationships among sets.

Example 1:

At Lincoln Middle School, every student is required to take a music class. Seventy-five students play an instrument and take a band or orchestra class. The remaining 300 students take a general music class. Students who take a band or orchestra class do not take the general music class.

You can draw a Venn diagram to illustrate this situation. The circles are drawn so that they do not overlap—students who take a band or orchestra class do not take a general music class, and students who take a general music class do not take a band or orchestra class.

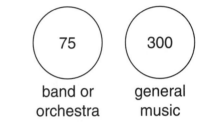

1. How many students are there at Lincoln Middle School? _____

Example 2:

Ms. Barrie teaches both math and science. There are 26 students in her math class and 24 students in her science class. Five of the students in her science class are also in her math class.

A Venn diagram of this situation shows overlapping circles. The overlapping part of the diagram represents the students who are in Ms. Barrie's math class and her science class.

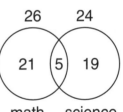

2. Ms. Barrie made a list of all the students in her math and science classes. How many *different* names are on her list? _____

3. Write a number story for the Venn diagram at the right.

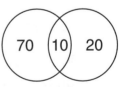

_____

_____

_____

_____

_____

More about Venn Diagrams

1. The sixth graders at Lincoln Middle School were asked whether they write with their left hand or right hand. A small number of students reported that they write equally well with either hand.

   The survey results are shown in the Venn diagram at the right.

   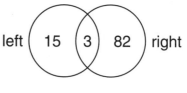

   left (15 (3) 82) right

   a. How many students were surveyed? _____

   b. How many are ambidextrous (write with either hand)? _____

   c. How many always write with their left hand? _____

   d. How many always write with their right hand? _____

   e. How many never write with their left hand? _____

2. Mr. Carlson has 30 students in his sixth grade homeroom. After receiving the final test scores for these students, he identified all students who scored 90% or above on each test.

   Mr. Carlson then drew this Venn diagram.

   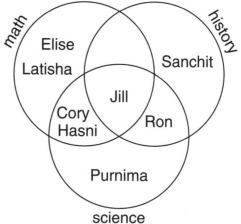

   a. Whose performance was best overall? _____

   b. Who scored 90% or above on at *least 2* tests? _____

   c. Who scored 90% or above on *exactly 1* test? _____

   d. Who scored 90% or above in *both* math and science? _____

   e. Which two tests had the least overlap? _____

   f. What percent of the students in Mr. Carlson's homeroom had a score of 90% or above on *exactly 2* tests? _____

Use with Lesson 75.

Tables and Venn Diagrams

Researchers chose 1000 adults at random and tested them to find out how many were right-handed and how many were left-handed. People who showed no preference were classified according to the hand they used most often in writing.

Each person was also tested to determine which eye was dominant—the right eye or left eye.

The results are shown in the table. For example, the table shows that 30 people were both left-handed and right-eyed.

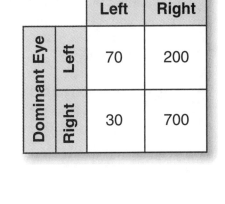

		Dominant Hand	
		Left	Right
Dominant Eye	Left	70	200
	Right	30	700

Refer to the table to answer the following questions.

1. The sum of the numbers in the table is _____

2. a. How many people in the sample were both right-handed and right-eyed? _____

   b. How many people were both right-handed and left-eyed? _____

   c. How many people were right-handed? _____

3. a. How many people in the sample were both left-handed and left-eyed? _____

   b. How many people were left-handed? _____

   c. How many people were left-eyed? _____

4. Use your answers in Problem 3 to complete the Venn diagram. Fill in the missing numbers.

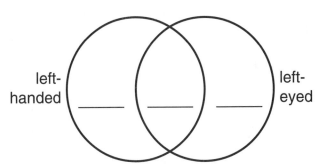

left-handed _____ _____ _____ left-eyed

5. What percent of the people in the sample have their dominant hand and dominant eye on the same side? _____

Math Boxes 75

1. Lou baked chocolate-chip cookies. He made 32 cookies with white chocolate chips. This was 4/9 of all the cookies. How many cookies

did he bake in all? _____

Explain how you found your answer.

_____

_____

_____

2. Complete each sentence with an algebraic expression.

a. If Maria earns x dollars per hour when she baby-sits, then

she earns _____ dollars when she baby-sits for $3\frac{1}{2}$ hours.

b. Bill's dog is 3 years older than his cat. If the dog is y years

old, then the cat is _____ years old.

156

3. Estimate the product by rounding the larger factor to the nearest million.

a. 46,882,003 * 4

_____

b. 831,247 * 27

_____

c. 3,589,221 * 15

_____

d. 20 * 13,402,655

130 _____

4. Write the following numbers with words. The first one has been done for you.

a. 0.89 *eighty-nine hundredths*

b. 249.2 _____

_____

c. 0.432 _____

_____

d. 0.00001 _____

42

5. Complete.   135

a. $16\frac{2}{3}$% of 36 = _____

b. $33\frac{1}{3}$% of 54 = _____

c. 75% of 88 = _____

d. 59% of 100 = _____

e. $12\frac{1}{2}$% of 48 = _____

6. Give this graph a title, label the axes, and describe a situation the graph might represent.

_____

_____

_____

Math Message: Fair and Unfair Games

A **fair game** is a game of chance in which a player has an equal chance of winning or losing. Any other game is an **unfair game.**

Each of the four games described below is for one player. Play Games 1, 2, and 3 a total of 6 times each. Tally the results. Later, you and your classmates will combine results for each game.

Game 1: Put 2 black counters and 1 white counter in a paper bag and shake the bag. Draw one counter. Then draw a second counter without putting the first counter back in the bag. If the 2 counters are the same color, you win. Otherwise, you lose. Play 6 games, and tally your results.

Tally for 6 games: Win _____ Lose _____

Do you think the game is fair?   _____

Combined class data: Win _____ Lose _____

Game 2: Use 2 black counters and 2 white counters. The rules are the same.

Tally for 6 games: Win _____ Lose _____

Do you think the game is fair?   _____

Combined class data: Win _____ Lose _____

Game 3: Use 3 black counters and 1 white counter. The rules are the same.

Tally for 6 games: Win _____ Lose _____

Do you think the game is fair?   _____

Combined class data: Win _____ Lose _____

Game 4: What if you use 4 black counters? The rules are the same.

Do you think the game is fair?   _____

Explain your answer.

_____

_____

_____

Fair Games and Probability

You can use a tree diagram to decide whether a game is fair or unfair. This tree diagram represents Game 1 on page 283.

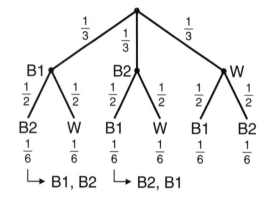

Before you draw the first counter, there are 3 counters in the bag. Although the 2 black counters look alike, they are not the same counters. They are labeled B1 and B2 to tell them apart. The probability of drawing either B1, B2, or W is $\frac{1}{3}$.

After the first draw, there are 2 counters left in the bag. Therefore, the probability of drawing either of the 2 remaining counters is $\frac{1}{2}$.

There are 6 possible ways to draw the counters. The probability of each outcome is $\frac{1}{3} * \frac{1}{2}$, or $\frac{1}{6}$. There are 2 ways to draw the same color counters: (1) B1 on the first draw and B2 on the second draw and (2) B2 on the first draw and B1 on the second draw. The chances of drawing 2 black counters is $\frac{1}{6} + \frac{1}{6}$, which is $\frac{2}{6}$, or $\frac{1}{3}$. Therefore, Game 1 is not a fair game.

Make tree diagrams to help you answer these questions.

1. **a.** What is the probability of winning Game 2? _____

    b. Is Game 2 a fair game? _____

2. **a.** What is the probability of winning Game 3? _____

    b. Is Game 3 a fair game? _____

Making a Fair Game

The directions for the game below need to be more specific.

Sum Game

Materials: ☐ Four number cards or playing cards: 1 (ace), 3, 6, and 10

Directions: Mix the cards and place them facedown on the playing surface. Turn over one of the cards. Then turn over a second card. Add the points on the two cards. The 1-card (ace) is worth 1 point, the 3-card is worth 3 points, and so on. This is your score for the game.

You win this game if you score at least a certain number of points. Otherwise, you lose.

Your job is to figure out this "winning number" so that the game will be fair. In other words, you must find the answer to the following question:

* If this is to be a fair game, what is the least number of points you must score to win?

Answer: You win if you score at least _____ points.

Explain how you found the answer.

_____

_____

_____

_____

_____

_____

_____

_____

_____

Math Boxes 76

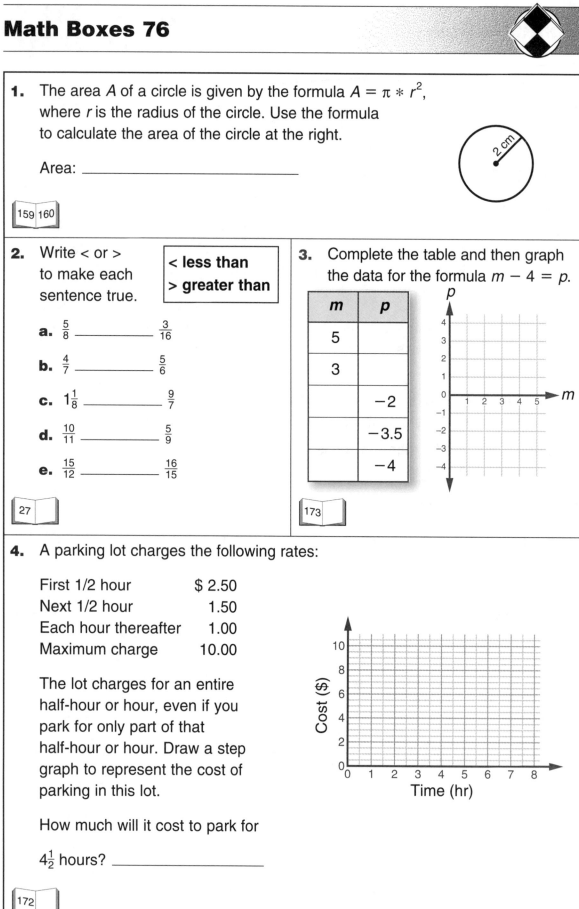

1. The area A of a circle is given by the formula $A = \pi * r^2$, where r is the radius of the circle. Use the formula to calculate the area of the circle at the right.

    Area: _____

    2 cm

    159 160

2. Write < or > to make each sentence true.

    | < less than |
    | > greater than |

    a. $\frac{5}{8}$ _____ $\frac{3}{16}$

    b. $\frac{4}{7}$ _____ $\frac{5}{6}$

    c. $1\frac{1}{8}$ _____ $\frac{9}{7}$

    d. $\frac{10}{11}$ _____ $\frac{5}{9}$

    e. $\frac{15}{12}$ _____ $\frac{16}{15}$

    27

3. Complete the table and then graph the data for the formula $m - 4 = p$.

m	p
5	
3	
	−2
	−3.5
	−4

    173

4. A parking lot charges the following rates:

    | First 1/2 hour | $ 2.50 |
    | Next 1/2 hour | 1.50 |
    | Each hour thereafter | 1.00 |
    | Maximum charge | 10.00 |

    The lot charges for an entire half-hour or hour, even if you park for only part of that half-hour or hour. Draw a step graph to represent the cost of parking in this lot.

    How much will it cost to park for

    $4\frac{1}{2}$ hours? _____

    172

286

Math Message: An Amazin' Contest

The sixth grade class at Bailey School wants to raise money on Parents' Night to buy a microscope. The students have created the maze shown below, which they will use for a contest. Each contestant pays a fee to enter the contest. A contestant who goes from Start to Exit without retracing his or her steps and without ending up at a dead end wins a prize.

Notice that the paths at each intersection are numbered. When a contestant reaches an intersection, the contestant chooses the next path at random by using the random-number generator on a calculator.

Suppose that you are going to try to get through the maze. There are 3 different paths at Start. To decide which to follow, use the key sequence [1] [2nd] [RAND] [3] [=].

If the number 1 comes up, follow Path 1. This leads to a dead end, so you lose.

If the number 2 comes up at Start, follow Path 2. This leads to an intersection that divides into 4 different paths. Use the random-number generator to choose which path to follow next. You win if you follow Path 3.

If the number 3 comes up at Start, follow Path 3. This leads to an intersection that divides into 2 different paths. Use the random-number generator to choose which path to follow next. You win if you follow Path 2.

Work with a partner. Take turns trying to get through the maze. Each of you should try a total of 6 times. What fraction of the time did you and your partner reach the Exit?

Analyzing the Amazin' Contest

Solve the following problems. Make a tree diagram in the space below.

1. Suppose that the prize is $12. If 60 people pay an entry fee of $5, how much can the class expect to make?   _____

2. Suppose that the class charges $5 to enter the contest. If 60 people enter, how much should the prize be if the class wants to break even?   _____

3. The class estimates that 80 people will pay $5 to enter the contest. Their goal is to make $100. How much should the prize be?   _____

My tree diagram:

Analyzing the Amazin' Contest (cont.)

4. Explain how you solved Problem 1 on page 288.

_____

_____

_____

_____

_____

5. Explain how you solved Problem 2 on page 288.

_____

_____

_____

_____

_____

6. Explain how you solved Problem 3 on page 288.

_____

_____

_____

_____

_____

Math Boxes 77

1. Cherise made a deal with her mother. If Cherise could mow the lawn in 1 hour or less, she would get paid double. In 45 minutes, Cherise finished mowing 7/10 of the lawn. If she continues to mow at the same rate, will she finish mowing the lawn in time to be paid double?

_____

Explain how you found your answer.

_____

_____

_____

_____

3. Estimate each product by rounding the larger factor to the nearest ten thousand.

a. 313,457 * 5 _____

b. 2,773,029 * 2 _____

c. 49,221 * 30 _____

d. 12 * 402,655 _____

2. Complete the following statements with an algebraic expression.

a. If each bag of potatoes weighs at least P pounds, then 6 bags weigh at least

_____ pounds.

b. Jack is 6 inches taller than Michael. If Jack is h inches tall, then Michael is _____ inches tall.

4. Write the following numbers with words.

a. 0.001 _____

_____

b. 0.017 _____

_____

c. 0.0001 _____

_____

d. 2.603 _____

_____

5. Complete.

a. 80% of 50 = _____

b. 10% of 83 = _____

c. 25% of 48 = _____

d. 35% of 100 = _____

e. 50% of 72 = _____

6. Give this graph a title, label the axes, and describe a situation the graph might represent.

_____

_____

_____

Use with Lesson 77.

Math Message: Guessing on Multiple-Choice Tests

Imagine that you are taking a multiple-choice test. Three possible answers are given for each question. You are to circle the correct answer.

1. Suppose that there are 15 questions for which you don't know the correct answer. You decide to guess at an answer for each of these questions.

   a. What is the probability (chance) of choosing the correct answer? _____

   b. How many of the 15 questions would you expect to answer correctly by guessing? _____

   Why? _____

   _____

   _____

2. In scoring the test, each correct answer is worth 1 point. To discourage guessing, there is a small penalty for each incorrect answer. What do you think would be a fair penalty for an incorrect answer? _____

   Explain. _____

   _____

   _____

Narrowing Your Choices on Multiple-Choice Tests

When you play board games or card games or answer fun quizzes where there is no penalty for guessing incorrectly, guessing can be a valuable tool for improving a score. You will improve your chances of guessing correctly if you can eliminate some of the choices before you guess. On the following pages, you will investigate the benefits (or disadvantages) that can result from guessing on multiple-choice tests.

Guessing is usually *not* encouraged for school tests or achievement tests, even if a penalty is not assessed for incorrect answers. A score that is inflated by guessing gives a misleading view of the test taker's skills and knowledge.

Guessing on Multiple-Choice Tests

1. For each question on the following test, first draw a line through each answer that you know is not correct. Then circle one answer for each question. If you do not know the correct answer, guess. Number correct: _____

---

1. A nautical mile is equal to
- **A.** 1 foot
- **B.** 1 yard
- **C.** 1832 meters
- **D.** 1852 meters

2. In 1994, the population of Nevada was
- **A.** 1 billion
- **B.** 1,475,028
- **C.** 1,457,028
- **D.** 14,628

3. Which region receives the greatest average annual rainfall?
- **A.** Atlanta, Georgia
- **B.** New Orleans, Louisiana
- **C.** Mojave Desert, California
- **D.** Sahara Desert, Africa

4. The addition sign (+) was introduced into mathematics by
- **A.** Johann Widman
- **B.** Johann Rahn
- **C.** Bill Clinton
- **D.** Martin Luther King, Jr.

5. How many diagonals does a 13-sided polygon (13-gon) have?
- **A.** 1
- **B.** 54
- **C.** 65
- **D.** 13,000

6. The leading cause of death in the United States is
- **A.** bungee jumping
- **B.** cancer
- **C.** drowning
- **D.** heart disease

---

2. When you can narrow the choices for a question to two possible answers, what is the chance of guessing the correct answer? _____

   a. How many of the six questions do you think you answered correctly? _____

   b. Is it likely that you will get all six correct? _____

   c. Is it likely that you will get all six wrong? _____

3. Suppose that each correct answer is worth 1 point and each incorrect answer carries a penalty of $\frac{1}{3}$ point. Complete the "Total Points" column of the table. You will complete the Class Tally column later.

Number Correct	Number Incorrect	Total Points	Class Tally
6	0	*6*	
5	1		
4	2		
3	3		
2	4	$2 - \frac{4}{3} = \frac{2}{3}$	
1	5		
0	6		

 Use with Lesson 78.

Guessing on Multiple-Choice Tests (cont.)

4. For each question on the following test, first draw a line through each answer that you know is not correct. Then circle one answer for each question. If you do not know the correct answer, guess. Number correct: _____

---

1. The neck of a 152-pound person weighs about

    A. 100 pounds

    B. $12\frac{1}{2}$ pounds

    C. $11\frac{1}{2}$ pounds

    D. $10\frac{1}{2}$ pounds

2. The average height of a full grown weeping willow tree is

    A. 50 feet

    B. 45 feet

    C. 35 feet

    D. 2 feet

3. The normal daily high temperature for July in Cleveland, Ohio, is

    A. 84°F

    B. 82°F

    C. 80°F

    D. 0°F

4. The circumference of Earth at the equator is about

    A. 24,901.6 miles

    B. 24,801.6 miles

    C. 24,701.6 miles

    D. 2000 miles

5. In 1994, the average American consumed about 141 pounds of which food?

    A. sugar

    B. spinach

    C. potatoes

    D. rice

6. A slice of white bread has about how many calories?

    A. 3

    B. 65

    C. 70

    D. 75

Source: *Numbers.*

---

5. When you can narrow the choices for a question to three possible answers, what is the chance of guessing the correct answer? _____

    a. How many of the six questions do you think you answered correctly? _____

    b. Is it likely that you will get all six correct? _____

    c. Is it likely that you will get all six wrong? _____

6. Suppose that each correct answer is worth 1 point and each incorrect answer carries a penalty of $\frac{1}{3}$ point. Complete the "Total Points" column of the table at the right.

Number Correct	Number Incorrect	Total Points	Class Tally
6	0	*6*	
5	1		
4	2		
3	3		
2	4	$2 - \frac{4}{3} = \frac{2}{3}$	
1	5		
0	6		

Guessing on Multiple-Choice Tests (cont.)

7. First draw a line through each answer that you know cannot be correct. Then circle one answer for each question. If you do not know the answer, guess. Make sure to answer all questions.

Scoring is the same as on previous tests: 1 point for each correct answer and $\frac{1}{3}$ point off for each incorrect answer. Number correct: _____

1. The area of a standard playing card is about
   - **A.** 25 in^2
   - **B.** 7.9 in^2
   - **C.** 7.6 in^2
   - **D.** 1 in^2

2. The fastest speed a base runner has circled the bases in baseball is almost
   - **A.** 2 km/hr
   - **B.** 30 km/hr
   - **C.** 28 km/hr
   - **D.** 32 km/hr

3. It took about 33,000 worker-years (number of workers * number of years) to complete which of the following?
   - **A.** Yankee Stadium
   - **B.** first McDonald's Restaurant in the U.S.
   - **C.** Great Pyramid at Giza, Egypt
   - **D.** Great Wall of China

4. The average number of quills on a porcupine is about
   - **A.** 30,000
   - **B.** 25,000
   - **C.** 100
   - **D.** 10

5. The size of the smallest dust particles is about
   - **A.** 0.01 cm
   - **B.** 5 cm
   - **C.** 50 cm
   - **D.** 100 cm

6. What is the fastest crawling insect, with a speed of almost 3 mph?
   - **A.** cockroach
   - **B.** ladybug
   - **C.** inchworm
   - **D.** carpenter ant

7. At age 120, the oldest person alive in 1995 was
   - **A.** Ronald Reagan
   - **B.** Shigeychico Izumi
   - **C.** Michael Jordan
   - **D.** Hillary Clinton

8. A modern light bulb lasts about 2500 hours. About how long did Edison's first successful light bulb last?
   - **A.** 5000 hours
   - **B.** 60 hours
   - **C.** 50 hours
   - **D.** 40 hours

9. About how much water can a camel drink in 10 minutes?
   - **A.** 1 cup
   - **B.** 1 pint
   - **C.** 30 gal
   - **D.** 35 gal

Source: *Sizesaurus.*

Use with Lesson 78.

Guessing on Multiple-Choice Tests (cont.)

8. How many questions could you answer without guessing? _____

9. a. For how many questions did you have 2 realistic choices? _____

   b. What would be your maximum score for these questions? _____

   c. What would be your minimum score for these questions? _____

   d. What would be your expected score for these questions? _____

10. a. For how many questions did you have 3 realistic choices? _____

   b. What would be your maximum score for these questions? _____

   c. What would be your minimum score for these questions? _____

   d. What would be your expected score for these questions? _____

11. a. Overall, what is the highest possible score you could achieve? _____

   b. Overall, what is the lowest possible score you could achieve? _____

   c. What would your expected score be? _____

   d. How did you calculate your expected score? _____

   _____

   _____

12. If you were not instructed to guess on the problems you weren't sure about,

   would you have skipped some? _____

   Explain. _____

   _____

Challenge

13. If the scoring was changed to 1 point for each correct answer and
    $\frac{1}{2}$ off for each incorrect answer, would you have answered
    all the questions on the test, guessing when necessary? _____

   Explain. _____

   _____

Math Boxes 78

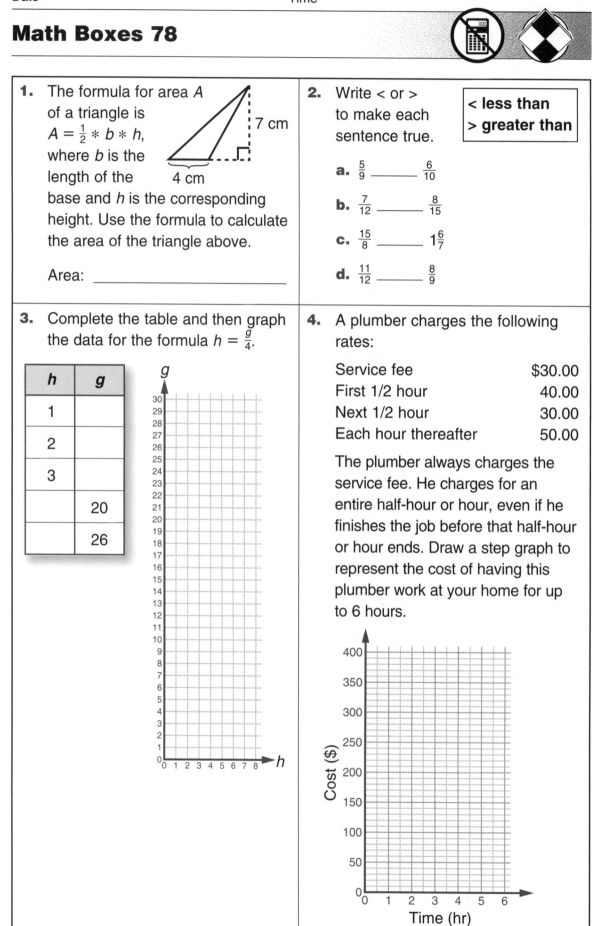

1. The formula for area A of a triangle is $A = \frac{1}{2} * b * h$, where b is the length of the base and h is the corresponding height. Use the formula to calculate the area of the triangle above.

7 cm

4 cm

Area: _____

2. Write < or > to make each sentence true.

| < less than |
| > greater than |

a. $\frac{5}{9}$ _____ $\frac{6}{10}$

b. $\frac{7}{12}$ _____ $\frac{8}{15}$

c. $\frac{15}{8}$ _____ $1\frac{6}{7}$

d. $\frac{11}{12}$ _____ $\frac{8}{9}$

3. Complete the table and then graph the data for the formula $h = \frac{g}{4}$.

h	g
1	
2	
3	
	20
	26

4. A plumber charges the following rates:

Service fee	$30.00
First 1/2 hour	40.00
Next 1/2 hour	30.00
Each hour thereafter	50.00

The plumber always charges the service fee. He charges for an entire half-hour or hour, even if he finishes the job before that half-hour or hour ends. Draw a step graph to represent the cost of having this plumber work at your home for up to 6 hours.

Use with Lesson 78.

Math Message: Time to Reflect

1. Here are some statements that describe chance events.

- It is likely that the Cougars will win the game.

- The probability of rain tomorrow is 30%.

- If I don't know which of two answers to a multiple-choice question is correct and I guess, I have a 50–50 chance of being right.

Make up at least two other statements that describe a chance event.

_____

_____

_____

_____

_____

_____

_____

_____

2. Think about the work you did in this unit. What did you like best? Why?

_____

_____

_____

_____

_____

_____

_____

_____

_____

Math Boxes 79

1. Add or subtract. Do not use your calculator.

   a. $55 + (-78) =$ _____

   b. $94 - (-23) =$ _____

   c. $-36 - (-65) =$ _____

   d. $-18 - 27 =$ _____

   e. $-138 + 89 =$ _____

2. The volume V of a rectangular prism is given by the formula

$$V = l * w * h$$

where l is the length of the prism, w is the width, and h is the height. Use the formula to calculate the volume of the rectangular prism below.

Volume: _____

3. Multiply. Write each answer in simplest form.

   a. $\frac{5}{6} * 4 =$ _____

   b. $3\frac{2}{3} * 2\frac{7}{8} =$ _____

   c. $\frac{12}{10} * \frac{11}{5} =$ _____

   d. $\frac{4}{3} * 3\frac{6}{7} =$ _____

   e. $6\frac{1}{4} * 3\frac{11}{8} =$ _____

4. The following formula can be used to convert temperatures from Fahrenheit to Celsius:

$$C = (F - 32) * 5/9$$

where C is the temperature in degrees Celsius and F is the temperature in degrees Fahrenheit. Calculate the temperature in degrees Celsius for the following Fahrenheit temperatures:

   a. $68°F =$ _____ $°C$

   b. $41°F =$ _____ $°C$

   c. $131°F =$ _____ $°C$

5. Franklin read 120 pages of a 160-page book. If it took him 3 hours to read that far, about how much longer will it take him to finish the book if he reads at the same rate? _____

Explain how you found your answer. _____

_____

_____

Use with Lesson 79.

Math Message: Multiplication and Division Properties

1. **a.** If you multiply a number by 1, what number do you get? _____

    b. Give 3 examples. Choose a whole number, a fraction, and a decimal.

    Whole number: _____ *5 * 1 = 5* _____   Fraction: _____

    Decimal: _____

    c. Complete: If y is a whole number, fraction, or decimal,

    then $y * 1 =$ _____ and $1 * y =$ _____.

2. **a.** If you divide a number by 1, what number do you get? _____

    b. Give 3 examples.

    Whole number: _____   Fraction: _____

    Decimal: _____

    c. Complete: If y is a whole number, fraction, or decimal,

    then $y/1 =$ _____ and $\frac{y}{1} =$ _____.

3. **a.** If you divide any number, except 0, by itself, what number do you get? _____

    b. Give 3 examples.

    Whole number: _____   Fraction: _____

    Decimal: _____

    c. Complete: If y is any whole number, fraction, or decimal, except 0,

    then $y/y =$ _____ and $\frac{y}{y} =$ _____.

4. Suppose you wanted to explain to a third grader how to solve the problem $\frac{2}{3} * \frac{3}{5}$. What would you say? Be sure to use words he or she already knows or define any words the child may not know.

    _____

    _____

    _____

    _____

Reuprocals

Reciprocal Property

If a and b are any numbers, except 0, then $\frac{a}{b} * \frac{b}{a} = 1$.

$\frac{a}{b}$ and $\frac{b}{a}$ are called reciprocals of each other.

$a * \frac{1}{a} = 1$, so a and $\frac{1}{a}$ are reciprocals of each other.

20 | 191

1. Find the reciprocal of each number. Then check your answers with a calculator.

    a. 6 _____

    b. $\frac{3}{8}$ _____

    c. 0.1 _____

    d. $4\frac{2}{3}$ _____

    e. π _____

    f. -2 _____

2. What sequence of calculator keys would you press to find the reciprocal of the reciprocal of $\frac{7}{8}$? _____

    What number will be shown in the display? _____

36 | 37

Multiply. Write your answers in simplest form. When you and your partner have finished solving the problems, compare your answers. If you disagree on an answer, check it with a calculator.

3. $\frac{5}{6} * \frac{3}{10} =$ _____

4. $6 * \frac{2}{3} =$ _____

5. $\frac{7}{8} * \frac{8}{7} =$ _____

6. $2\frac{3}{4} * \frac{4}{1} =$ _____

7. $2\frac{3}{5} * 1\frac{2}{3} =$ _____

8. $\frac{7}{3} * \frac{1}{3} =$ _____

9. $\frac{1}{4} * \frac{2}{5} =$ _____

10. $3\frac{3}{8} * \frac{3}{4} =$ _____

11. $1\frac{5}{6} * 4\frac{2}{3} =$ _____

12. $\frac{7}{10} * 2\frac{3}{5} =$ _____

Use with Lesson 80.

Math Boxes 80

1. For each of the following, tell which measure is needed: perimeter, circumference, area, or volume.

   a. Jean is going to tile her kitchen floor. She needs to know how many square-foot tiles to buy. _____

   b. Tyrone needs to add 1 drop of anti-chlorine solution to his aquarium for every 2 liters of water. He wants to know how many drops to add. _____

   c. Mrs. Vui plans to build a circular fence around her garden. She wants to know how much fencing to buy. _____

   116 118 122

2. Add or subtract.

   a. $23 + (-32) =$ _____

   b. $-14 + (-78) =$ _____

   c. $-800 + 275 =$ _____

   d. _____ $= 45 - 155$

   e. _____ $= -195 - (-223)$

   56 57

3. Write each number in standard notation.

   a. 72 billion = _____

   b. 0.3 trillion = _____

   c. 42.78 million = _____

   d. 89.6 billion = _____

   e. 0.5 million = _____

   5

4. Draw an acute angle *QRS*. Then measure it.

   Measure of $\angle QRS$ is about _____.

   72

5. Fill in the missing equivalents.

Fraction	Decimal	Percent
$\frac{3}{4}$		
	0.24	
		65%
	0.365	
$\frac{45}{90}$		

   44 47

Math Message: "Fraction of" Problems

If you wanted to find out how many 12-inch segments there are on a yardstick, you could simply count by 12 inches from one end of the yardstick to the other: 12, 24, 36. There are three 12-inch segments.

Or you could ask yourself: "How many 12s are there in 36?" and write the division number model $36/12 = 3$. To check that 3 is the correct answer, you could write the multiplication number model $3 * 12 = 36$.

Solve as many of the problems on this page as you can. Write a division number model for each problem. Write a multiplication number model to check the answer.

At first you may want to solve the problems by counting on an inch ruler. Look for patterns. The answer to one problem may help you solve the next problem.

		Division Model	**Check**
Example:			
How many $\frac{1}{2}$-inch segments are there in 1 inch?	2	$1 \div \frac{1}{2}$	$2 * \frac{1}{2}$
1. How many $\frac{1}{2}$-inch segments are there in 2 inches?			
2. How many $\frac{1}{2}$-inch segments are there in $1\frac{1}{2}$ inches?			
3. How many $\frac{1}{4}$s are there in 1?			
4. How many $\frac{1}{4}$s are there in 2?			
5. How many $\frac{1}{4}$s are there in $1\frac{1}{2}$?			
6. How many $\frac{3}{8}$s are there in $1\frac{1}{2}$?			
7. How many $\frac{3}{8}$s are there in $\frac{3}{4}$?			
8. How many $\frac{2}{4}$s are there in 1?			
9. How many $\frac{2}{4}$s are there in $1\frac{1}{2}$?			
10. How many $\frac{2}{4}$s are there in $1\frac{1}{4}$?			
11. How many $\frac{2}{3}$s are there in 2?			
12. How many $\frac{2}{3}$s are there in 1?			
13. How many $\frac{2}{3}$s are there in $\frac{1}{2}$?			

302

Division of Fractions and Mixed Numbers

Division of Fractions Algorithm

$$\frac{a}{b} \div \frac{c}{d} = \frac{a}{b} * \frac{d}{c}$$

Divide. Show your work. Write your answers in simplest form.

1. $\frac{3}{8} \div \frac{5}{6} =$ _____ $\frac{3}{8} * \frac{6}{5}$ _____   **2.** $\frac{4}{7} \div \frac{2}{3} =$ _____

Answer: _____ $\frac{9}{20}$ _____   Answer: _____

3. $\frac{3}{10} \div \frac{3}{8} =$ _____   **4.** $\frac{11}{12} \div \frac{8}{5} =$ _____

Answer: _____   Answer: _____

5. $\frac{7}{8} \div \frac{4}{9} =$ _____   **6.** $\frac{7}{12} \div \frac{1}{3} =$ _____

Answer: _____   Answer: _____

7. $\frac{5}{9} \div \frac{1}{10} =$ _____   **8.** $\frac{3}{4} \div \frac{7}{8} =$ _____

Answer: _____   Answer: _____

Division of Fractions and Mixed Numbers (cont.)

Divide. Show your work. Write your answers in simplest form.

9. $\frac{5}{3} \div \frac{3}{5} =$ _____ **10.** $\frac{9}{10} \div \frac{2}{3} =$ _____

Answer: _____ Answer: _____

11. $1\frac{5}{8} \div \frac{4}{9} =$ _____ **12.** $\frac{3}{8} \div \frac{8}{2} =$ _____

Answer: _____ Answer: _____

13. $\frac{5}{4} \div \frac{16}{8} =$ _____ **14.** $1\frac{2}{3} \div 2\frac{1}{4} =$ _____

Answer: _____ Answer: _____

15. $\frac{1}{4} \div \frac{8}{9} =$ _____ **16.** $3\frac{7}{8} \div 1\frac{3}{4} =$ _____

Answer: _____ Answer: _____

Use with Lesson 81.

Math Boxes 81

1. The spreadsheet shows Evelyn's and Ann's scores on their first three spelling tests.

	A	B	C	D	E
1	Student	Test 1	Test 2	Test 3	Average Score
2	Evelyn	95	90	85	
3	Ann	80	75	100	

   a. What information is shown in Cell C2? _____

   b. Calculate the values for Cells E2 and E3 and enter them in the spreadsheet.

   c. Circle the correct formula for Evelyn's average score on Tests 1–3.

   (A2 + B2 + C3)/3   (B1 + B2 + B3)/3   (B2 + C2 + D2)/3 | 174 |

2. Rename each fraction as a mixed number or a whole number.

   a. $\frac{5}{3}$ = _____

   b. $\frac{8}{4}$ = _____

   c. _____ = $\frac{13}{7}$

   d. _____ = $\frac{9}{5}$

   e. _____ = $\frac{16}{6}$ | 24 |

3. Fill in the missing numbers. | 64 |

   a. 947 * 23 * 16 =

      16 * 23 * _____

   b. 18 * 7 * 3 = 21 * _____

   c. _____ * 51 * 97 = 51 * 97 * 82

   d. _____ * 14 * 182 = 28 * 182

   e. _____ * 29 * 30 = 150 * 29

4. Multiply.
   a. 602 * 59 = _____

   b. 218 * 193 = _____

| 12 |

5. Estimate each product by rounding the larger factor to the nearest million.

   a. 19,304,767 * 3

      _____

   b. 5 * 29,789,124

      _____

   c. 867,259 * 7

      _____

   d. 25,483,001 * 40

| 130 | 131 | _____

Math Message: Signed Numbers on a Calculator

Read the section "Positive and Negative Numbers" at the bottom of page 183 in your *Student Reference Book.* Then use your calculator to solve the problems below.

1. Enter each number into your calculator. Record the calculator display. Clear.

Enter -236 -4.85 -2π $-(\frac{2}{3})$ -0.006 $(-4)^2$ $(-8)^5$

Display   _____ _____ _____ _____ _____ _____ _____

2. To enter the opposite of a number, first enter the number and then press the [↔] key. For example, to enter the opposite of 12, enter 12 and press the [↔] key. The display shows -12. Now press the [↔] key again. The display shows 12, the opposite of -12. Try it.

We can write "the opposite of -12" as "$-(-12)$" or as "(op) (-12)." The symbol (op) is read "the opposite of."

Enter each number into your calculator. Record the calculator display. Clear.

Enter   (op) 75   (op) (-89) (op) (-312) (op) 27 * 16 $-(-18 + 56)$

Display   _____ _____ _____ _____ _____

3. Add or subtract with a calculator.

a. $-26 - 17 =$ _____

$-26 + (op)\ 17 =$ _____

b. $-34 - 68 =$ _____

$-34 + (-68) =$ _____

c. $56 - 24 =$ _____

$56 + (op)\ 24 =$ _____

d. $18 - 84 =$ _____

$18 + (-84) =$ _____

e. $43 - (-97) =$ _____

$43 + (op)\ (-97) =$ _____

$43 + 97 =$ _____

f. $31 - (-13) =$ _____

$31 + (-(-13)) =$ _____

$31 + 13 =$ _____

g. $-130 - (-62) =$ _____

$-130 + (op)\ (-62) =$ _____

$-130 + 62 =$ _____

h. $-2 - (-22) =$ _____

$-2 + (-(-22)) =$ _____

$-2 + 22 =$ _____

306

Subtraction of Positive and Negative Numbers

One way to subtract one number from another number is to change the subtraction problem into an addition problem.

> **Subtraction Rule**
> To subtract a number b from a number a, add the opposite of b to a.
> Thus, for any numbers a and b, $a - b = a + (\text{op}) b$, or $a - b = a + (-b)$.

Examples:

$6 - 9 = 6 + (\text{op}) 9 = 6 + (-9) = -3$

$-15 - (-23) = -15 + (\text{op}) (-23) = -15 + 23 = 8$

$-8 - 7 = -8 + (\text{op}) 7 = -8 + (-7) = -15$

Rewrite each subtraction problem as an addition problem. Then solve the problem.

1. $22 - (15) =$ _____ $22 + (op) \ 15 = 22 + (-15) = 7$ _____

2. $-35 - 20 =$ _____

3. $-3 - (-4.5) =$ _____

4. $-27 - (-27) =$ _____

5. $-16 - (16) =$ _____

6. $0 - (-\pi) =$ _____

Subtract.

7. $-23 - (-5) =$ _____   **8.** $9 - (-54) =$ _____

9. $-(\frac{4}{5}) - 1\frac{1}{5} =$ _____   **10.** $\$1.25 - (-\$6.75) =$ _____

11. $-76 - (-56) =$ _____   **12.** $-27 - 100 =$ _____

Fill in the missing numbers.

13. _____ $+ 5 = -10$ **14.** _____ $+ (-5) = -10$ **15.** $-9 +$ _____ $= 0$

     $-10 - 5 =$ _____ $-10 - (-5) =$ _____ $0 - (-9) =$ _____

16. $16 +$ _____ $= -7$ **17.** $-25 +$ _____ $= 15$ **18.** _____ $+ 13 = -8$

     $-7 - 16 =$ _____ $15 - (-25) =$ _____ $-8 - 13 =$ _____

Math Boxes 82

1. Do the following on the grid.

   a. Mark point (4,−2). Label it *A*.

   b. Mark point (−4,2). Label it *B*.

   c. Draw line segment *AB*.

   d. Find the coordinates of the midpoint of $\overline{AB}$. (__, __)

87

2. Reshi's brother was 8 when Reshi was born. Reshi's brother is now twice as old as Reshi.
How old is Reshi now? _____
Explain how you got your answer.

_____

_____

_____

_____

156

3. Write the value of the digit 4 in each numeral.

   a. 364,091 _____

   b. 2,043,877 _____

   c. 20.004 _____

   d. 51.047 _____

   e. 139,047 _____

5   41

4. Add or subtract.

   a. 42.8 + 5.2 = _____

   b. 1.206 + 0.58 = _____

   c. $3.85 − $1.17 = _____

   d. _____ = 105.33 − 97.5

   e. _____ = 13.659 + 3.6

48   49

5. Divide.

   a. 826/34 → _____

   b. 7968/75 → _____

15

Math Message: Multiplication Patterns

In each of Problems 1–4, complete the patterns in Part a. Check your answers with a calculator. Then circle the word in parentheses that correctly completes the statement in Part b.

1. **a.** $6 * 4 = 24$
    $6 * 3 = 18$
    $6 * 2 =$ _____
    $6 * 1 =$ _____
    $6 * 0 =$ _____

    b. **Positive * Positive Rule:**
    When a positive number is multiplied by a positive number, the product is a

    (positive or negative) number.

2. **a.** $5 * 2 = 10$
    $5 * 1 = 5$
    $5 * 0 = 0$
    $5 * (-1) =$ _____
    $5 * (-2) =$ _____

    b. **Positive * Negative Rule:**
    When a positive number is multiplied by a negative number, the product is a

    (positive or negative) number.

3. **a.** $2 * 3 = 6$
    $1 * 3 = 3$
    $0 * 3 = 0$
    $-1 * 3 =$ _____
    $-2 * 3 =$ _____

    b. **Negative * Positive Rule:**
    When a negative number is multiplied by a positive number, the product is a

    (positive or negative) number.

4. **a.** $-4 * 1 = -4$
    $-4 * 0 = 0$
    $-4 * (-1) = 4$
    $-4 * (-2) =$ _____
    $-4 * (-3) =$ _____

    b. **Negative * Negative Rule:**
    When a negative number is multiplied by a negative number, the product is a

    (positive or negative) number.

5. **a.** Solve.
    $-1 * 6 =$ _____
    $-1 * (-7.7) =$ _____
    $-1 * -(-\frac{1}{2}) =$ _____
    $-1 * m =$ _____

    b. **Multiplication Property of −1:**
    For any number a,
    $-1 * a = a * -1 = $ (op) a, or $-a$.
    Since the number a can be a negative number, (op) a or $-a$ can be a positive number. For example, if $a = -5$, then $-a = $ (op) $-5 = 5$.

Fact Families for Multiplication and Division

A **fact family** is a group of four basic related multiplication and division facts.

Example: The fact family for 6 * 3 = 18 is made up of the following multiplication and division facts:

6 * 3 = 18   3 * 6 = 18   18/6 = 3   18/3 = 6

As you already know, when a positive number is divided by a positive number, the quotient is a positive number. Problems 1 and 2 will help you discover the rules for division with negative numbers.

Complete the fact families. Check your answers to the division facts with a calculator. Then complete each rule.

1. a. 5 * (−3) = _____   **b.** 6 * (−8) = _____   **c.** 5 * (−5) = _____

   −3 * 5 = _____   −8 * 6 = _____   _____

   −15/(−3) = _____   −48/(−8) = _____   _____

   −15/5 = _____   −48/6 = _____   _____

d. Negative/Negative Rule: When a negative number is divided by a negative number, the quotient is a _____ (positive or negative) number.

e. Negative/Positive Rule: When a negative number is divided by a positive number, the quotient is a _____ (positive or negative) number.

2. a. −4 * (−3) = _____   **b.** −7 * (−5) = _____   **c.** −2 * (−10) = ____

   −3 * (−4) = _____   _____   _____

   12/(−3) = _____   _____   _____

   12/(−4) = _____   _____   _____

d. Positive/Negative Rule: When a positive number is divided by a negative number, the quotient is a _____ (positive or negative) number.

3. Fill in the missing numbers. Check your answers with a calculator.

   a. _____ * (−4) = 24 (*Think:* What number multiplied by −4 is equal to 24?)

   b. _____ * 9 = −81   **c.** −6 * _____ = 48   **d.** _____ * (−3) = −27

   e. −81/9 = _____   **f.** 48/(−6) = _____   **g.** −27/(−3) = _____

310

Multiplication/Division of Signed Numbers

Multiplication Property	Division Property
For all numbers *a* and *b,* if the values of *a* and *b* are both positive or both negative, then the product *a* ∗ *b* is a positive number. If one of the values is positive and the other is negative, then the product *a* ∗ *b* is a negative number.	For all numbers *a* and *b,* if the values of *a* and *b* are both positive or both negative, then the quotient *a/b* is a positive number. If one of the values is positive and the other is negative, then the quotient *a/b* is a negative number.

Fill in the missing numbers. Use a calculator to check your answers.

1. $-7 * 8 = $ _____

2. $73 * (-45) = $ _____

3. $-10 * $ _____ $ = 70$

4. $\frac{1}{2} * (-\frac{3}{4}) = $ _____

5. $0.5 * (-15) = $ _____

6. _____ $ * 3.3 = -3.3$

7. $-3 * 4 * (-7) = $ _____

8. _____ $ * (-8) * (-3) = -48$

9. $-54/9 = $ _____

10. $36/(-12) = $ _____

11. $-\frac{3}{5}/(-\frac{4}{5}) = $ _____

12. $45/(-5)/(-3) = $ _____

13. _____ $/15 = -6$

14. $72/(-8) = $ _____

15. $-99/$ _____ $ = 11$

16. $\frac{1}{2}/(-\frac{3}{4}) = $ _____

17. $-3 * (-4 + 6) = $ _____

18. $32/(-5 - 3) = $ _____

19. $(-9 * 4) + 6 = $ _____

20. $(-75/5) + (-20) = $ _____

21. $(-6 * 3) + (-6 * 5) = $ _____

22. $(4 * (-7)) - (4 * (-3)) = $ _____

Evaluate each expression for $y = -4$.

23. $3 * (-y) = $ _____

24. $-y/(-6) = $ _____

25. $y * (-7 + 3) = $ _____

26. $y - (y + 2) = $ _____

27. $(-8 * y) - 6 = $ _____

28. $(-8 * 6) - (-8 * y) = $ _____

Use with Lesson 83.

Date   Time

Math Boxes 83

1. For each of the following, tell which measure is needed: perimeter, circumference, area, or volume.

   a. Warren plans to install wood molding where his living room walls meet the ceiling. He needs to know how much wood to buy. _____

   b. Tina runs on a circular track. She knows the diameter of the track. She wants to find the distance around. _____

   c. Fertilizer is to be added to Flo's garden at the rate of 1 cup for every 20 square feet. Flo wants to know how much fertilizer to add. _____

2. Add or subtract.

   a. _____ $= -303 + (-28)$

   b. _____ $= 245 - 518$

   c. _____ $= -73 + 89$

   d. $176 + (-95) =$ _____

   e. $280 - (-31) =$ _____

3. Write each number in standard notation.

   a. 14.05 billion =

   _____

   b. 2.3 trillion =

   _____

   c. 389.1 million =

   _____

   d. 5.07 billion =

   _____

   e. 88.08 trillion =

   _____

4. Draw a reflex angle *LNE*. Then measure it.

   Measure of
   ∠*LNE* is about _____ .

5. Fill in the missing equivalents.

Fraction	Decimal	Percent
$\frac{7}{8}$		
	0.73	
		30%
	0.675	
$\frac{28}{40}$		

312

Use with Lesson 83.

Math Boxes 84

1. The spreadsheet shows Cecilia's utility bills for two months.

	A	B	C	D	E
1	Month	Phone	Electric	Gas	Total
2	January	$17.95	$38.50	$120.50	
3	February	$34.70	$35.60	$148.96	

a. If Cecilia entered the wrong electric bill for February, which cell should she correct? _____

b. Calculate the values for Cells E2 and E3 and enter them in the spreadsheet.

c. Circle the correct formula for the total cost of utilities in February.

A2 + B2 + C2 + D2   B3 + C3 + D3   (B2 + C2 + D2)/3

---

2. Rename each fraction as a mixed number or a whole number.

a. $\frac{15}{2}$ = _____

b. $\frac{18}{3}$ = _____

c. $\frac{12}{1}$ = _____

d. _____ = $\frac{1000}{1000}$

e. _____ = $\frac{29}{6}$

3. Fill in the missing numbers.

a. 58 * 91 * 27 = 27 * 58 * _____

b. 24 * 16 * 10 = 240 * _____

c. _____ * 35 * 94 = 35 * 94 * 87

d. _____ * 500 = 25 * 20 * 153

e. _____ * 426 * 81 = 81 * 945 * 426

---

4. Multiply.

a. 431 * 87 = _____

b. 956 * 306 = _____

5. Estimate each product by rounding the larger factor to the nearest million.

a. 65,002,389 * 2

_____

b. 300,894,115 * 3

_____

c. 15,224,025 * 5

_____

d. 501,444 * 7

_____

e. 9,657,077 * 9

_____

Order of Operations

<u>P</u>lease <u>E</u>xcuse <u>M</u>y <u>D</u>ear <u>A</u>unt <u>S</u>ally
<u>P</u>arentheses <u>E</u>xponents <u>M</u>ultiplication <u>D</u>ivision <u>A</u>ddition <u>S</u>ubtraction

Evaluate each expression. Then compare your answers to those of your partner. If you don't agree on an answer, check it with a calculator.

Easy

1. $4 * 6 + 3 = $ _____

2. $33 - 16/4 = $ _____

3. $4 * 7 - (3 + 5) = $ _____

4. $24/6 * 4 = $ _____

Moderate

5. $7 - 5 + 13 - 23 - 17 = $ _____

6. $12 * 2^2 - 3^3 = $ _____

7. $7/7 * 4 + 3^2 = $ _____

8. $5 - 15 + 3 * 2 = $ _____

Use with Lesson 85.

Order of Operations (cont.)

Please Excuse My Dear Aunt Sally

Parentheses Exponents Multiplication Division Addition Subtraction

Evaluate each expression. Then compare your answers to those of your partner. If you don't agree on an answer, check it with a calculator.

Difficult

9. $10^{-1} + 16 - 0.5 * 12 =$ _____

10. $((\frac{1}{2}/\frac{1}{4}) + 3) * 6 - 3^3 =$ _____

11. $-(-8) - (-4) * 6 - (-12)/4 =$ _____

12. $-4 + -18/6 + (-3 * -3 - 5) =$ _____

Challenging

13. $-5(-6-(-3))/7.5 =$ _____

14. $-(\frac{3}{4}/\frac{1}{2}) + \frac{1}{2} - (\frac{1}{2} * -\frac{1}{2}) =$ _____

15. Evaluate the following expressions for $x = -2$:

   a. $x * -x + 14/2 =$ _____

   b. $-x * (6 + x) - 3^3/9 =$ _____

Math Boxes 85

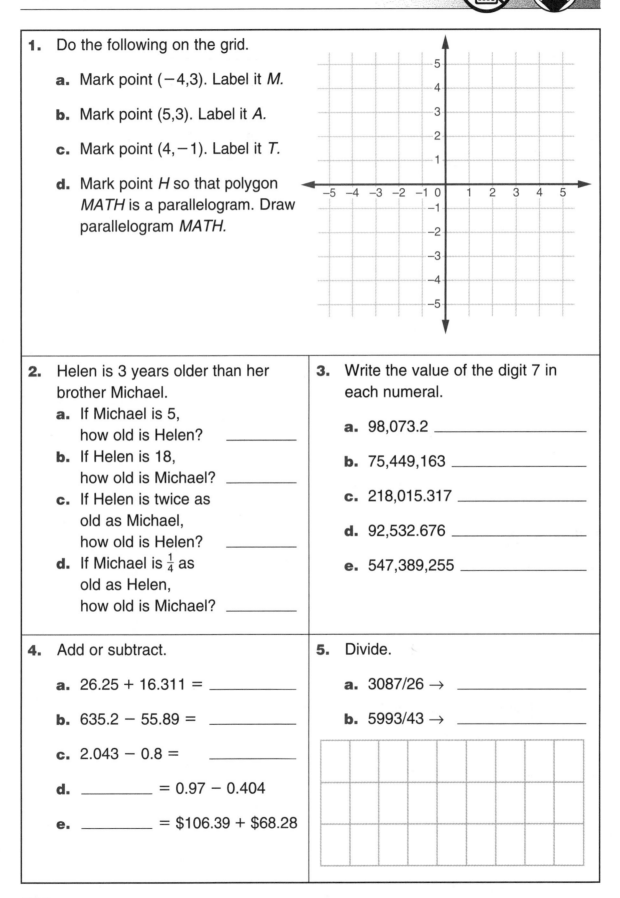

1. Do the following on the grid.

   a. Mark point (−4,3). Label it *M*.

   b. Mark point (5,3). Label it *A*.

   c. Mark point (4,−1). Label it *T*.

   d. Mark point *H* so that polygon *MATH* is a parallelogram. Draw parallelogram *MATH*.

2. Helen is 3 years older than her brother Michael.

   a. If Michael is 5, how old is Helen? _____

   b. If Helen is 18, how old is Michael? _____

   c. If Helen is twice as old as Michael, how old is Helen? _____

   d. If Michael is $\frac{1}{4}$ as old as Helen, how old is Michael? _____

3. Write the value of the digit 7 in each numeral.

   a. 98,073.2 _____

   b. 75,449,163 _____

   c. 218,015.317 _____

   d. 92,532.676 _____

   e. 547,389,255 _____

4. Add or subtract.

   a. 26.25 + 16.311 = _____

   b. 635.2 − 55.89 = _____

   c. 2.043 − 0.8 = _____

   d. _____ = 0.97 − 0.404

   e. _____ = $106.39 + $68.28

5. Divide.

   a. 3087/26 → _____

   b. 5993/43 → _____

Number Sentences

1. Translate the English sentences below into number sentences.
   The first one has been done for you.

   a. Three times five is equal to fifteen.   _____ $3 * 5 = 15$ _____

   b. Nine increased by seven is less than twenty-nine. _____

   c. Thirteen is not equal to nine more than twenty. _____

   d. The product of eight and six is less than
      or equal to the sum of twenty and thirty. _____

   e. Thirty-seven increased by twelve is greater
      than fifty decreased by ten. _____

   f. Nineteen is less than or equal to nineteen. _____

2. Tell whether each number sentence is true or false.

   a. $3 * 21 = 63$ _____

   b. $(3 * 4) + 7 = 19$ _____

   c. $42 - 12/6 > 5$ _____

   d. $8 \geq 7 + 1$ _____

   e. $24/4 + 2 = 8$ _____

   f. $9/(8 - 5) \leq 3$ _____

   g. $21 > (7 * 3) + 5$ _____

   h. $8 * 7 \leq 72$ _____

   i. $63/7 \neq 8$ _____

   j. $35 + 5 * 8 = 320$ _____

3. Insert parentheses so that each number sentence is true.

   a. $5 * 8 + 4 - 2 = 42$

   b. $7 * 9 - 6 = 21$

   c. $10 + 2 * 6 < 24$

   d. $9 - 7 / 7 = 8$

   e. $33 - 24 / 3 \geq 25$

   f. $36 / 7 + 2 * 3 = 12$

   g. $3 * 4 + 3 > 5 * 3 + 3$

   h. $48 / 8 + 4 \neq 10^2 / 10$

Number Sentences (cont.)

4. Write 3 true and 3 false number sentences. Trade journals with your partner and determine which sentences are true and which are false.

a. _____   _____

b. _____   _____

c. _____   _____

d. _____   _____

e. _____   _____

f. _____   _____

Challenge

5. The word HOPE is printed in block letters inside a 15-foot-by-5-foot rectangular billboard. What is the area of the unshaded portion of the billboard?

_____

6. Square corners, 6 centimeters on a side, are removed from a 36-centimeter-by-42-centimeter piece of paper.

The paper is then folded to form an open box. What is the surface area of the inside of the box?

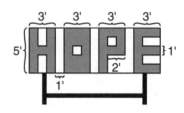

_____

7. Pennies tossed at the gameboard at the right have an equal chance of landing anywhere on the board. If 60% of the pennies tossed land inside the smaller square, what is the length of a side *s* of the smaller square, to the nearest inch?

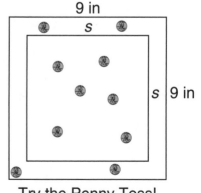

Try the Penny Toss!

_____

Math Boxes 86

1. The formula $d = rt$ gives the distance d traveled at speed r in time t. Use this formula to solve the problems below. `159 160`

   a. Ms. Ruiz is driving at an average speed of 60 miles per hour. At this speed, how far can she drive in 4.5 hours? _____

   b. Jill walks at an average speed of 5 miles per hour. At this speed, how far can she walk in 2.5 hours? _____

   c. The distance from San Francisco to Los Angeles is about 420 miles. About how many hours will it take to drive from San Francisco to Los Angeles at an average speed of 55 miles per hour? _____

2. Give three special cases for the pattern $\frac{1}{a} * \frac{b}{c} = \frac{b}{(a*c)}$.

_____

_____

_____

`63`

3. A circle has an area of 314.16 cm^2. Circle the best estimate for its circumference.

about 20 cm   about 40 cm

about 60 cm   about 80 cm

Explain why you chose this estimate.

_____

_____

_____

_____

`118`

4. Solve.   Solution

   a. $\frac{22}{m} = \frac{1}{2}$ _____

   b. $0.25 * s = 64$ _____

   c. $d * 10^2 = 420.5$ _____

   d. $f * \frac{1}{8} = \frac{3}{16}$ _____

   e. $\sqrt{h} = 20$ _____

`158`

5. Multiply or divide. Write your answers in simplest form.

   a. $1\frac{3}{7} * 2\frac{1}{5} =$ _____

   b. $3\frac{6}{8} * \frac{28}{6} =$ _____

   c. $5\frac{1}{10} \div 2\frac{5}{4} =$ _____

   d. $\frac{46}{3} \div 20 =$ _____

   e. $5\frac{3}{5} * \frac{1}{8} =$ _____

`37 38`

Use with Lesson 86.   **319**

Solving Equations

Use with Lesson 87.

1. Find the solution of each equation. Write a number sentence with the solution in place of the variable. Check that the number sentence is true.

Equation	Solution	Number sentence
a. $12 + x = 32$	20	$12 + 20 = 32$
b. $y + 89 = 93$		
c. $e - 32 = 15$		
d. $m * 8 = 35 - 19$		
e. $p + (4 * 9) = 55$		
f. $42 = 7 * (a - 4)$		
g. $(9 + w)/2 = 6 + (6/6)$		
h. $4 + (3n - 6) = 1 + (3 * 6)$		

2. Find the solution to each equation.

a. $4 * 6 = 35 - t$ _____   b. $9 * (11 - c) = 81$ _____

c. $17 - 11 = k/8$ _____   d. $(m + 14)/4 = 6$ _____

e. $36/9 = 2 + p$ _____   f. $23 - a = 15$ _____

g. $(3 * p) + 5 = 26$ _____   h. $2 - d = 3 * 4$ _____

3. Make up four equations whose solutions are whole numbers. Ask your partner to solve each equation.

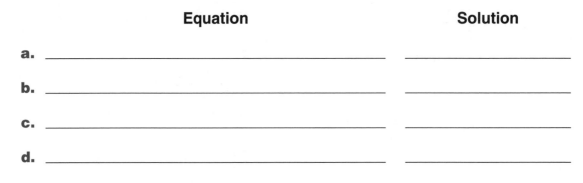

Equation	Solution
a.	
b.	
c.	
d.	

Solving Equations (cont.)

Challenge Problems

4.　$x - x = 0$　　　　$n + 5 = 1$　　　　$a + 8 < 3$　　　　$y \neq y$　　　　$\frac{0}{g} \geq 1$

Which of the above sentences have

a. no solution? _____

b. more than one solution? _____

c. a solution that is a negative number? _____

5. Find the solution to each equation.

a. $x + (x + 1) + (x + 2) = 90$ _____

(*Hint:* Think of this equation as a sum of three numbers.)

b. $a + (a + 1) + (a + 2) + (a + 3) + (a + 4) = 90$ _____

6. Whole numbers are said to be **consecutive** if they follow one another in an uninterrupted pattern. For example, 5, 6, 7, 8, 9, and 10 are six consecutive whole numbers.

a. What are 3 consecutive whole numbers whose sum is 90? (*Hint:* Replace each variable x in Problem 5a with the solution of the equation.)

_____ + _____ + _____ = 90

b. What are 5 consecutive whole numbers whose sum is 90?

_____ + _____ + _____ + _____ + _____ = 90

c. What are 4 consecutive whole numbers whose sum is 90?

_____ + _____ + _____ + _____ = 90

7. Each letter in the subtraction problem below represents a different digit from 0 through 9. The digits 3 and 5 do not appear in the problem. Replace each letter so that the answer to the subtraction problem is correct.

```
  G R A P E
− P L U M
  A P P L E
```

G = _____　R = _____　A = _____　P = _____

E = _____　L = _____　U = _____　M = _____

Math Boxes 87

1. Solve.   Solution

a. $\frac{3}{4} = \frac{x}{28}$ _____

b. $\frac{12}{16} = \frac{x}{32}$ _____

c. $\frac{14}{1} = \frac{42}{x}$ _____

d. $\frac{7}{16} = \frac{x}{28}$ _____

e. $\frac{250}{20} = \frac{2.5}{x}$ _____

158

2. Write five names for the number in the name-collection box so that each name contains the fraction $\frac{1}{3}$ and includes multiplication.

8

3. Insert the decimal point in the product.

a. $3.6 * 5.35 = 1\ 9\ 2\ 6$

b. $-299 * -0.03 = 8\ 9\ 7$

c. $218 * 2.15 = 4\ 6\ 8\ 7$

d. $-6.59 * 3.03 = -1\ 9\ 9\ 6\ 7\ 7$

e. $25 * -0.025 = -\ 6\ 2\ 5$

52

4. Complete.

a. 19 qt = _____ pt

b. 9 gal 3 pt = _____ c

c. _____ pt _____ c = 27 c

d. _____ c = 43 pt

e. 560 c = _____ qt

339

5. Janine watches about 12 hours of television per week. Complete the table. Then use your protractor to make a circle graph of the information.

Type of Show	Number of Hours	Percent of Hours	Degrees
Comedy	4		
Educational	1		
News	2		
Sports	3		
Cartoons	2		
Total			

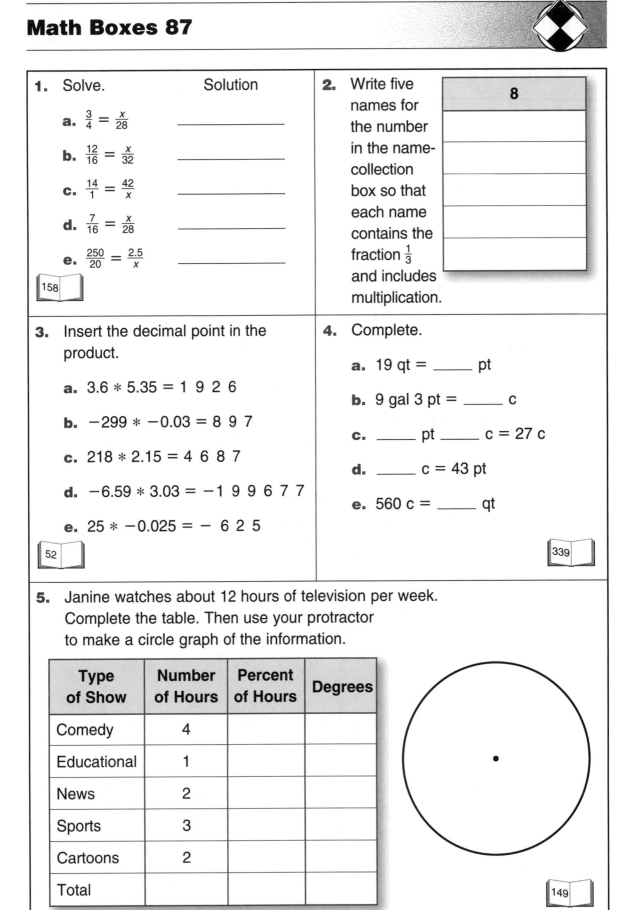

149

Pan-Balance Problems

A pan balance can be used to compare the weights of objects or to weigh objects. If the objects in one pan weigh as much as the objects in the other pan, then the pans will be balanced.

In this unit, a balanced pan balance will be represented as shown at the right.

Example: In each of the diagrams below, the two pans are in perfect balance. Your job is to figure out how many marbles weigh as much as an orange. The best way to do this is to move oranges and marbles so that a single orange is in one pan and only marbles are in the other pan. When moving the oranges and marbles, you must follow this simple rule:

Whatever you do, the pans must always remain balanced.

The pan balance shows that 3 oranges weigh as much as 1 orange and 12 marbles.

If you remove 1 orange from each pan, the pans remain balanced.

If you then remove half of the objects from each pan, the pans will still be balanced.

Success!! One orange weighs as much as 6 marbles.

Try to solve the following pan-balance problems with your partner. Be prepared to share your strategy with the class.

1. One pencil weighs

as much as _____ paper clips.

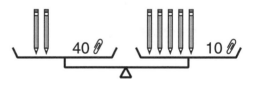

2. One *P* (pencil) weighs

as much as _____ *C*'s (paper clips).

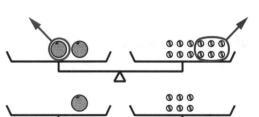

Pan-Balance Problems (cont.)

Solve these pan-balance problems. In each figure, the two pans are in perfect balance.

Warm-up Problems

1. One banana weighs

   as much as _____ marbles.

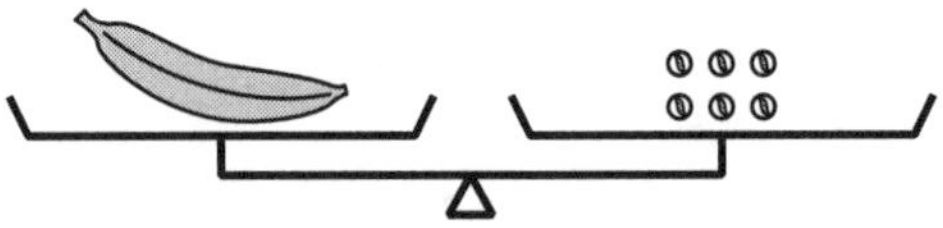

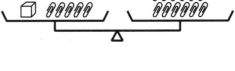

2. One cube weighs

   as much as _____ paper clips.

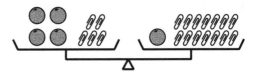

3. One cube weighs

   as much as _____ marbles.

Slightly Sweaty Problems

4. One triangle weighs

   as much as _____ squares.

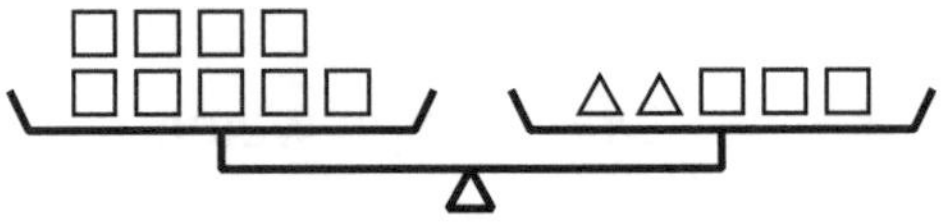

5. One orange weighs

   as much as _____ paper clips.

6. One and $\frac{1}{2}$ cantaloupes weigh

   as much as _____ apples.

Pan-Balance Problems (cont.)

Reminder: 4 ⬜ or 4 ∗ ⬜ is just another way to write ⬜ + ⬜ + ⬜ + ⬜.

Heart Rate Is Really Soaring Now Problems

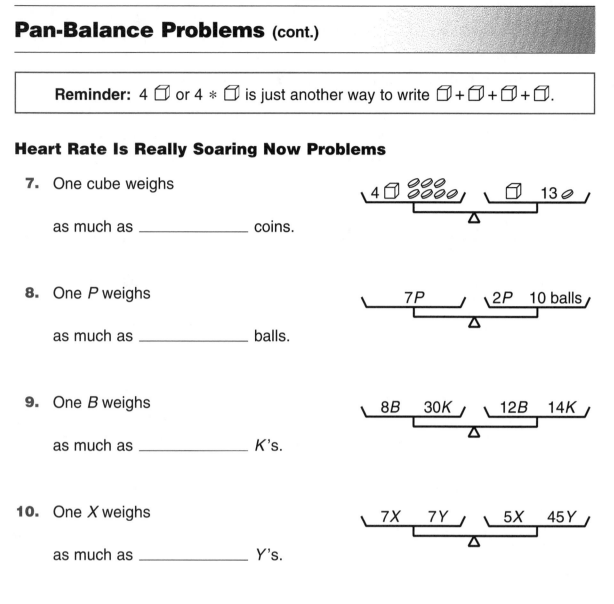

7. One cube weighs

as much as _____ coins.

8. One *P* weighs

as much as _____ balls.

9. One *B* weighs

as much as _____ *K*'s.

10. One *X* weighs

as much as _____ *Y*'s.

Check your answers.

- The sum of the answers to Problems 1 and 4 is equal to the square root of 81.

- The answer to Problem 10 is a prime number greater than 17 and less than 5^2.

- The product of the answers to Problems 6 and 7 is 36.

- The sum of the answers to Problems 1 and 10 is the solution of the equation $4n = 10^2$.

- The product of the answers to Problems 5, 7, and 9 is 24.

Use with Lesson 88.

Pan-Balance Problems (cont.)

"Iron Mathematician" Triathlon Challenge Problems

Problems 11 and 12 each consist of two parts. You need to solve one of the parts before you have enough information to solve the other part. You must figure out which statement to complete first—it may be either the first or the second statement.

In each of the figures, the two pans are in perfect balance.

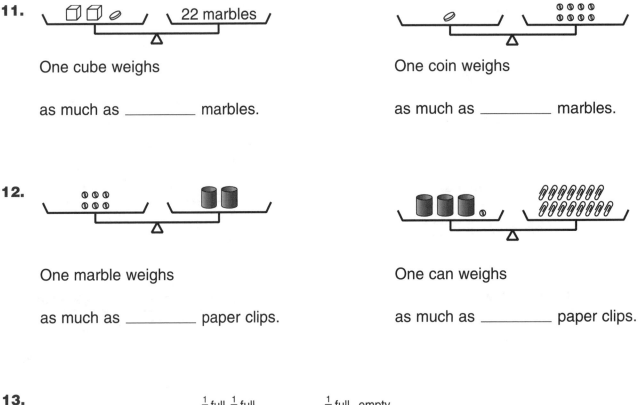

11.

One cube weighs

as much as _____ marbles.

One coin weighs

as much as _____ marbles.

12.

One marble weighs

as much as _____ paper clips.

One can weighs

as much as _____ paper clips.

13.

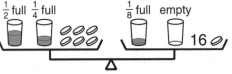

An empty juice glass weighs as much as 5 coins.

If the juice glass is full, the juice in the glass weighs as much as _____ coins.

If the juice glass is full, the juice plus the glass weigh as much as _____ coins.

Use with Lesson 88.

Math Boxes 88

1. The area of triangle *FOG* is 12 cm^2.
What is the perimeter of rectangle *FROG*? _____ cm

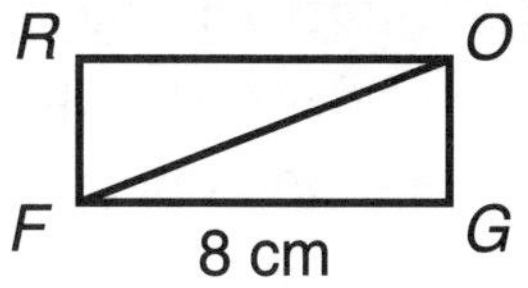

Explain how you found the perimeter of rectangle *FROG*.

_____

_____

_____

| 116 | 121 |

2. Evaluate each expression. Use the rules for order of operations.

a. $3 * 8/4 + 7 =$ _____

b. $9 + 3 * 5 - 7 =$ _____

c. $6 * 5 + 7 * 3 =$ _____

d. $8/(2 + 8) * 3^3 + 5 =$ _____

e. $28 - 7 * 4 * 0 + 2 =$ _____

| 161 |

3. Multiply or divide.

a. $-8 * 6 =$ _____

b. $550/(-11) =$ _____

c. _____ $= -125/(-5)$

d. _____ $= -930/31$

e. _____ $= -500 * 40$

| 59 |

4. Without using a protractor, find the measure in degrees of each numbered angle. Write each measure on the drawing. (Lines that appear parallel are parallel.)

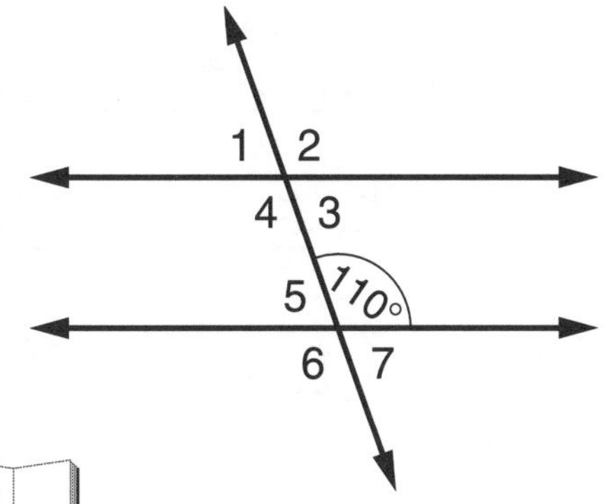

| 71 |

5. Multiply or divide. Write your answer in simplest form.

a. $\frac{8}{9} \div \frac{4}{5} =$ _____

b. $3\frac{6}{5} * \frac{2}{3} =$ _____

c. _____ $= 5\frac{1}{2} \div \frac{11}{12}$

d. _____ $= \frac{29}{4} * \frac{15}{6}$

e. _____ $= \frac{3}{7} * 18$

| 36 | 38 |
| 37 | 39 |

Pan-Balance Equations

1. Start with the original pan-balance equation. Do the first operation on both sides of the pan balance, and write the result on the second pan balance. Do the second operation on both sides of the second pan balance, and write the result on the third pan balance. Fill in the fourth pan balance in the same way.

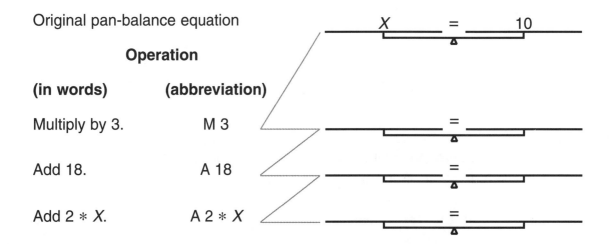

Original pan-balance equation

Operation

(in words)   **(abbreviation)**

Multiply by 3.   M 3

Add 18.   A 18

Add 2 ∗ X.   A 2 ∗ X

Equations that have the same solution are called **equivalent equations.**

2. Check that the pan-balance equations above are equivalent equations, that is, that 10 is the solution to each equation.

3. Now do the opposite of what you did in Problem 1. Record the operation that was used to obtain the results on each pan balance.

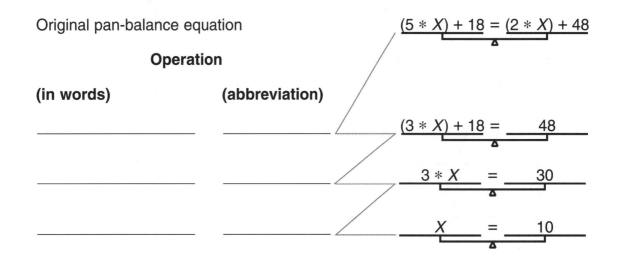

Original pan-balance equation

Operation

(in words)   **(abbreviation)**

_____   _____

_____   _____

_____   _____

Pan-Balance Equations (cont.)

4. Record the results of the operation on each pan, as you did in Problem 1.

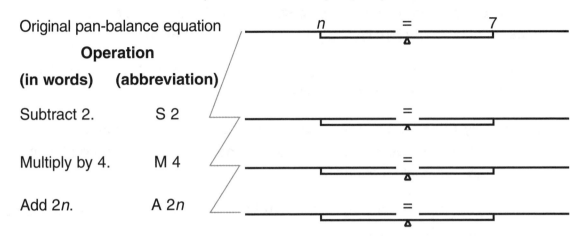

Original pan-balance equation n = 7

Operation

(in words)   (abbreviation)

Subtract 2.   S 2   =

Multiply by 4.   M 4   =

Add 2n.   A 2n =

5. Check that the solution to each pan-balance equation in Problem 4 is 7.

In Problems 6 and 7, record the operation that was used to obtain the results on each pan balance, as you did in Problem 3.

6. Original pan-balance equation

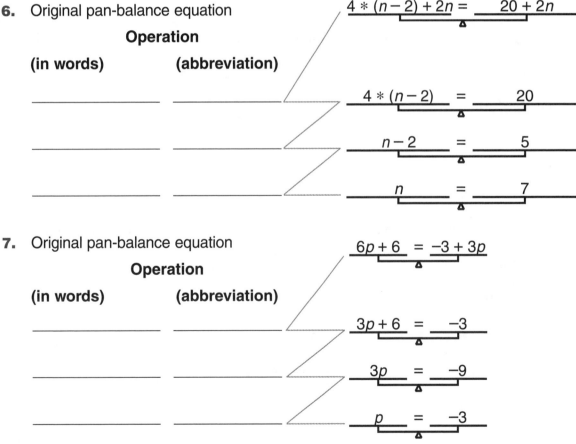

Operation

(in words)   (abbreviation)

_____   _____ $4 * (n - 2) + 2n = 20 + 2n$

_____   _____ $4 * (n - 2) = 20$

_____   _____ $n - 2 = 5$

_____   _____ $n = 7$

7. Original pan-balance equation

Operation

(in words)   (abbreviation)

_____   _____ $6p + 6 = -3 + 3p$

_____   _____ $3p + 6 = -3$

_____   _____ $3p = -9$

_____   _____ $p = -3$

8. Check that 7 is the solution to each pan-balance equation in Problem 6 and that -3 is the solution to each pan-balance equation in Problem 7.

Inventing and Solving Equations

Work in groups of three. Each of you will invent two equations and then ask the other two members of your group to solve them. You will show your solutions on page 331. Here is what you do for each equation.

Step 1: Choose any positive or negative integer and record it on the first line to complete the original equation.

Step 2: Apply any operation you wish to both sides of the equation. Record the operation you used and write the new (equivalent) equation on the lines below the original equation.

Step 3: Repeat this step one more time. Apply a new operation and show the new equation that results.

Step 4: Check your work. The value of X in the original equation should be the solution to each equation you have written.

Step 5: Give the other members of your group the final equation to solve.

1. Make up an equation from 2 equivalent equations.   Selected integer

    Original equation _____ X _____ = _____

    Operation

    _____ _____ = _____

    _____ _____ = _____

2. Make up an equation from 3 equivalent equations.   Selected integer

    Original equation _____ X _____ = _____

    Operation

    _____ _____ = _____

    _____ _____ = _____

    _____ _____ = _____

Use with Lesson 89.

Inventing and Solving Equations (cont.)

Use this page to solve your partners' equations.

First, record the equation. Then solve it. For each step, record the operation you use and the equation that results. Check your solution by substituting it for the variable in your partner's equation. Finally, compare the steps you used to solve your partner's equation to the steps your partner used in inventing the equation.

1. Partner's equation _____ = _____

Operation

_____   _____ = _____

_____   _____ = _____

_____   _____ = _____

2. Partner's equation _____ = _____

Operation

_____   _____ = _____

_____   _____ = _____

_____   _____ = _____

3. Partner's equation _____ = _____

Operation

_____   _____ = _____

_____   _____ = _____

_____   _____ = _____

4. Partner's equation _____ = _____

Operation

_____   _____ = _____

_____   _____ = _____

_____   _____ = _____

Use with Lesson 89.   **331**

Math Boxes 89

1. The formula $d = rt$ gives the distance d traveled at speed r in time t. Use this formula to solve the problems below.

   a. The distance from Chicago to Los Angeles is about 2190 miles. About how many hours will it take to drive from Chicago to Los Angeles at an average speed of 55 miles per hour? _____

   b. About how long will an airplane flying at an average speed of 500 miles per hour take to travel this distance? _____

   c. Circle the formula that is equivalent to $d = rt$.

   $r = d/t$ $r = d - t$ $r = t/d$ $r = t + d$

2. Give three special cases for the pattern.

   $5 * (a - b) = (5 * a) - (5 * b)$

   _____

   _____

   _____

3. Solve.   Solution

   a. $w * 10^{-2} = 28.2$ _____

   b. $420 * k = 140$ _____

   c. $\frac{5}{2} - p = \frac{7}{4}$ _____

   d. $18/a = -6$ _____

   e. $2^d = 64$ _____

4. A circle has a radius of 3 cm. Circle the best estimate for its area.

   1.8 cm^2 2.7 cm^2

   18 cm^2 27 cm^2

   Explain why you chose this estimate.

   _____

   _____

   _____

5. Multiply or divide. Write your answers in simplest form.

   a. $3\frac{8}{9} * 4\frac{5}{6} =$ _____

   b. _____ $= \frac{1}{5} * \frac{38}{3}$

   c. _____ $= \frac{24}{15} \div \frac{1}{2}$

   d. _____ $= \frac{3}{7} * \frac{22}{3}$

   e. $\frac{24}{8} \div \frac{12}{7} =$ _____

Use with Lesson 89.

Date _____   Time _____

Solving Equations

Solve the following equations.

Example: $3x + 5 = 14$

Original equation $3x + 5 = 14$
Operation

| $\cancel{S}\,5$ | $3x = 9$ |
| $\cancel{D}\,3$ | $x = 3$ |

Check $(3 * 3) + 5 = 14;$ *true*

1. $11y - 4 = 9y$

Original equation _____

Operation

_____   _____

_____   _____

_____   _____

Check _____

2. $16t + 7 = 19t + 10$

Original equation _____

Operation

_____   _____

_____   _____

_____   _____

Check _____

3. $12n - 5 = 9n - 2$

Original equation _____

Operation

_____   _____

_____   _____

_____   _____

Check _____

4. $8e - 6 = 10e + 6$

Original equation _____

Operation

_____   _____

_____   _____

_____   _____

Check _____

5. $3b + 7.1 = 2.5b + 11.5$

Original equation _____

Operation

_____   _____

_____   _____

_____   _____

Check _____

Solving Equations (cont.)

6. $8 - 3h = 5h + 1$

Original equation

_____

Operation

_____ _____

_____ _____

_____ _____

Check

_____

7. $-2p - 6 = 12 - 4p$

Original equation

_____

Operation

_____ _____

_____ _____

_____ _____

Check

_____

8. $\frac{1}{4}r + 9 = 10 - \frac{3}{4}r$

Original equation

_____

Operation

_____ _____

_____ _____

Check

_____

9. $\frac{2}{3}u - 7 = 9 - \frac{2}{3}u$

Original equation

_____

Operation

_____ _____

_____ _____

_____ _____

Check

_____

10. Two equations are equivalent if they have the same solutions. Circle each pair of equivalent equations. Write the solution of the equations, if they are equivalent.

a. $z = 5$

   $3z - 8 = 2z - 3$

   Solution: _____

b. $d + 5 = 8$

   $6 - 2d = 9 - 3d$

   Solution: _____

c. $v + 1 = 2v + 2$

   $3v - 8 = 2v - 3$

   Solution: _____

d. $t = 4$

   $(5t + 3) - 2(t + 3) = 29 - 5t$

   Solution: _____

               Use with Lesson 90.

Math Boxes 90

---

1. Solve.   Solution

   a. $\frac{42}{18} = \frac{x}{3}$ _____

   b. $\frac{125}{x} = \frac{5}{1}$ _____

   c. $\frac{36}{x} = \frac{18}{2}$ _____

   d. $\frac{x}{150} = \frac{3}{5}$ _____

   e. $\frac{90}{3} = \frac{9}{x}$ _____

2. Write five names for the number in the name-collection box so that each name contains the number -2 and includes subtraction.

10

---

3. Insert the decimal point in the product.

   a. $4.02 * 85 = 3\ 4\ 1\ 7$

   b. $-9.6 * 38.82 = -\ 3\ 7\ 2\ 6\ 7\ 2$

   c. $67 * 1.004 = 6\ 7\ 2\ 6\ 8$

   d. $0.89 * -5.1 = -\ 4\ 5\ 3\ 9$

   e. $-2.307 * -1.9 = 4\ 3\ 8\ 3\ 3$

4. Complete.

   a. 10 qt = _____ pt

   b. 7 gal 3 qt = _____ pt

   c. _____ pt _____ c = 48 c

   d. _____ gal _____ qt = 43 pt

   e. 40 c = _____ gal

---

5. Peabody's Bookstore had a sale. Complete the table. Then use your protractor to make a circle graph of the information.

Book Category	Number Sold	Percent of Total	Degrees
Fiction	280		
Sports	283		
Children's	125		
Travel	212		
Computer	100		
Total			

Math Message: Introduction to Inequalities

1. Translate each inequality into an English sentence. $\boxed{157\,|\,158}$

   a. $15 \neq 3 * 7$ _____

   _____

   b. $(9/9) + 13 \leq 14$ _____

   _____

   c. $7 > 1 * \frac{2}{3}$ _____

   _____

   d. $23 < 6 * 3$ _____

   _____

   e. $20 \geq 5^2$ _____

   _____

2. Are all of the inequalities in Problem 1 true? _____

   If not, which are false? _____

3. Some of the inequalities below are true, and some are false.
   Write "true" or "false" after each one.

   a. $5 * 4 < 20$ _____ b. $(7 + 3) * 6 \neq 60$ _____

   c. $54/9 > 7$ _____ d. $9 - (3 * 2) < 10$ _____

   e. $45 \geq 9 * 5$ _____ f. $3 \leq -1 + 6$ _____

   g. $15 \leq 12 + 2$ _____ h. $17 - 6 \geq 9$ _____

4. a. Write an inequality that is neither true nor false. _____

   _____

   b. Explain how you could change it into an inequality that is true.

   _____

   _____

   _____

336

Inequalities

1. Name two solutions of each inequality.

   a. $15 > r$ _____   **b.** $8 < m$ _____

   c. $t \geq 56$ _____   **d.** $15 - 11 \leq p$ _____

   e. $21/7 \geq y$ _____   **f.** $w > -3$ _____

   g. $6.5 \geq 3 * d$ _____   **h.** $g \leq 0.5$ _____

2. Name two numbers that are not solutions of each inequality.

   a. $(7 + 3) * q \geq 40$ _____   **b.** $\frac{1}{2} + \frac{1}{4} < t$ _____

   c. $y \leq 2.6 + 4.3$ _____   **d.** $6/g > 12$ _____

3. Describe the solution set of each inequality.

   Example: $t + 5 < 8$

   Solution set: All numbers less than 3.

   a. $8 - y > 3$ Solution set: _____

   b. $4b \geq 8$ Solution set: _____

4. Graph the solution set of each inequality.

   a. $x < 5$

   b. $6 > b$

   c. $1\frac{1}{2} \geq h$

Inequalities (cont.)

Challenge

5. Graph all solutions of each inequality.

   a. $8 > x \geq -1$ (*Hint:* "$8 > x \geq -1$" means "$8 > x$" and "$x \geq -1$." In order for a number to be a solution, it must make both number sentences true.)

   b. $3 < y + 2 \leq 7$

   c. $m \neq -2$

   d. $x^2 \geq 9$

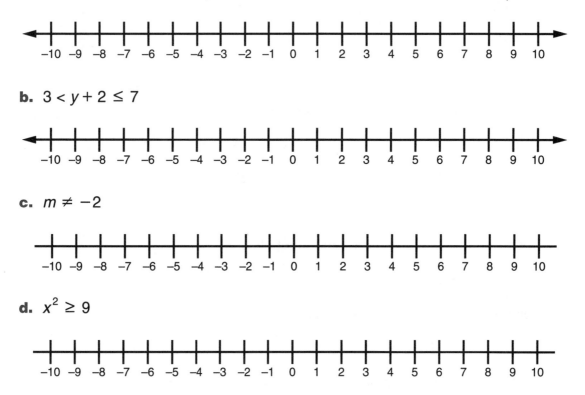

6. Write an inequality for each graph.

   a. _____

   b. _____

   c. _____

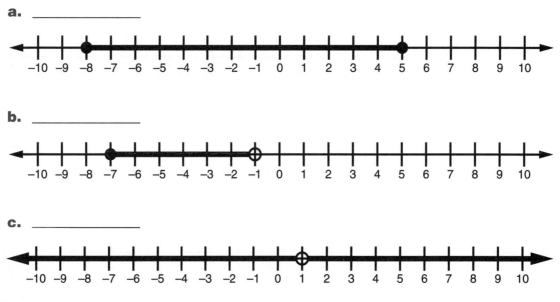

338

Math Boxes 91

1. The area of square *CAMP* is 25 cm². Squares *CAMP* and *MADE* are congruent. What is the area of triangle *APE*? _____ cm²

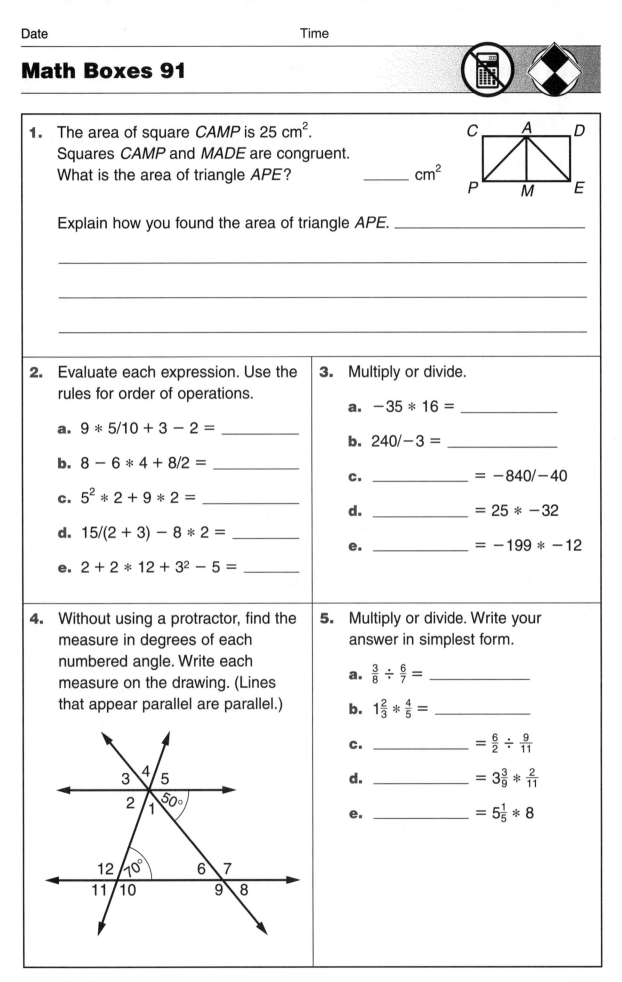

Explain how you found the area of triangle *APE*. _____

_____

_____

_____

2. Evaluate each expression. Use the rules for order of operations.

a. $9 * 5/10 + 3 - 2 =$ _____

b. $8 - 6 * 4 + 8/2 =$ _____

c. $5^2 * 2 + 9 * 2 =$ _____

d. $15/(2 + 3) - 8 * 2 =$ _____

e. $2 + 2 * 12 + 3^2 - 5 =$ _____

3. Multiply or divide.

a. $-35 * 16 =$ _____

b. $240/-3 =$ _____

c. _____ $= -840/-40$

d. _____ $= 25 * -32$

e. _____ $= -199 * -12$

4. Without using a protractor, find the measure in degrees of each numbered angle. Write each measure on the drawing. (Lines that appear parallel are parallel.)

5. Multiply or divide. Write your answer in simplest form.

a. $\frac{3}{8} \div \frac{6}{7} =$ _____

b. $1\frac{2}{3} * \frac{4}{5} =$ _____

c. _____ $= \frac{6}{2} \div \frac{9}{11}$

d. _____ $= 3\frac{3}{9} * \frac{2}{11}$

e. _____ $= 5\frac{1}{5} * 8$

Math Message: Time to Reflect

1. In this unit, you have been studying algebra concepts and practicing algebra skills. Pretend you had to explain to someone what algebra is. What would you tell the person?

_____

_____

_____

_____

_____

_____

_____

_____

_____

2. Describe something in this unit that you found interesting.

_____

_____

_____

_____

_____

_____

_____

_____

Use with Lesson 92.

Math Boxes 92a

1. Mr. and Mrs. Gauss keep a record of expenses on a spreadsheet.

a. If the Gausses entered the wrong amount for car expenses in July, which cell should they correct? _____

b. In which month were the total expenses greater? _____

How much greater? _____

c. Circle the correct formula for the total for June.

	A	B	C
1	Type of Expense	June	July
2	Rent and Utilities	$755	$723
3	Food	$125	$189
4	Car Expenses	$179	$25
5	Clothing	$65	$0
6	Miscellaneous	$45	$23
7	Total		

A7 + B7 + C7   B2 + B3 + B4 + B5 + B6   (B2+ B3 + B4 + B5 + B6)/5

2. Do the following on the grid.

a. Mark point (1,1). Label it *M*.

b. Mark point (3,2). Label it *A*.

c. Mark point *X* so that triangle *MAX* is an isosceles triange. Draw triangle *MAX*.

3. The circumference of a circle is given by the formula $C = \pi d$, where *C* is the circumference and *d* is the diameter. Circle an equivalent formula.

$d = C/\pi$ $d = C * \pi$

$d = \pi/C$ $d = \pi + C$

4. Solve.   Solution

a. $\frac{15}{2} = \frac{x}{6}$ _____

b. $\frac{x}{99} = \frac{10}{11}$ _____

c. $\frac{144}{3} = \frac{x}{1}$ _____

d. $\frac{24}{x} = \frac{80}{100}$ _____

e. $\frac{50}{x} = \frac{18}{72}$ _____

Date _____ Time _____

Math Boxes 92b

1. Estimate the answers.

    a. 7 L is about _____ qt.

    b. 9 km is about _____ mi.

    c. 30 cm is about _____ in.

    d. 50 yd is about _____ m.

    e. 15 kg is about _____ lb.

2. Complete.

    a. $\frac{1}{9}$ of 54 = _____

    b. $\frac{3}{8}$ of 48 = _____

    c. $\frac{4}{7}$ of 49 = _____

    d. $\frac{4}{5}$ of 1600 = _____

    e. $\frac{3}{4}$ of 96 = _____

3. Write each in scientific notation.

    a. 8000 = _____

    b. _____ = 700,000

    c. 350,000 = _____

    d. 5680 = _____

    e. _____ = 40,600

4. Write each in standard notation.

    a. $6 * 10^3$ = _____

    b. _____ = $4 * 10^5$

    c. $15 * 10^4$ = _____

    d. $23.7 * 10^2$ = _____

    e. _____ = $4.51 * 10^6$

5. Complete.

    a. 7 ft = _____ in

    b. 9 ft 5 in = _____ in

    c. 79 in = _____ ft _____ in

    d. 95 ft = _____ yd _____ ft

    e. 106 ft = _____ yd _____ ft

6. Find the probability of each event when rolling a 12-sided die.

    a. Roll a number less than or equal to 7. _____

    b. Roll an even composite number. _____

    c. Roll an odd composite number. _____

    d. Roll a square number. _____

    e. Roll a number that is neither prime nor composite. _____

Use with Lesson 92.

Math Message: Area of a Rectangle

What is the area of rectangle A? _____ square units

We can express the area of rectangle A with a number sentence in four ways:

5 * (3 + 7) = 50   (5 * 3) + (5 * 7) = 50

(3 + 7) * 5 = 50   (3 * 5) + (7 * 5) = 50

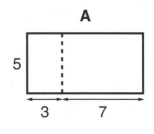

Two Methods for Finding Areas of Rectangles

1. Write a number sentence for the area of rectangle B in two ways.

    _____ * (_____ + _____) = _____

    (_____ * _____) + (_____ * _____) = _____

2. The area of rectangle C is 144 square units.

    a. What is the value of x? _____

    b. Write a number sentence for the area of rectangle C in two ways.

    _____ * (_____ + _____) = 144

    (_____ * _____) + (_____ * _____) = 144

3. Each of the following expressions describes the area of one of the rectangles below. Write the letter of the rectangle next to the expression.

    a. 6 * (5 + 4) _____ℰ_____   **b.** (4 + 6) * 5 _____

    c. 44 _____   **d.** 24 + 30 _____

    e. (6 * 4) + (5 * 4) _____   **f.** 50 _____

    g. (5 * 6) + (4 * 6) _____   **h.** 24 + 20 _____

    i. (6 + 5) * 4 _____   **j.** (5 * 6) + (5 * 4) _____

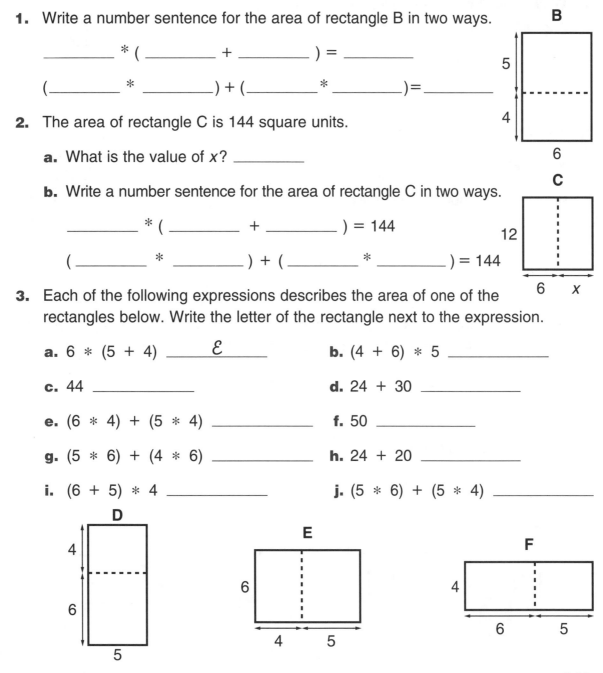

Two Methods for Finding Areas of Rectangles (cont.)

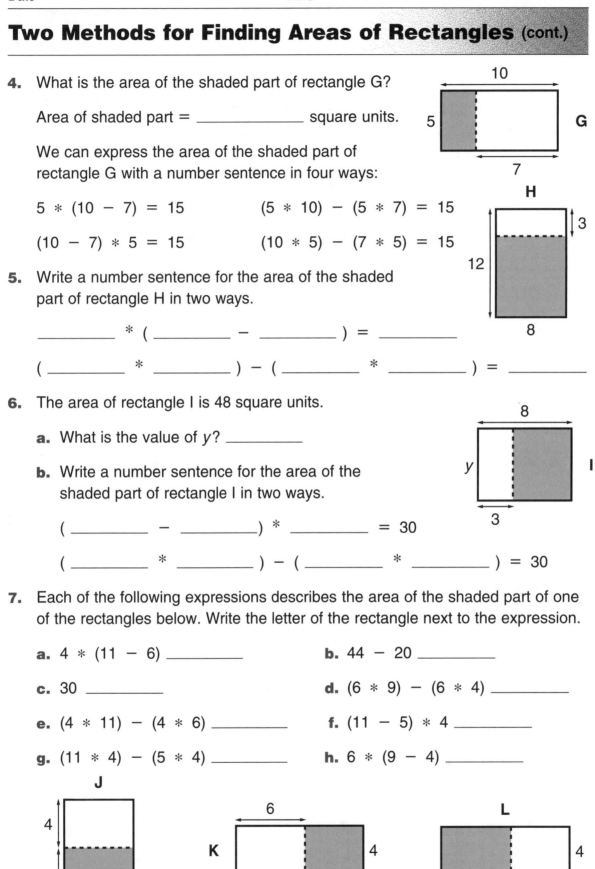

4. What is the area of the shaded part of rectangle G?

   Area of shaded part = _____ square units.

   We can express the area of the shaded part of
   rectangle G with a number sentence in four ways:

   5 * (10 − 7) = 15   (5 * 10) − (5 * 7) = 15

   (10 − 7) * 5 = 15   (10 * 5) − (7 * 5) = 15

5. Write a number sentence for the area of the shaded
   part of rectangle H in two ways.

   _____ * (_____ − _____) = _____

   (_____ * _____) − (_____ * _____) = _____

6. The area of rectangle I is 48 square units.

   a. What is the value of y? _____

   b. Write a number sentence for the area of the
      shaded part of rectangle I in two ways.

      (_____ − _____) * _____ = 30

      (_____ * _____) − (_____ * _____) = 30

7. Each of the following expressions describes the area of the shaded part of one
   of the rectangles below. Write the letter of the rectangle next to the expression.

   a. 4 * (11 − 6) _____   b. 44 − 20 _____

   c. 30 _____   d. (6 * 9) − (6 * 4) _____

   e. (4 * 11) − (4 * 6) _____   f. (11 − 5) * 4 _____

   g. (11 * 4) − (5 * 4) _____   h. 6 * (9 − 4) _____

Use with Lesson 93.

Math Boxes 93

1. Measure the reflex angles.

a.

∠*AMY* is about _____.

112 113

b.

∠*PAM* is about _____.

---

2. Divide.

a. $\frac{3}{2} \div \frac{3}{9} =$ _____

b. $\frac{7}{8} \div \frac{2}{3} =$ _____

c. $\frac{5}{6} \div \frac{1}{5} =$ _____

d. $\frac{4}{7} \div \frac{9}{12} =$ _____

e. $6 \div \frac{3}{8} =$ _____

38

---

3. Solve.   Solution

a. $15 * x = 60$ _____

b. $\frac{q}{10} = 150$ _____

c. $m + (-28) = -5$ _____

d. $\frac{36}{s} + 5 = 9$ _____

e. $-1 * t = -15$ _____

158

---

4. Circle the equation that describes the relationship between the numbers in the table.

x	y
10	$\frac{1}{5}$
14	1
19	2
49	8

$(x - 9) * 5 = y$

$\frac{x - 9}{5} = y$

$(y + 5) * 9 = x$

$5 * (y + 5) = x$

165

---

5. Find the following measures for a circle with a radius of 3 cm.

diameter _____ cm

circumference   about _____ cm

area   about _____ cm²

Explain how you found the area.

_____

_____

_____

_____

118

The Distributive Property

The **distributive property** is a number property that combines multiplication with addition or multiplication with subtraction. The distributive property can be stated in four different ways:

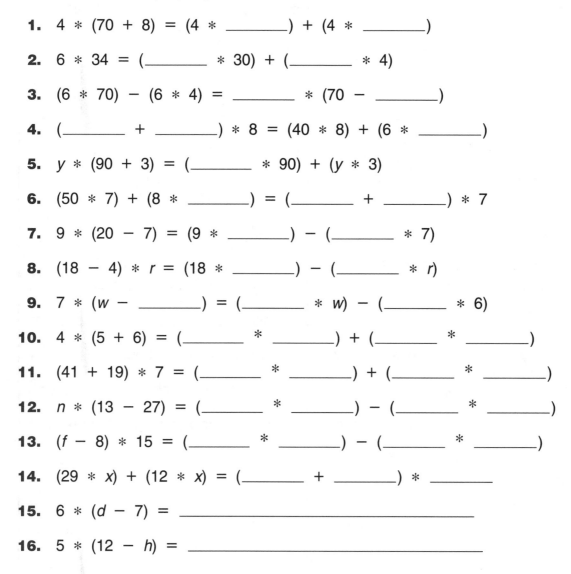

Multiplication over Addition For any numbers *a*, *x*, and *y:* $a * (x + y) = (a * x) + (a * y)$ $(x + y) * a = (x * a) + (y * a)$	**Multiplication over Subtraction** For any numbers *a*, *x*, and *y:* $a * (x - y) = (a * x) - (a * y)$ $(x - y) * a = (x * a) - (y * a)$

Use the distributive property to fill in the blanks.

1. $4 * (70 + 8) = (4 * \underline{\hspace{1.5cm}}) + (4 * \underline{\hspace{1.5cm}})$

2. $6 * 34 = (\underline{\hspace{1.5cm}} * 30) + (\underline{\hspace{1.5cm}} * 4)$

3. $(6 * 70) - (6 * 4) = \underline{\hspace{1.5cm}} * (70 - \underline{\hspace{1.5cm}})$

4. $(\underline{\hspace{1.5cm}} + \underline{\hspace{1.5cm}}) * 8 = (40 * 8) + (6 * \underline{\hspace{1.5cm}})$

5. $y * (90 + 3) = (\underline{\hspace{1.5cm}} * 90) + (y * 3)$

6. $(50 * 7) + (8 * \underline{\hspace{1.5cm}}) = (\underline{\hspace{1.5cm}} + \underline{\hspace{1.5cm}}) * 7$

7. $9 * (20 - 7) = (9 * \underline{\hspace{1.5cm}}) - (\underline{\hspace{1.5cm}} * 7)$

8. $(18 - 4) * r = (18 * \underline{\hspace{1.5cm}}) - (\underline{\hspace{1.5cm}} * r)$

9. $7 * (w - \underline{\hspace{1.5cm}}) = (\underline{\hspace{1.5cm}} * w) - (\underline{\hspace{1.5cm}} * 6)$

10. $4 * (5 + 6) = (\underline{\hspace{1.5cm}} * \underline{\hspace{1.5cm}}) + (\underline{\hspace{1.5cm}} * \underline{\hspace{1.5cm}})$

11. $(41 + 19) * 7 = (\underline{\hspace{1.5cm}} * \underline{\hspace{1.5cm}}) + (\underline{\hspace{1.5cm}} * \underline{\hspace{1.5cm}})$

12. $n * (13 - 27) = (\underline{\hspace{1.5cm}} * \underline{\hspace{1.5cm}}) - (\underline{\hspace{1.5cm}} * \underline{\hspace{1.5cm}})$

13. $(f - 8) * 15 = (\underline{\hspace{1.5cm}} * \underline{\hspace{1.5cm}}) - (\underline{\hspace{1.5cm}} * \underline{\hspace{1.5cm}})$

14. $(29 * x) + (12 * x) = (\underline{\hspace{1.5cm}} + \underline{\hspace{1.5cm}}) * \underline{\hspace{1.5cm}}$

15. $6 * (d - 7) = \underline{\hspace{6cm}}$

16. $5 * (12 - h) = \underline{\hspace{6cm}}$

                                              Use with Lesson 94.

Math Boxes 94

1. Complete the Venn diagram.

18   27

Name at least two ways in which the numbers 18 and 27 are alike.

Name at least two ways in which they are different.

153

2. Fill in the blanks. (*Hint:* For decimals, think fractions.)

a. $\frac{3}{5} * \underline{\hspace{3cm}} = 1$

b. $\frac{8}{9} * \underline{\hspace{3cm}} = 1$

c. $\frac{7}{3} * \underline{\hspace{3cm}} = 1$

d. $0.01 * \underline{\hspace{2.5cm}} = 1$

e. $0.5 * \underline{\hspace{1.5cm}} = 1$

20

3. Write in standard notation.

a. $\underline{\hspace{4cm}} = 4^2$

b. $3^3 = \underline{\hspace{3cm}}$

c. $10^7 = \underline{\hspace{3cm}}$

d. $9^2 = \underline{\hspace{3cm}}$

e. $\underline{\hspace{3cm}} = 5^3$

6

4. The table shows the results of a survey that asked people where they keep their computers at home. Fill in the missing information in the table. Use a protractor to make a circle graph of the results. Do not use the Percent Circle.

Location	Number of People	Percent of Total
Family room	20	
Bedroom	10	
Living room	8	
Home office	8	
Kitchen	2	
Basement	2	
Total		

149

Combining Like Terms

Algebraic expressions are made up of **terms.** For example, the expression $4y + 2x - 7y$ is made up of the terms $4y$, $2x$, and $7y$. We say that $4y$ and $7y$ are **like terms,** because they are multiples of the same variable, y.

Algebraic expressions are often difficult to work with, because they are not written in a simple way. To **simplify an expression** that contains a sum or difference of like terms, **combine like terms** and rewrite the expression as a single term.

Reminder: The multiplication symbol ($*$) is usually not written. For example, $4 * y$ is usually written as $4y$, and $(x + 3) * 5$ is often written as $(x + 3)5$.

Example 1:   Simplify the expression $5x - (-8)x$. Use the distributive property.
$$5x - (-8)x = (5 * x) - (-8 * x)$$
$$= (5 - (-8)) * x$$
$$= (5 + 8) * x$$
$$= 13 * x, \text{ or } 13x$$

For each problem, check your answer by substituting several values for the variable.
Check: Substitute 5 for the variable.
$$5x - (-8)x = 13x$$
$$(5 * 5) - (-8 * 5) = 13 * 5$$
$$25 - (-40) = 65$$
$$65 = 65$$

If there are more than two like terms, you can add or subtract the terms in the order they occur and keep a running total.

Example 2:   Simplify the expression $2n - 7n + 3n - 4n$.
$$2n - 7n = -5n$$
$$-5n + 3n = -2n$$
$$-2n - 4n = -6n$$
Therefore, $2n - 7n + 3n - 4n = -6n$

1. Simplify each expression by rewriting it as a single term.

   a. $6y + 13y =$ _____   **b.** $7g - 12g =$ _____

   c. _____ $= 5\frac{1}{2}x - 1\frac{1}{2}x$ **d.** $3c - (-5)c =$ _____

2. Simplify each expression by rewriting it as a single term.

   a. $5y - 3y + 11y =$ _____   **b.** $6g - 8g + 5g - 4g =$ _____

   c. $n + n + n + n + n =$ _____   **d.** $n + 3n + 5n - 7n =$ _____

   e. $2x + 4x - (-9)x =$ _____   **f.** $-7x + 2x + 3x =$ _____

Combining Like Terms (cont.)

An expression like $2y + 6 + 4y - 8 - 9y + (-3)$ is difficult to work with, because it is made up of six different terms that are added and subtracted.

There are two sets of like terms in the expression. The terms $2y$, $4y$, and $9y$ are like terms. The number terms in the expression—6, 8, and (-3)—are a second set of like terms.

Each set of like terms can be combined into a single term. To simplify an expression that has more than one set of like terms, you must combine each set of like terms into a single term.

Example 3:   Simplify $2y + 6 + 4y - 8 - 9y + (-3)$ by combining like terms.

             Step 1:   Combine the y-terms. $2y + 4y - 9y = 6y - 9y = -3y$

             Step 2:   Combine the number terms. $6 - 8 + (-3) = -2 + (-3) = -5$
                         So $2y + 6 + 4y - 8 - 9y + (-3) = -3y + (-5) = -3y - 5$

             Check: Substitute 2 for y in the original expression and the simplified expression.

$$2y + 6 + 4y - 8 - 9y + (-3) = -3y - 5$$

$$(2 * 2) + 6 + (4 * 2) - 8 - (9 * 2) + (-3) = (-3 * 2) - 5$$

$$4 + 6 + 8 - 8 - 18 + -3 = -6 - 5$$

$$-11 = -11$$

Simplify each expression by combining like terms. Check each answer by substituting several values for the variable.

3. $4 + 7y + 20 =$ _____

4. $5x - 3x + 8 =$ _____

5. $5n + 6 - 8n - 2 - 3n =$ _____

6. $n + \pi + 2n - \frac{1}{2}\pi =$ _____

7. $-2.5x + 9 + 1.4x + 0.6 =$ _____

8. $9d + 2a - (-6a) + 3d - 15d =$ _____

Simplifying Algebraic Expressions

Use the distributive property to remove the parentheses from the expression. Then simplify the expression by combining like terms. Check the answer by substituting several values for the variable.

Example: Simplify $20 * (3 + 2x) + 30x$.

        Step 1: Remove the parentheses.
$$20 * (3 + 2x) + 30x = (20 * 3) + (20 * 2x) + 30x$$
$$= 60 + 40x + 30x$$

        Step 2: Simplify the expression by combining like terms.
$$60 + 40x + 30x = 60 + 70x$$

Simplify each expression. Check each answer by substituting several values for the variable.

1. $7 + (5 - 3) * x + 1 =$ _____

2. $2(g - 1) + 1 - 5g =$ _____

3. $\frac{1}{2}(2m + 1) + \frac{1}{2} =$ _____

4. $n + 2n + 3n + (4 + 5)n + 6(7 + 2n) =$ _____

Challenge

5. $6(p - 7) - 5p + 15 + (3p + 2)4 =$ _____

Use with Lesson 95.

Math Boxes 95

1. Write each number in standard notation. Then round each number to the nearest tenth.

 a. four and sixty-two thousandths

 standard notation _____

 rounded _____

 b. three and eighty-eight hundredths
 standard notation _____

 rounded _____

 c. two hundred seventy thousandths
 standard notation _____

 rounded _____ `41`

2. Divide.

 a. $\frac{387}{24} \rightarrow$ _____

 b. 4306/36 $\rightarrow$ _____

`15`

3. Vickie bought a new baseball for $8.95, a new bat for $13.49, and a new basketball for $25.78. How much did she spend for the baseball and bat? _____

How much more did she spend on the basketball than on the baseball and bat? _____ `48 49`

4. Evaluate each expression. Use the rules for order of operations.

 a. $4 * \frac{7}{2} =$ _____

 b. $8 + 5 * 6 =$ _____

 c. $\frac{6^2}{9} + 3 * 4 =$ _____

 d. $8 + 7 - 2 * 5 =$ _____

 e. $\frac{12}{6} + 9 * 3 =$ _____ `161`

5. Fran collects pennies. Fifteen pennies in her collection have the wheat design on the back. These pennies are $\frac{3}{7}$ of her collection. How many pennies does she have in all? _____

Explain. _____
_____
_____ `141 142`

6. Rename each mixed number as a fraction.

 a. $12\frac{3}{4} =$ _____

 b. $8\frac{5}{7} =$ _____

 c. _____ $= 35\frac{2}{3}$

 d. _____ $= 10\frac{11}{15}$

 e. _____ $= 6\frac{7}{8}$ `23`

Simplifying and Solving Equations

Simplify both sides of the following equations. You need not solve them.

1. $5h + 13h = 20 - 2$

2. $2 + x + 2x + 4 = x + 16$

_____

_____

3. $2(y + 2) = 4(y + 3)$

4. $(4 - 1)m - m = (m - 1) * 4$

_____

_____

5. $4y + 6 = 8(1 + y)$

6. $5(x + 3) - 2x = 35 + x$

_____

_____

7. $3 * (3.2 - 2c) = 4.6 + 4c$

8. $\frac{2z + 4}{5} = z - 1$

(*Hint:* Both sides $* 5$)

_____

_____

Simplify each equation. Then solve it. Record the operations you used to solve the equations. Check your solutions.

9. $8d - 3d = 27$

10. $3m - 1 + m + 6 = 2 - 9$

_____

_____

Solution: _____

Solution: _____

Use with Lesson 96.

Simplifying and Solving Equations (cont.)

11. $3(1 + 2y) = y + 2y + 4y$

12. $8 - 12x = 6 * (1 + x)$

_____

Solution: _____

_____

Solution: _____

13. $-4.8 + b + 0.6b = 1.8 + 3.6b$

14. $\frac{t - 3}{4} = \frac{t + 6}{8}$

_____

Solution: _____

_____

Solution: _____

15. $5y + 3 = -6y + 4 + 12y$ $5y + 3 = -6y + 4(1 + 3y)$

Are the two equations above equivalent? _____

Explain your answer. _____

_____

_____

16. $5(f - 2) + 6 = 16$ $f - 1 = 3$

Are the two equations above equivalent? _____

Explain your answer. _____

_____

_____

Math Boxes 96

1. Measure the angles.

a.

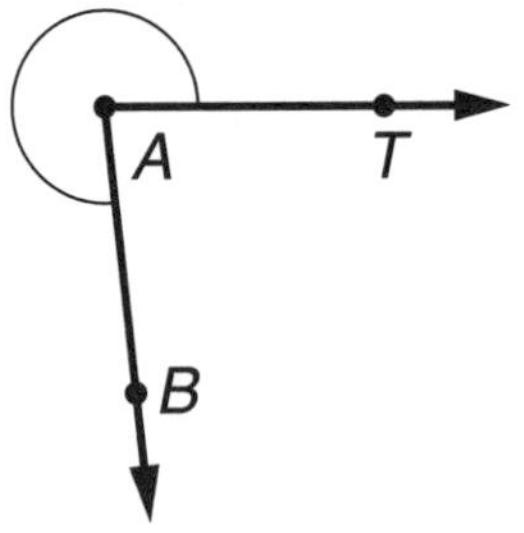

Reflex ∠*BAT* is about _____.

b.

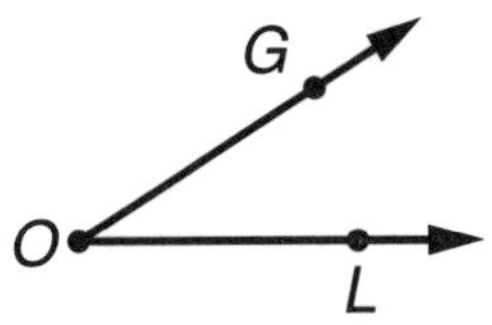

∠*LOG* is about _____.

2. Divide.

a. $\frac{4}{5} \div \frac{2}{7} =$ _____

b. $\frac{1}{9} \div \frac{5}{6} =$ _____

c. $\frac{2}{3} \div \frac{10}{7} =$ _____

d. $\frac{4}{9} \div \frac{8}{5} =$ _____

e. $8 \div \frac{8}{7} =$ _____

3. Solve.   Solution

a. $n - 54 = -29$ _____

b. $25 * y = 5$ _____

c. $v * 0.01 = 0.54$ _____

d. $\frac{376}{w} = 94$ _____

e. $\frac{12}{b} = -4$ _____

4. Circle the equation that describes the relationship between the numbers in the table.

x	y
$\frac{1}{4}$	−2
$\frac{1}{2}$	−1
4	13
10	37

$(x * 4) - 3 = y$

$(4 * x) + 3 = y$

$(y * 5) - 3 = x$

$(4 * y) + 3 = x$

5. Find the following measures for a circle with a radius of 4 cm.

diameter _____ cm

circumference about _____ cm

area   about _____ cm^2

Explain how you found the circumference.

_____

_____

_____

_____

            Use with Lesson 96.

Solving Mobile Problems

The mobile shown in each problem is in balance.
The **fulcrum** is the center point of the rod.
A mobile will balance if $W * D = w * d$.

fulcrum
(at center
of rod)

145 146

Write and solve an equation to answer
each question.

1. What is the distance from the fulcrum to the
   object on the right of the fulcrum?

   $W =$ _____ $D =$ _____ $w =$ _____ $d =$ _____

   Equation: _____   Solution: _____

   Distance: _____ units

2. What is the weight of the object on the left of the fulcrum?

   $W =$ _____ $D =$ _____ $w =$ _____ $d =$ _____

   Equation: _____   Solution: _____

   Weight: _____ units

3. What is the distance from the fulcrum to each of the objects?

   $W =$ _____ $D =$ _____ $w =$ _____ $d =$ _____

   Equation: _____   Solution: _____

   Distance on the left of the fulcrum: _____ units

   Distance on the right of the fulcrum: _____ units

4. What is the weight of each object?

   $W =$ _____ $D =$ _____ $w =$ _____ $d =$ _____

   Equation: _____   Solution: _____

   Weight of the object on the left of the fulcrum: _____ units

   Weight of the object on the right of the fulcrum: _____ units

Solving Mobile Problems (cont.)

The mobile shown in each problem is in balance. The fulcrum is **not** the center point of the rod. In the diagrams below, the fulcrum is shown with a dot and the center point of the rod with a vertical mark. Such mobiles will balance if $(W * D) + (R * L) = w * d$.

Note: The *w* in this formula always refers to the weight of the object that is farthest from the center point, and *d* refers to that object's distance from the fulcrum.

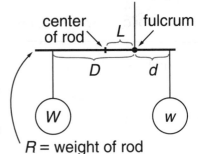

R = weight of rod

Write and solve an equation to answer each question.

5. What is the weight of the rod?

   $W =$ _____ $D =$ _____ $R =$ _____

   $L =$ _____ $w =$ _____ $d =$ _____

   Equation: _____

   Solution: _____   Weight of rod: _____ units

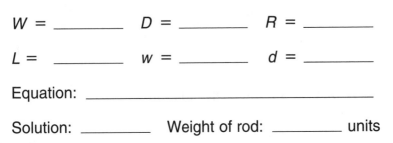

weight of rod = 10x

6. What is the length of the rod? What is the distance from the fulcrum to the object on the right of the fulcrum?

   $W =$ _____ $D =$ _____ $R =$ _____

   $L =$ _____ $w =$ _____ $d =$ _____

   Equation: _____

   Solution: _____   Length of rod: _____ units

   Distance on the right of the fulcrum: _____ units

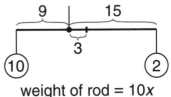

weight of rod = 5

7. What is the weight of each object?

   $W =$ _____ $D =$ _____ $R =$ _____

   $L =$ _____ $w =$ _____ $d =$ _____

   Equation: _____

   Solution: _____

   Weight on the left: _____ units   Weight on the right: _____ units

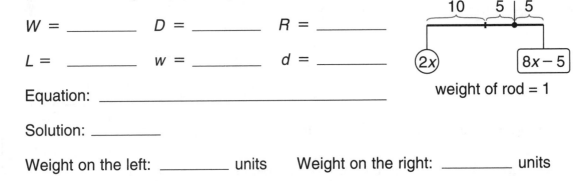

weight of rod = 1

Use with Lesson 97.

Math Boxes 97

1. Complete the Venn diagram.

21   14

Name at least two ways in which the numbers 21 and 14 are alike.

Name at least two ways in which they are different.

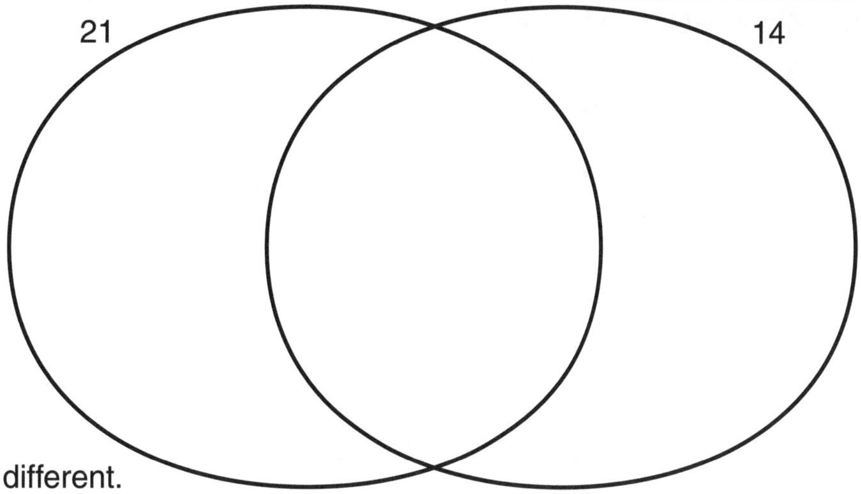

2. Fill in the blanks. (*Hint:* For decimals, think fractions.)

a. $\frac{4}{9}$ * _____ = 1

b. $\frac{11}{12}$ * _____ = 1

c. $\frac{16}{5}$ * _____ = 1

d. 0.3 * _____ = 1

e. 0.06 * _____ = 1

3. Write in standard notation.

a. 5^2 = _____

b. 2^5 = _____

c. _____ = 6^2

d. _____ = 4^3

e. _____ = 10^9

4. The table shows the results of a survey that asked Internet surfers how they most often find sites to visit. Fill in the missing information in the table. Use a protractor to make a circle graph of the results. Do not use the Percent Circle.

Method	Number of People	Percent of Total
Word-of-mouth	43	
Printed material	26	
Browsing	14	
Links	9	
Other	8	
Total		

Math Boxes 98

1. Write each number in standard notation. Then round each number to the nearest tenth.

   a. six and twenty-nine hundredths

      standard notation _____

      rounded _____

   b. four and thirteen ten-thousandths

      standard notation _____

      rounded _____

   c. fourteen and sixty-two hundredths

      standard notation _____

      rounded _____

2. Divide.

   a. $\frac{795}{67}$ → _____

   b. 3994/43 → _____

3. Fabian kept track of his lunch costs for one week. He bought a turkey sandwich for $1.35 on Monday and again on Tuesday. He bought a hamburger for $2.19 on Wednesday and a pizza for $1.89 on Thursday. He spent a total of $5.97 on Wednesday, Thursday, and Friday. Which did he buy on Friday—
a turkey sandwich,
a hamburger,
or a pizza? _____

4. Evaluate each expression. Use the rules for order of operations.

   a. $15 - 3 * 4 =$ _____

   b. $\frac{20}{4} * 5 + 8 * 2 =$ _____

   c. $7 * 3^2 - \frac{10}{2} =$ _____

   d. $8 * (2 + 5) - 4 =$ _____

   e. $0.01 + 0.01 * 10 + 0.01 =$ _____

5. Allen worked all summer mowing lawns, baby-sitting, and pulling weeds. He earned $50 mowing lawns. This was $\frac{2}{5}$ of the money he earned. How much did he earn in all? _____

Explain. _____

_____

_____

6. Rename each mixed number as a fraction.

   a. $9\frac{5}{6} =$ _____

   b. $11\frac{4}{9} =$ _____

   c. $20\frac{5}{8} =$ _____

   d. _____ $= 15\frac{1}{4}$

   e. _____ $= 25\frac{7}{10}$

A Picnic Budget Spreadsheet

The following spreadsheet gives budget information for a class picnic:

	A	B	C	D
		Class Picnic ($)		
1		budget for class picnic		
2				
3	quantity	food items	unit price	cost
4	6	packages of hamburgers	2.79	16.74
5	5	packages of hamburger buns	1.29	6.45
6	3	bags of potato chips	3.12	9.36
7	3	quarts of macaroni salad	4.50	13.50
8	4	bottles of soft drinks	1.69	6.76
9			subtotal	52.81
10			8% tax	4.23
11			total	57.04

1. What information is shown in row 8? _____

2. What kind of information is shown in
    Column A (labels, numbers, or formulas)? _____

3. Cell D6 holds the formula D6 = A6 * C6.

    a. What formula is stored in Cell D4? _____

    b. What formula is stored in Cell D8? _____

4. Circle the formula stored in Cell D9.

    D9 = C4 + C5 + C6 + C7 + C8   D9 = D4 + D5 + D6 + D7 + D8

5. a. What is calculated by the formula stored in Cell D10? _____

    b. Circle the formula stored in Cell D10.

       D10 = 0.08 * C9   D10 = 0.08 * D9   D10 = 8 * D9

6. a. What is calculated by the formula stored in Cell D11? _____

    b. Write the formula stored in D11. _____

7. a. Which cells in the spreadsheet would change if you
        changed the number of bags of potato chips to 4? _____

    b. Calculate the number that would be shown in each of these cells.

Stopping Distance for an Automobile

The driver of an automobile may need to stop quickly. The time it takes to stop depends on the speed at which the car is traveling. It will take the driver about $\frac{3}{4}$ second to react before actually stepping on the brake pedal. Once the brake has been depressed, it will take additional time before the car comes to a complete stop.

The spreadsheet below shows the minimum stopping distances for various vehicle speeds.

1. The spreadsheet is not completely filled in. Calculate and record the numbers for the cells in rows 9, 10, and 11. (*Hint:* Use the formulas given in Cells B4, C4, and D4.)

	A	B	C	D
			Stopping Distances	
1	minimum stopping distance on a dry, level, concrete surface			
2				
3	speed (mph)	reaction-time distance (ft)	braking distance (ft)	total stopping distance (ft)
4		distance = 1.1 $*$ speed	distance = 0.06 $*$ speed^2	distance = 1.1 $*$ speed + 0.06 $*$ speed^2
5	10	11	6	17
6	20	22	24	46
7	30	33	54	87
8	40	44	96	140
9	50			
10	60			
11	70			

2. Circle the cell(s) that contain labels.

   A3　　　　　　　B10　　　　　　　C6　　　　　　　D4

3. Circle the cell(s) that contain numbers used in calculations but not in formulas.

   B4　　　　　　　A5　　　　　　　D5　　　　　　　C10

4. Circle the cell(s) in which formulas are stored.

   D9　　　　　　　B5　　　　　　　A11　　　　　　　C4

5. Write the formula stored in each cell.

   B7 = _____　　　D11 = _____

6. If you change the number in Cell A7 to 35, will the numbers in any other

   cells change? _____　　　If so, which cells? _____

360

Stopping Distance for an Automobile (cont.)

7. Use the data in the spreadsheet on page 360.

    a. Graph the number pairs for **speed** and **reaction-time distance** on the first grid below. Make a line graph by connecting the points.

    b. Graph the number pairs for **speed** and **braking distance** on the second grid below. Make a line graph by connecting the points.

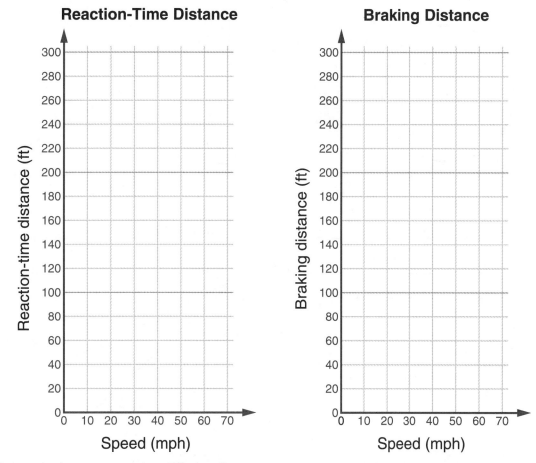

Reaction-Time Distance   **Braking Distance**

8. How are the two graphs different?

_____

_____

_____

9. Complete the statement. At speeds of 50 miles per hour or more,

_____

_____

_____

Math Message: Area Formulas

Calculate the area of each figure below. A summary of useful area formulas appears on pages 118–121 of the *Student Reference Book*.

Measure any dimensions you need to the nearest tenth of a centimeter. Record the dimensions next to each figure. You may need to draw and measure one or two line segments on a figure. Round your answers to the nearest square centimeter.

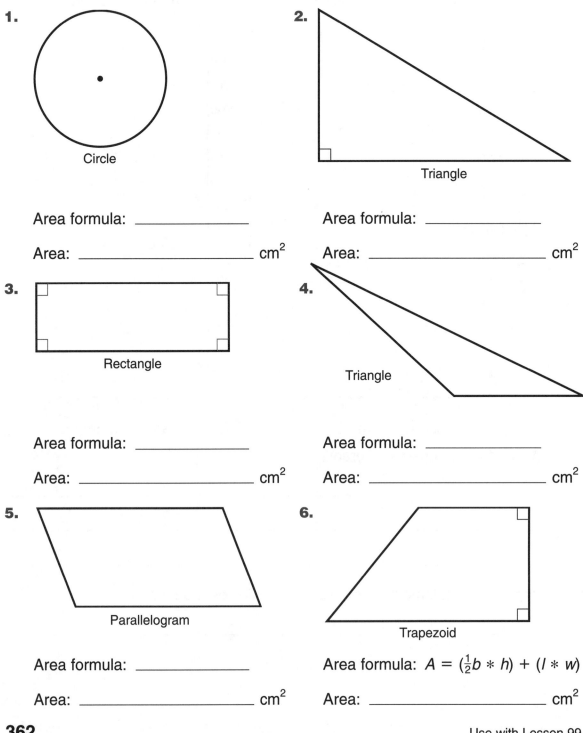

1.

Circle

2.

Triangle

3.

Rectangle

4.

Triangle

5.

Parallelogram

6.

Trapezoid

Area formula: _____

Area: _____ cm^2

Area formula: _____

Area: _____ cm^2

Area formula: _____

Area: _____ cm^2

Area formula: _____

Area: _____ cm^2

Area formula: _____

Area: _____ cm^2

Area formula: $A = (\frac{1}{2}b * h) + (l * w)$

Area: _____ cm^2

Perimeter, Circumference, and Area Problems

Solve each problem. Explain your answers.

1. Rectangle *PERK* has a perimeter of 40 feet.

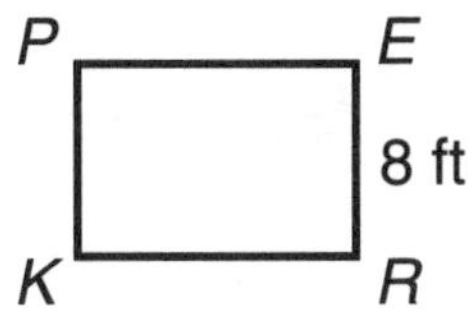

Length of side *PE:* _____ ft

Area of rectangle *PERK:* _____ ft^2

P ⌐————————┐ E
  | | 8 ft
K └—————————┘ R

_____

_____

_____

_____

_____

2. The area of triangle *ABC* is 300 meters^2.
What is the length of side *AB*?

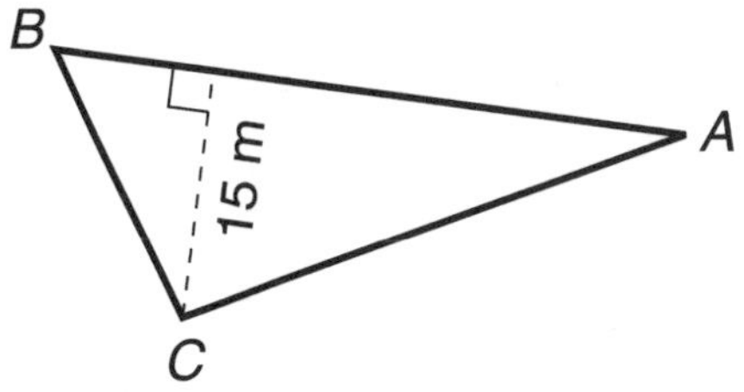

Length of side *AB:* _____ m

_____

B, 15 m, A, C

_____

_____

_____

_____

3. The area of parallelogram *KLMN* is 72 square inches.
The length of side *LX* is 6 inches, and the length of
side *KY* is 3 inches.

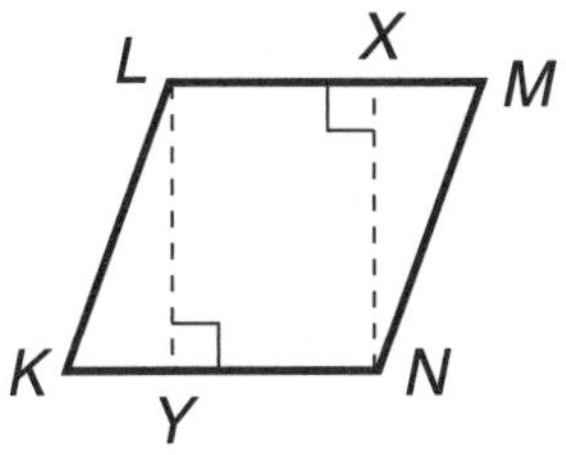

What is the length of $\overline{LY}$?

Length of $\overline{LY}$: _____ in

L, X, M, K, Y, N

_____

_____

_____

_____

Perimeter, Circumference, and Area Problems (cont.)

4. The area of triangle *ACE* is 42 square yards. What is the area of rectangle *BCDE*?

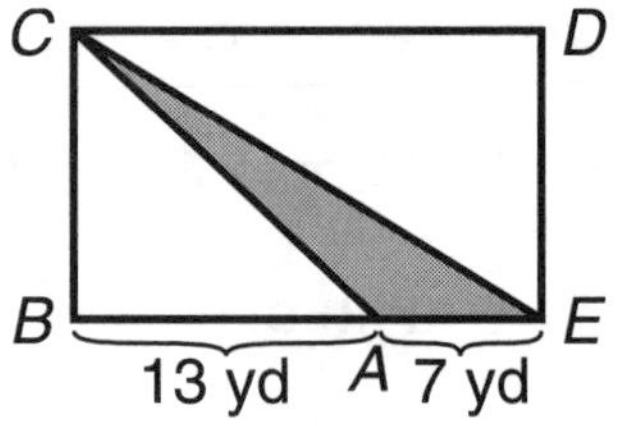

Area of rectangle *BCDE:* _____ yd²

_____

_____

_____

_____

_____

C ———————————— *D*

B ⌐————————————⌐ *E*

13 yd   *A*   7 yd

5. To the nearest percent, about what percent of the area of the square is covered by the area of the circle?

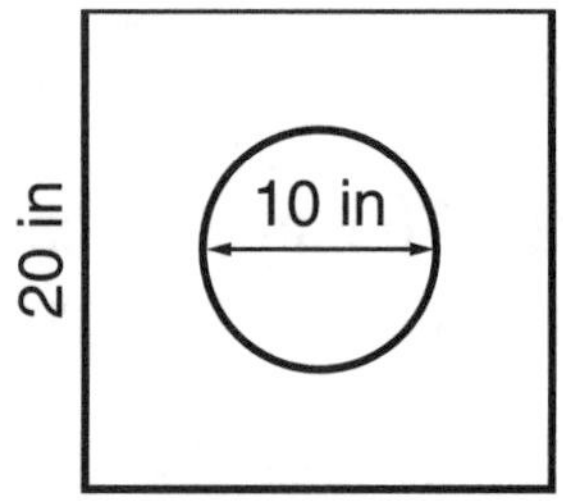

Answer: _____%

_____

_____

_____

_____

20 in

10 in

6. Which path is longer: once around the figure 8— from *A,* to *B,* to *C,* to *B,* and back to *A*—or once around the large circle? _____

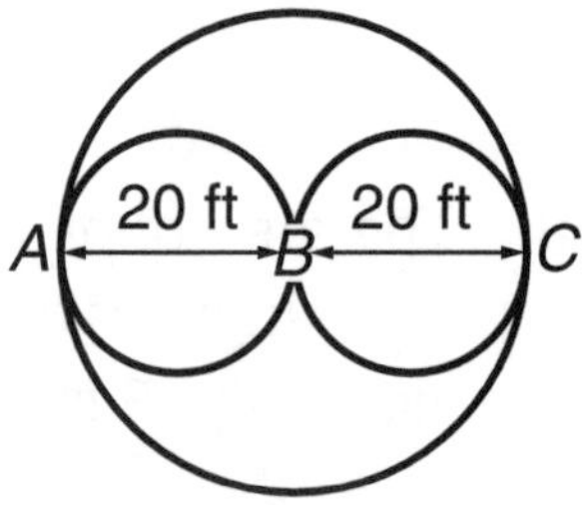

_____

_____

_____

_____

_____

_____

A   20 ft   *B*   20 ft   *C*

Use with Lesson 99.

Math Boxes 99

1. Multiply or divide.

   a. $-150/15$ = _____

   b. $-16 * (-4)$ = _____

   c. $20 * (-9)$ = _____

   d. $-180/30$ = _____

   e. $360/(-4)$ = _____

59

2. Insert parentheses to make each number sentence true.

   a. $0.01 * 7 + 9 / 4 = 0.04$

   b. $\frac{4}{5} * 25 - 10 / 2 = 15$

   c. $\sqrt{64} / 5 + 3 * 3 = 3$

   d. $5 * 10^2 + 10^2 * 2 = 2000$

   e. $5 * 10^2 + 10^2 * 2 = 700$

157

3. Measure angle *ELF* with your full-circle protractor.

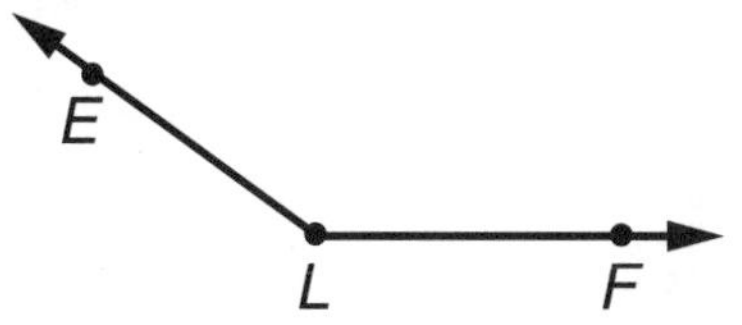

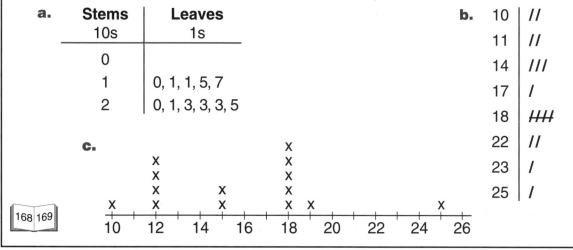

Measure of $\angle ELF$ is about _____°.

$\angle ELF$ is which kind of angle? (Circle one.)

acute obtuse reflex right straight

72 113

4. Complete.

   a. $\frac{1}{3}$ of 216 = _____

   b. $\frac{5}{8}$ of 160 = _____

   c. $\frac{9}{10}$ of 300 = _____

   d. $\frac{3}{20}$ of 420 = _____

   e. $\frac{5}{7}$ of 777 = _____

36

5. Which data set displayed below has the following landmarks: maximum 25, minimum 10, mode 18, median 18? (Circle its letter.)

a.

Stems 10s	Leaves 1s
0	
1	0, 1, 1, 5, 7
2	0, 1, 3, 3, 3, 5

b.

10	//
11	//
14	///
17	/
18	ЖЖ
22	//
23	/
25	/

c.

```
                        X
        X               X
        X               X
        X       X       X
  X     X       X       X   X             X
 ──┼────┼────┼────┼────┼────┼────┼────┼────┼──
  10    12   14   16   18   20   22   24   26
```

168 169

Calculating the Volume of the Human Body

An average adult human male is about 69 inches (175 centimeters) tall and weighs about 170 pounds (77 kilograms). The drawings below show how a man's body may be approximated by 7 cylinders, 1 rectangular prism, and 1 sphere.

The drawings use the scale 1 mm:1 cm. This means that every length of 1 millimeter in the drawing represents 1 centimeter of actual body length. The drawing below is 175 millimeters high. Therefore, it represents a male who is 175 centimeters tall.

head
(sphere)

neck
(cylinder)

torso
(rectangular
prism)

2 arms
(cylinders)

2 upper legs
(cylinders)

2 lower legs
(cylinders)

scale is 1 mm:1 cm

torso
(rectangular
prism)
(side view)

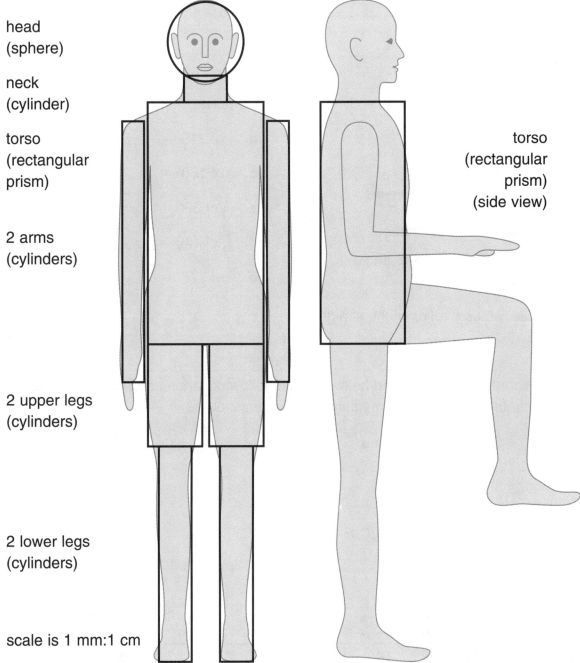

Calculating the Volume of the Human Body (cont.)

1. **a.** Use a centimeter ruler to estimate the diameters of the cylinders and sphere and the dimensions of the rectangular prism shown on page 366. Record your estimates on the drawing. Then record the radius of each cylinder and the sphere and the dimensions of the rectangular prism in the table below. (To find the radius, divide the diameter by 2.)

   Be sure to record the actual body dimensions. For example, if you measure the length of an arm as 72 millimeters, record this as 72 centimeters, because the scale of the drawings is 1 mm:1 cm.

   b. Calculate the volume of each body part and record it in the table. You will find a summary of useful volume formulas on pages 122–126 in your *Student Reference Book*. (Volume of a sphere: $V = \frac{4}{3}\pi r^3$)

   For the arm, upper leg, and lower leg, multiply the volume by 2. Add to find the total volume of an average adult male's body. Your answer will be in cubic centimeters.

Body Part and Shape	Actual Body Dimensions (cm)		Volume (cm³) (Round to the nearest 1000 cm³.)
head (sphere)	radius:		* 1 =
neck (cylinder)	radius:	height:	* 1 =
torso (rectangular prism)	length: height:	width:	* 1 =
arm (cylinder)	radius:	height:	* 2 =
upper leg (cylinder)	radius:	height:	* 2 =
lower leg (cylinder)	radius:	height:	* 2 =
	Total volume:		about

2. One liter is equal to 1000 cubic centimeters. Use this fact to complete the following statement: I estimate that the total volume of an average adult male's body is about _____ liters.

3. John weighs about 136 pounds. What is the ratio of John's weight to the average adult male's weight of about 170 pounds? Ratio:_____ to 1

   Use the ratio to estimate the volume of John's body. The volume of John's body is about _____ cm³, or about _____ liters.

Perimeter and Area Problems

Study the example. Then solve the problems.

Example: The area of triangle *ABC* is 21 square inches.

Find the length of side *AB*.

Solution: 1. Write the formula for the area of a triangle: Area $= \frac{1}{2} * b * h$
2. Substitute the dimensions in the formula: $21 = \frac{1}{2} * 6 * (3x + 1)$
3. Solve the equation: $21 = 3 * (3x + 1)$
$21 = 9x + 3$
$18 = 9x$, so $2 = x$
$3x + 1 = (3 * 2) + 1$, or 7
4. Answer the question: Side *AB* is 7 inches long.
5. Check the answer: Area $= \frac{1}{2} * 6 * 7 = \frac{1}{2} * 42 = 21$ in^2

1. The area of rectangle *RPQT* is 14 ft^2. Find the length of side *RP*.

Formula: Area $=$ _____

Substitute: _____ $=$ _____

Solve:

Length of $\overline{RP}$: _____

Check: _____

2. The area of parallelogram *FLOW* is 15 in^2. Find the length of side *FL*.

Formula: Area $=$ _____

Substitute: _____ $=$ _____

Solve:

Length of $\overline{FL}$: _____

Check: _____

3. The perimeter of triangle *MNO* is 29 centimeters. Find the length of each side.

Formula: Perimeter $=$ sum of lengths of sides

Substitute: _____ $=$ _____

Solve:

Length of $\overline{MN}$:_____ $\overline{NO}$: _____ $\overline{MO}$: _____

Check: _____

368

Math Boxes 100

1. Add or subtract.

a. $5\frac{5}{6} + 3\frac{2}{3} =$ _____

b. $\frac{3}{10} + 8\frac{5}{4} =$ _____

c. $12\frac{1}{9} - 7\frac{1}{6} =$ _____

d. $2\frac{4}{7} + 6\frac{5}{9} =$ _____

e. $3\frac{7}{8} - 2\frac{5}{12} =$ _____

$\begin{array}{|c|} \hline 33 \\ 34 \end{array} \begin{array}{|c|} \hline 35 \\ \hline \end{array}$

2. **a.** Divide: 9755/82 → _____

b. Write a number story for the division problem in Part a.

_____

_____

_____

_____

$\boxed{15}$

3. Use your calculator to complete the table. $\boxed{7 \mid 8}$

Problem	Calculator Display	Scientific Notation	Standard Notation
$8{,}200{,}000^2$			
$30^8 - 70^6$			
$80^6 + 600^4$			
$50^3 * 50^3$			
$\frac{490^3}{7^2}$			

4. The high temperature in Chicago on January 3 was 38°F, and the low temperature was 24°F. Then a cold front moved in. The low temperature on January 4 was −5°F.

By how many degrees did the temperature drop from the high on January 3 to the low on January 4?

Write a number model to show how you found your answer.

_____

$\boxed{58}$

Solving Equations by Trial and Error

If you substitute a number for the variable in an equation and the result is a true number sentence, then that number is a solution of the equation. One way to solve an equation is to try several **test numbers** until you find the solution. Each test number can help you "close in" on the exact solution. Using this **trial-and-error method** for solving equations, you may not find the exact solution, but you can come very close to the exact solution.

Example: Find a solution of the equation $\frac{1}{x} + x = 4$ by trial and error. If you can't find an exact solution, try to find a number that is very close to an exact solution.

The table shows the results of substituting several test numbers for x.

x	$\frac{1}{x}$	$\frac{1}{x} + x$	Compare ($\frac{1}{x} + x$) to 4
1	1	2	less than 4
2	0.5	2.5	still less than 4, but closer
3	$0.\overline{3}$	$3.\overline{3}$	less than 4, but even closer
4	0.25	4.25	greater than 4

These results suggest that we try testing numbers for x that are between 3 and 4.

x	$\frac{1}{x}$	$\frac{1}{x} + x$	Compare ($\frac{1}{x} + x$) to 4
3.9	0.256...	4.156...	> 4
3.6	$0.2\overline{7}$	$3.8\overline{7}$	< 4

We're getting closer. Your turn. Try other test numbers. See how close you can get to 4 for the value of $\frac{1}{x} + x$.

x	$\frac{1}{x}$	$\frac{1}{x} + x$	Compare ($\frac{1}{x} + x$) to 4

My closest solution: _____

Solving Equations by Trial and Error (cont.)

Find the numbers that are closest to the solutions of the equations. Use the suggested test numbers to get started.

1. Equation: $\sqrt{y} + y = 10$

y	$\sqrt{y}$	$\sqrt{y} + y$	Compare ($\sqrt{y} + y$) to 10
0	0	0	< 10
5	2.24	7.24	
9	3		

My closest solution: _____

2. Equation: $x^2 - 3x = 8$

x	$3x$	x^2	$x^2 - 3x$	Compare ($x^2 - 3x$) to 8
4				
6				
5				

My closest solution: _____

Use with Lesson 101.

Using Formulas to Solve Problems

To solve a problem using a formula, you can substitute the known quantities for variables in the formula and solve the resulting equation.

Example: A formula for converting between Celsius and Fahrenheit temperatures is $F = 1.8C + 32$, where C represents the Celsius and F the Fahrenheit temperature.

- Use the formula to convert 30°C to degrees Fahrenheit.
  $F = 1.8C + 32$
  Substitute 30 for C in the formula: $F = (1.8 * 30) + 32$
  Solve the equation: $F = 86$
  Answer: 30°C = 86°F

- Use the formula to convert 50°F to degrees Celsius.
  $F = 1.8C + 32$
  Substitute 50 for F in the formula: $50 = (1.8 * C) + 32$
  Solve the equation: $10 = C$
  Answer: 50°F = 10°C

1. The formula $W = 570A - 850$ expresses the relationship between the average number of words small children know and their ages (for ages 2 to 8). The variable W represents the number of words known and A the age in years.

   a. About how many words might a $3\frac{1}{4}$-year-old child know? _____

   b. About how old might a child be who knows about 1700 words? _____

2. A bowler whose average score is less than 200 is given a handicap. The **handicap** is a number of points that is added to a bowler's score for each game. A common handicap formula is $H = 0.8 * (200 - A)$, where H is the handicap and A the average score.

   a. What is the handicap of a bowler whose average score is 160? _____

   b. What is the average score of a bowler whose handicap is 68 points? _____

3. An adult human female's height can be estimated from the length of her tibia (shinbone) by using the formula $h = 2.4 * t + 75$, where h is the height in centimeters and t is the length of the tibia in centimeters.

   a. Estimate the height of a female
   whose tibia is 31 centimeters long.   _____ cm

   b. Estimate the length of a female's
   tibia if she is 175 centimeters tall.   _____ cm

Math Boxes 101

1. Multiply.

   a. $5.67 * 2.02 = $ _____

   b. $443.6 * 0.08 = $ _____

   c. $12.7 * 6.63 = $ _____

   d. _____ $= 773.5 * 5.5$

   e. _____ $= 25.1 * 0.3$

52

2. Circle the equation that describes the relationship between the numbers in the table.

x	y
1	$\frac{3}{8}$
2	$\frac{3}{4}$
8	3
24	9

$\frac{y}{8} * 3 = x$

$(3 * y) + 8 = x$

$\frac{x}{8} * 3 = y$

$(3 * x) + 8 = y$

165

3. Frederick and Lucille conducted a survey to find out how many of their classmates had brothers and sisters. They surveyed 31 students and learned that 18 had at least one sister and 21 had at least one brother.

Draw a Venn diagram to represent the results of Frederick and Lucille's survey.

How many students had at least one brother and one sister? _____

153

4. Write the following numbers with words.

   a. 0.043 _____

   b. 27.28 _____

   c. 0.0064 _____

   d. 2.909 _____

   e. 442.77 _____

42

A Box Problem

You are given a square piece of cardboard that measures 8 inches along each side. To construct an open box out of the cardboard, you can cut same-sized squares from the 4 corners of the cardboard and then turn up and tape the sides.

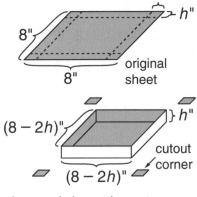

box made by cutting out square corners and folding up sides

1. John cut small squares to make his box. Amy cut large squares to make her box.

    a. Whose box was taller? _____

    b. Whose box had a
       greater area of the base? _____

The volume of the box depends on the size of the squares cut from the corners.

2. Find the dimensions of a box with the greatest possible volume. Use a trial-and-error method to solve the problem. Keep a record of your results in the spreadsheet below.

    a. Three test values for h (the height of the box) are listed in Column A. Complete Rows 4, 5, and 6.

	A	B	C	D
			Boxes	
1	Problem: Find the length that maximizes the box volume.			
2	box height (in)	box length, width (in)	base area of box (in^2)	volume of box (in^3)
3	h	$8 - 2h$	$(8 - 2h)^2$	$(8 - 2h)^2 * h$
4	1	6	36	
5	2			
6	3			
7				
8				
9				

    b. Use the results in your spreadsheet to select new test values for h that are likely to give a box of greater volume.

       The box that I found with the greatest volume has a height of

       _____ inches and a volume of _____ cubic inches.

Date _____ Time _____

Perimeter, Area, and Volume Problems

Solve each problem. You may need to look up formulas in your
Student Reference Book. Check your answers.

116 123 126

1. ∠*ABC* is a right angle. What is the degree measure of
    ∠*CBD*? Of ∠*ABD*?

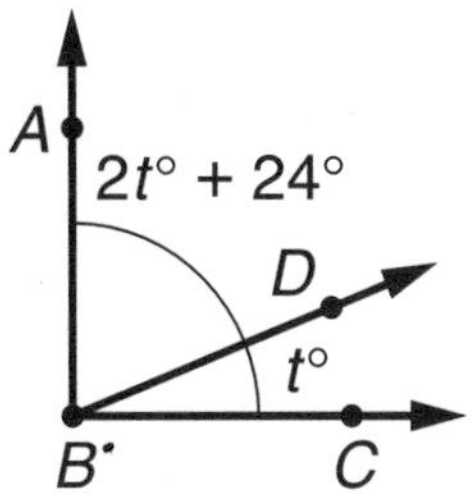

    Equation: _____

    Solve:

    Measure of ∠*CBD* = _____°. Measure of ∠*ABD* = _____°.

2. The **capacity** (volume) of the desk drawer is 1365 in³.
    Find the depth (*d*) of the drawer.

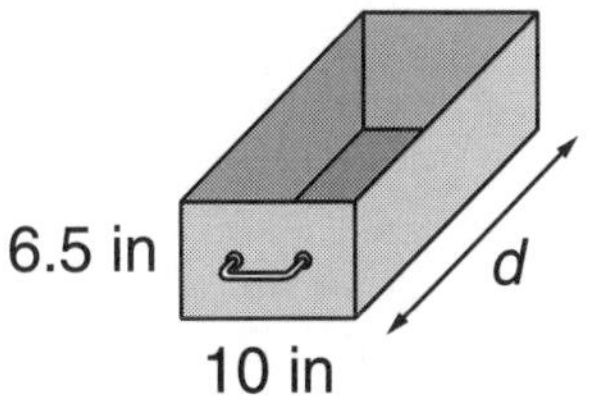

    Formula: _____

    Substitute: _____

    Solve:

    Depth of drawer = _____

3. Triangle *MJQ* and square *EFGH*
    have the same perimeter. The
    dimensions are given in millimeters.
    What are the lengths of sides *MQ*
    and *MJ* in triangle *MJQ*?

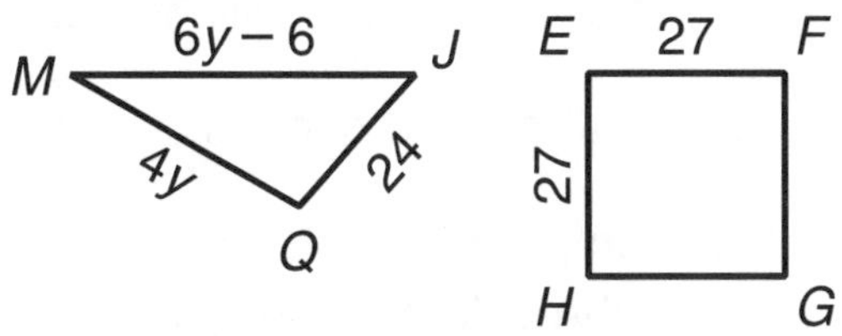

    Equation: _____

    Solve:

    Length of $\overline{MQ}$ = _____. Length of $\overline{MJ}$ = _____.

Use with Lesson 102.

375

Perimeter, Area, and Volume Problems (cont.)

4. The cylindrical can has a capacity of 4 liters
(4 liters = 4000 cm^3). Find the height (*h*) of the
can, to the nearest centimeter.

8 cm

h

Formula: _____

Substitute: _____

Solve:

Height = _____.

5. The area of the shaded part of rectangle *RSTU* is 78 ft^2.
Find the length of side *TU*.

Solve:

R   *S*

6 ft   7 ft   10 ft

U (2*x* + 2) ft *T*

Length of side *TU* = _____.

6. A soccer ball has a 9-inch diameter.

9 in

a. What is the shape of the
smallest box that will hold the ball? _____

b. What are the dimensions of the box? _____

c. Compare the volume of the box to the volume of the ball.
Is the volume of the box more or
less than twice the volume of the ball? _____
(*Reminder:* A formula for finding the volume of a sphere is $V = \frac{4}{3} * \pi * r^3$.)

Explain your answer. _____

_____

_____

Date

Time

Math Boxes 102

1. Multiply or divide.

a. _____ = 4 ∗ 15

b. _____ = −70 ∗ (−300)

c. _____ = −380/19

d. _____ = 35 ∗ (−4)

e. _____ = −72/8

2. Insert parentheses to make each equation true.

a. $\frac{1}{2}$ ∗ 18 + 2 ∗ 15 = 150

b. $\frac{1}{2}$ ∗ 18 + 2 ∗ 15 = 39

c. 5 / 3 + 3 ∗ 5 = $4\frac{1}{6}$

d. 0.8 ∗ 20 + 10 ∗ 0.7 = 23

e. 4 / 9 + 3 ∗ 6 = 2

3. Measure angle *NOG* with your full-circle protractor.

Measure of ∠*NOG* is about _____°.

∠*NOG* is which kind of angle? (Circle one.)

acute obtuse reflex right straight

4. Complete.

a. $\frac{3}{4}$ of 280 = _____

b. $\frac{4}{12}$ of 303 = _____

c. $\frac{5}{6}$ of 420 = _____

d. $\frac{2}{9}$ of 360 = _____

e. $\frac{3}{5}$ of 1200 = _____

5. Which data set below has the following landmarks: range 29, maximum 48, mode 22, median 34? (Circle its letter.)

a.

Stems 10s	Leaves 1s
0	
1	9, 9
2	1, 2, 2, 2, 2, 5, 7
3	4, 6, 6, 8, 9, 9
4	2, 7, 8, 8

b.

20	/
22	///
24	//
25	/
34	//
35	//
36	/
37	/
39	//
42	/
48	/

c.

Use with Lesson 102.

377

Date _____ Time _____

Math Message: Square Roots

You know that the **square of a number** is equal to the number multiplied by itself. For example, $5^2 = 5 * 5 = 25$.

The **square root** of a number n is a number whose square is n. For example, a square root of 25 is 5, because $5^2 = 5 * 5 = 25$.

The square root of 25 is also equal to -5, because $(-5) * (-5) = (-5)^2 = 25$. So every positive number has two square roots, which are opposites of each other.

We use the symbol $\sqrt{}$ to write positive square roots. $\sqrt{25}$ is read as *the positive square root of 25*.

1. Write the square root of each number.

    a. $\sqrt{81}$ = _____   **b.** $\sqrt{100}$ = _____   **c.** $\sqrt{100^2}$ = _____

2. What is the square root of zero? _____

3. Can a negative number have a square root? _____

    Explain. _____

    _____

To find the positive square root of a number with a calculator, enter the number and press the [$\sqrt{}$] key. (If necessary, press the [2nd] key before [x^2].) For example, to find the square root of 25, enter 25 and press the [$\sqrt{}$] key. The display will show 5.

4. Solve these problems on the calculator. Round your answers to a and d to the nearest hundredth.

    a. $\sqrt{17}$ = _____   **b.** $\sqrt{17} * \sqrt{17}$ = _____

    c. $\sqrt{\pi} * \sqrt{\pi}$ = _____   **d.** $\sqrt{\pi}$ = _____

    e. $(\sqrt{17})^2$ = _____   **f.** $\sqrt{\frac{1}{16}}$ = _____
       (Use the [$\sqrt{}$] and [x^2] keys.)

5. The length of a side of a square is $\sqrt{6.25}$ centimeters. What is the area of the square?   _____

6. The area of a square is 21 square inches. What is the length of a side, to the nearest tenth of an inch?   _____

7. The radius of a circle is $\sqrt{20}$ feet. What is its area?   about _____

Challenge

8. The area of a circle is 14 square meters. What is its radius?   about _____

Verifying the Pythagorean Theorem

In a right triangle, the side opposite the right angle is called the **hypotenuse.** The other two sides are called the **legs of the triangle.**

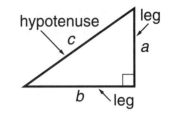

Think about the following statement:

If a and b are the lengths of the legs of a right triangle and c is the length of the hypotenuse, then $a^2 + b^2 = c^2$.

This statement is known as the **Pythagorean Theorem.**

1. To verify that the Pythagorean Theorem is true, use a blank sheet of paper that has square corners. Draw diagonal lines to form 4 right triangles, one at each corner. Then measure the lengths of the legs and the hypotenuse of each right triangle, to the nearest millimeter.

    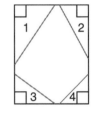

    Record the lengths in the table below. Then complete the table.

Triangle	Leg (a)	Leg (b)	Hypotenuse (c)	$a^2 + b^2$	c^2
1					
2					
3					
4					

2. Compare $(a^2 + b^2)$ to c^2 for each of the triangles you drew. Why might these two numbers be slightly different?

    _____

    _____

3. Use the Pythagorean Theorem to find c^2 for the triangle at the right. Then find the length c.

    $c^2 =$ _____ $c =$ _____

Using the Pythagorean Theorem

In Problems 1–6, use the Pythagorean Theorem to find each missing length.
Round your answer to the nearest tenth.

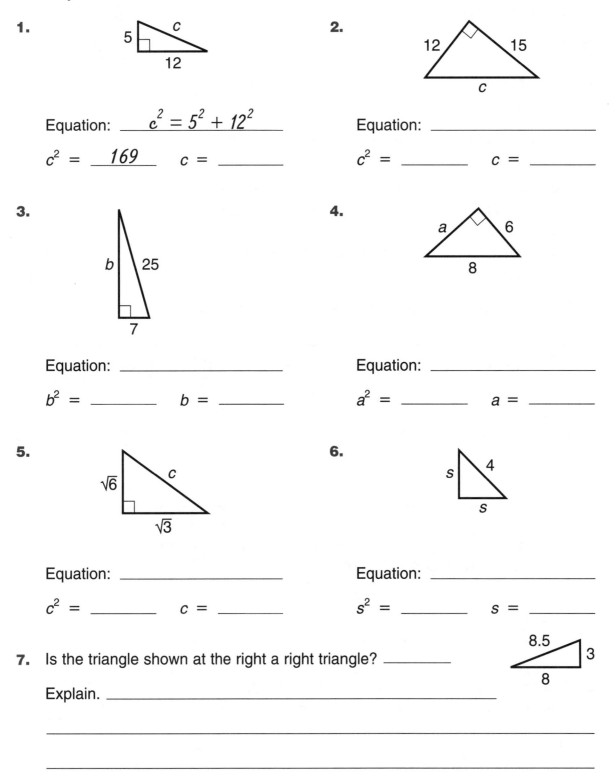

1.

Equation: $c^2 = 5^2 + 12^2$

$c^2 = \underline{\quad 169 \quad}$ $c = \underline{\qquad}$

2.

Equation: _____

$c^2 = \underline{\qquad}$ $c = \underline{\qquad}$

3.

Equation: _____

$b^2 = \underline{\qquad}$ $b = \underline{\qquad}$

4.

Equation: _____

$a^2 = \underline{\qquad}$ $a = \underline{\qquad}$

5.

Equation: _____

$c^2 = \underline{\qquad}$ $c = \underline{\qquad}$

6.

Equation: _____

$s^2 = \underline{\qquad}$ $s = \underline{\qquad}$

7. Is the triangle shown at the right a right triangle? _____

Explain. _____

_____

_____

Date _____ Time _____

Math Boxes 103

1. Add or subtract.

 a. $7\frac{3}{8} - 5\frac{9}{5} =$ _____

 b. $2\frac{4}{10} + \frac{11}{7} =$ _____

 c. $9\frac{4}{3} - 8\frac{1}{5} =$ _____

 d. $\frac{38}{12} + \frac{19}{4} =$ _____

 e. $15\frac{1}{9} - 2\frac{14}{5} =$ _____

2. **a.** Divide: $4791/24 \rightarrow$ _____

 b. Write a number story for the division problem in Part a.

 _____

 _____

 _____

 _____

3. Use your calculator to complete the table.

Problem	Calculator Display	Scientific Notation	Standard Notation
$760,000^2$			
$20^{10} - 300^5$			
$100^6 + 1000^4$			
$400^7 * 0.1^3$			
$\frac{900^9}{900^3}$			

4. When Marlene removed her dinner from the freezer, the temperature of the dinner was $-10°C$. She heated the dinner in the oven, and then put it on the table. It cooled to room temperature, $23°C$, while she was talking on the phone.

How many degrees warmer was the dinner at room temperature than it was when removed from the freezer? _____

Write a number model to show how you found your answer.

 _____

Use with Lesson 103.

381

Similar Figures and the Size-Change Factor

The two butterfly clamps shown below are similar because they each have the same shape.

One clamp is an enlargement of the other. The size-change factor tells the amount of enlargement.

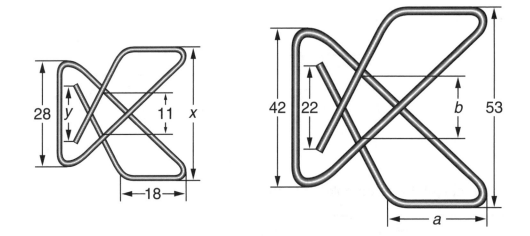

unit: millimeters (mm)

1. The size-change factor for the clamps shown above is _____.

In Problems 2–5, use the size-change factor to find the missing lengths.

2. a = _____ mm = _____ cm

3. b = _____ mm = _____ cm

4. x = _____ mm = _____ cm

5. y = _____ mm = _____ cm

6. If a butterfly clamp is straightened out, it forms a long, thin cylinder. When the small clamp is straightened out, it is 21 cm long, and the thickness (diameter) of the clamp is 0.15 cm. Its radius is 0.075 cm. Calculate the volume of the small clamp. Use the formula $V = \pi r^2 h$.

   Volume of small clamp = _____ cm^3 (to the nearest thousandth cm^3)

7. Find the length, thickness (diameter), and volume of the large clamp.

   Length = _____ cm   Diameter = _____ cm

   Volume of large clamp = _____ cm^3 (to the nearest thousandth cm^3)

Indirect Measure Problems

In the problems that follow, you are going to use **indirect methods** to determine the heights and lengths of objects that you cannot measure directly.

1. A tree is too tall to measure, but it casts a shadow that is 18 feet long. Ike is standing near the tree. He is 5 feet tall and casts a shadow that is 6 feet long.

    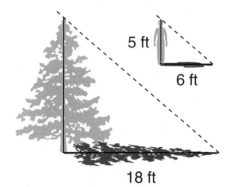

    The light rays, the tree, and its shadow form a triangle that is **similar** to the triangle formed by the light rays, Ike, and his shadow.

    What is the size-change factor of the triangles? _____

    About how tall is the tree? _____

2. Ike's dad is 6 feet tall. He is standing near the Washington Monument, which is 555 feet tall. Ike's dad casts a 7-foot shadow. About how long a shadow does the Washington Monument cast?
    (*Hint:* Draw sketches that include the above information.) _____

3. A surveyor wants to find the distance between points *A* and *B* on opposite ends of a lake. He sets a stake at point *C* so that angle *ABC* is a right angle. By measuring, he finds that $\overline{AC}$ is 95 meters long and $\overline{BC}$ is 76 meters long.

    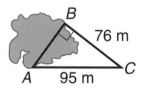

    How far across the lake is it from point *A* to point *B*? _____

Indirect Measure Problems (cont.)

4. Work with three other students. Your teacher has taped a target on the wall, near the ceiling. You will use an indirect method to determine the height of the target above the floor.

Study the diagram shown below. Each student has a special job.

Observer: Sit on the floor and face the target. Sit about 15 to 20 feet from the target.

Supporter: You and the observer hold a meter stick so that it is at the observer's eye level. Make sure the meter stick is parallel to the floor.

Pointer: Take a second meter stick and place the "0" end on top of the end of the meter stick the supporter is already holding. The supporter holds the ends of the sticks together. Make sure that you hold the meter stick vertically so that angle *ACB* is approximately a right angle (90°).

Observer: Place your eye near the end of the meter stick (point *A*) and look at the target (point *D*). Instruct the pointer to slide a finger up or down the vertical meter stick, until the finger appears to point to the target (point *D*). Record the length of $\overline{BC}$.

Measurer: Measure the height above the floor of the observer's meter stick (height of $\overline{AC}$ above floor). Also measure the distance from the observer's eye to the wall (length of $\overline{AE}$).

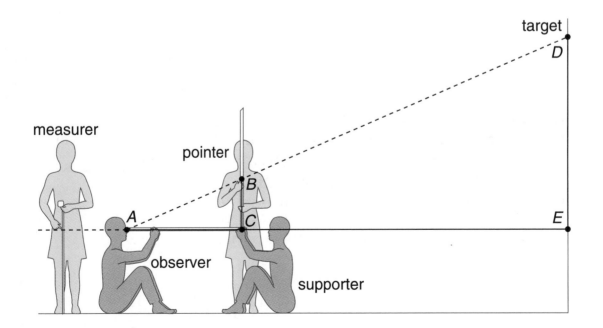

Use with Lesson 104.

Indirect Measure Problems (cont.)

5. Record your measurements:

$\overline{AC}$ = 100 cm $\overline{AE}$ = _____ cm (distance from observer's eye to wall)

$\overline{BC}$ = _____ cm   Distance from observer's eye to floor = _____ cm

6. Draw sketches of triangles *ACB* and *AED* that include your measurement information.

7. Triangles *ACB* and *AED* are similar figures. What is the size-change factor for these figures? _____

Use the size-change factor to calculate the length of $\overline{DE}$.

Length of $\overline{DE}$ = _____ cm

8. What is the height of the target above the floor? _____

Cornering Right Triangles

Any triangle whose sides have lengths of 3 units, 4 units, and 5 units is a right triangle. Here is a method for finding right triangles whose sides have whole-number lengths.

Choose any even number as the length of one leg of the triangle. Call it *n*. To find the length of the other leg, first take half of *n*. Then find two factors whose product is that number ($\frac{n}{2}$). Call the factors *s* and *t*. Square both *s* and *t*; then subtract the smaller square from the larger square. The difference is the length of the other leg. The length of the hypotenuse is the sum of the squares of *s* and *t*.

Example: Let the length of one leg = 36 units. To find the other leg, first take half of 36, or 18. Two factors whose product is 18 are 6 and 3. The squares of these factors are 36 and 9. The difference of the squares is 27. The length of the other leg is 27 units. The length of the hypotenuse is 36 + 9, or 45. Check: $36^2 + 27^2 = 45^2$.

Source: *How to Figure It.*

Math Boxes 104

---

1. Multiply.

   a. 6.76 ∗ 0.005 = _____

   b. 32.04 ∗ 49.6 = _____

   c. _____ = 78.1 ∗ 0.29

   d. _____ = 14.09 ∗ 2.25

   e. _____ = 93.6 ∗ 1.54

2. Circle the equation that describes the relationship between the numbers in the table.

x	y
0.55	$\frac{1}{2}$
0.6	1
1	5
1.5	10

   $(y + 0.1) * \frac{1}{2} = x$

   $(y * 0.1) + \frac{1}{2} = x$

   $\frac{0.1y}{2} = x$

   $(y + \frac{1}{2}) * 0.1 = x$

---

3. Mr. Wilson's 28 sixth graders had to read at least one nonfiction book—either a biography or a science book. At the end of the grading period, Mr. Wilson tallied the number of students who had read each kind of book. Nineteen had read at least one biography, and 18 had read at least one science book.

   Draw a Venn diagram to represent the number of students who read each kind of book.

   How many students read at least one biography and one science book?

   _____

---

4. Write the following numbers with words:

   a. 8.009 _____

   b. 0.432 _____

   c. 38.87 _____

   d. 1.111 _____

   e. 7.00004 _____

Use with Lesson 104.

Math Message: Time to Reflect

1. The following is an excerpt from the beginning of the poem "Mathematics" by Theoni Pappas. It is taken from the book *Math Talk: Mathematical Ideas in Poems for Two Voices*. The poem is designed to be read by two people. One person reads the left-hand column and the other the right-hand column, alternating between the two columns.

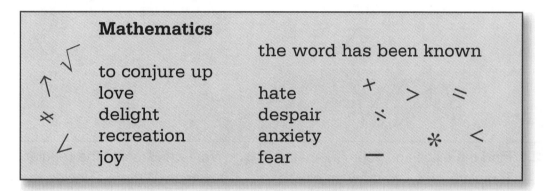

   Mathematics

to conjure up	the word has been known
love	hate
delight	despair
recreation	anxiety
joy	fear

   a. Which of the emotions above best describes your experiences with

   Unit 9? _____

   Explain. _____

   _____

   _____

   b. Which of the emotions above least describes your experiences with

   Unit 9? _____

   Explain. _____

   _____

   _____

2. Now think about mathematics in general, not just your experiences in Unit 9, as you answer the following question. If math were a way to travel,

   what means of travel would it be? _____

   Why? _____

   _____

   _____

Math Boxes 105

1. Fill in each shape so that it becomes a recognizable figure. For example:

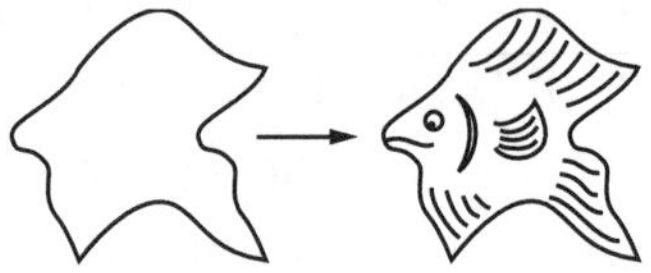

a.

b.

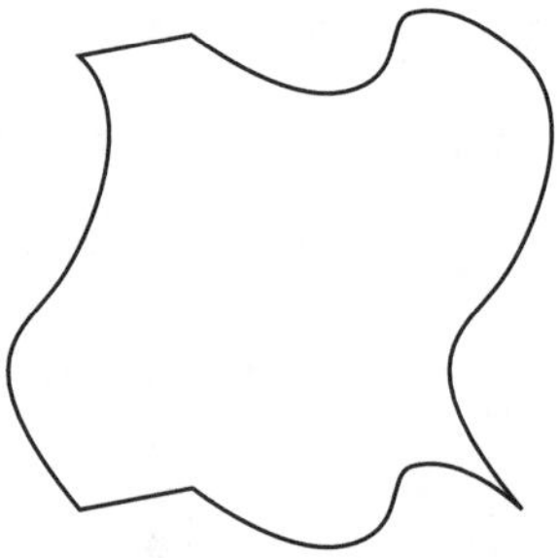

2. Find the ellipse on your Geometry Template. Use it to draw an ellipse below.

How would you describe an ellipse?

_____

_____

_____

69

3. Write an *H* inside the regular hexagon. Write a *P* inside the regular pentagon.

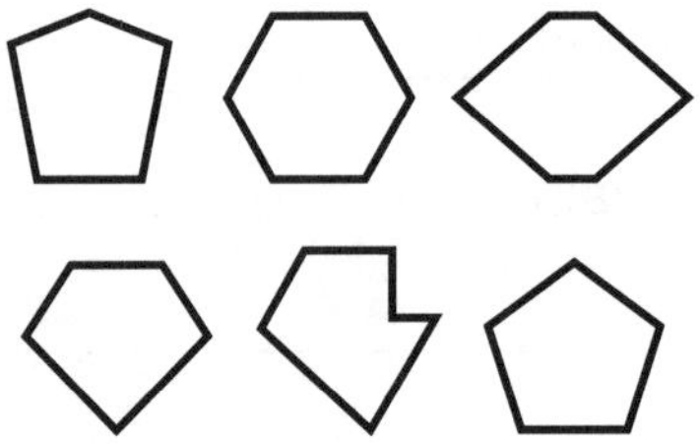

73

4. Draw the line(s) of symmetry for each figure below.

a.

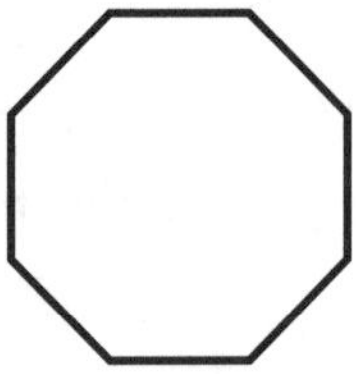

b.

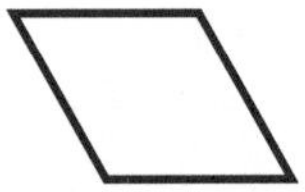

82

5. Draw an obtuse angle *HIJ*. Measure it.

Measure of ∠*HIJ* is about _____.

72

388

Semiregular Tessellations

A **semiregular tessellation** is shown below and on page 85 of your *Student Reference Book*.

84 85

A semiregular tessellation is made up of two or more kinds of regular polygons. Possible polygons are equilateral triangles, squares, regular hexagons, regular octagons, and regular dodecagons.

There are eight different semiregular tessellations. One is shown below.

Try to draw the other seven semiregular tessellations, using your Geometry Template and the template of a regular dodecagon that your teacher will provide. Experiment first on a separate piece of paper. Then draw the tessellations below and on the next page. Write the name of each tessellation.

1.

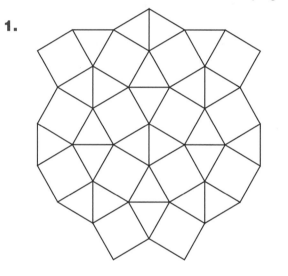

2.

Name: _____ *3.3.4.3.4* _____   Name: _____

3.   **4.**

Name: _____   Name: _____

Semiregular Tessellations (cont.)

5.

6.

Name: _____

Name: _____

7.

8.

Name: _____

Name: _____

Math Boxes 106

---

1. Divide.

   a. $\frac{3}{7} \div \frac{4}{5} =$ _____

   b. $\frac{8}{12} \div \frac{2}{3} =$ _____

   c. $\frac{9}{8} \div \frac{6}{5} =$ _____

   d. $\frac{7}{10} \div \frac{2}{1} =$ _____

   e. $7 \div \frac{4}{3} =$ _____

20

---

2. Use the distributive property. Show your work.

   a. $5 * (25 + 40) =$

   _____

   _____

   b. $11 * (50 - 3) =$

   _____

   _____

64

---

3. Tell what additional information you need to solve the following problem.

Ms. Putman's gym class ran the 50-yard dash. The average time was 14.5 seconds. Raoul's and Julia's times were only 0.5 second apart. What was Julia's time for the 50-yard dash?

_____

_____

129   _____

---

4. Without using a protractor, find the measure of each numbered angle. Write each measure on the drawing. Lines that appear parallel are.

112
113

---

5. Translate the word sentences below into number sentences. Do not solve or simplify them.

| < less than |
| > greater than |

   a. Thirty times one half is equal to fifteen. _____

   b. Ten more than the square root of sixty-four is equal to eighteen. _____

   c. Nine increased by twelve is less than thirty. _____

   d. Twenty-five more than three is greater than ten more than five. _____

   e. Sixteen is greater than six more than four. _____

157 158

Translations, Reflections, and Rotations

1. Plot and label the vertices of the image that would result from each translation. One vertex of each image has already been plotted and labeled.

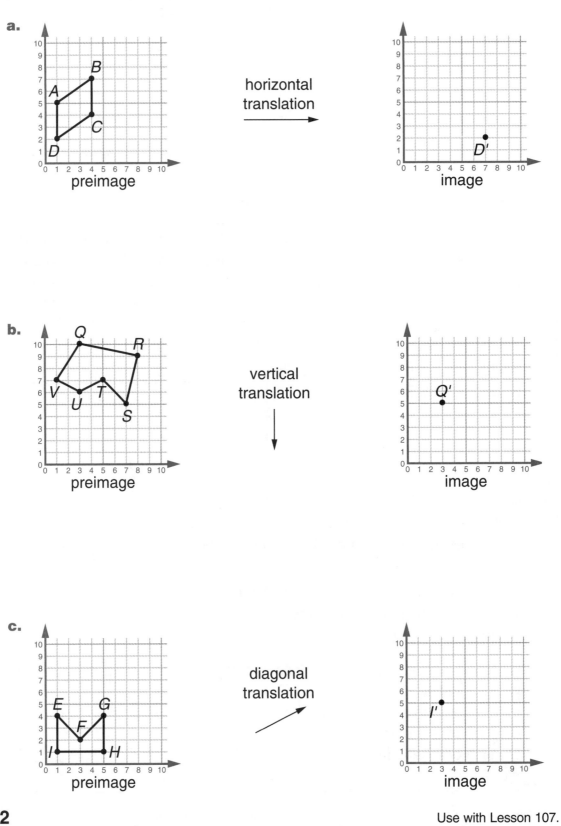

80 | 81

a.

horizontal translation →

preimage   image

b.

vertical translation ↓

preimage   image

c.

diagonal translation ↗

preimage   image

Use with Lesson 107.

Translations, Reflections, and Rotations (cont.)

2. Use your Geometry Template to draw the reflected image of each geometric design below. Line *AB* is the line of reflection.

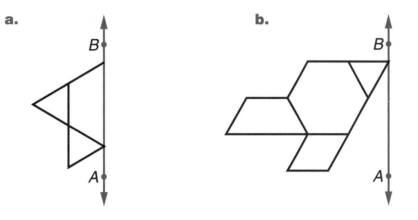

3. Tell the number of degrees of rotation that would produce each given image. The point of rotation is marked. You might find it helpful to copy the figures onto a piece of paper using your Geometry Template. Then rotate the paper the given number of degrees.

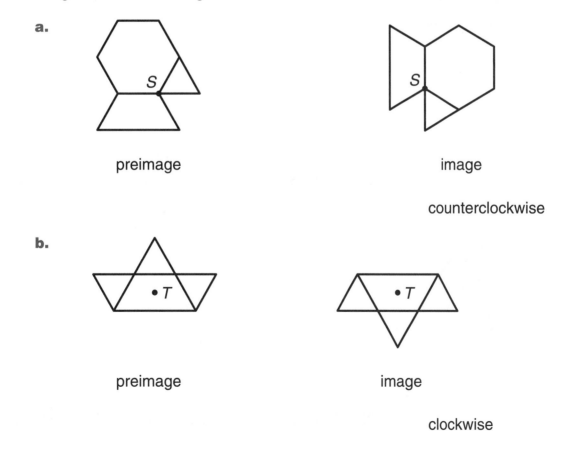

a.

preimage   image

counterclockwise

b.

preimage   image

clockwise

Translations, Reflections, and Rotations (cont.)

As in Problem 3, you might find it helpful to copy the figures onto a piece of paper.

4. Use your Geometry Template to draw the result of each rotation.
    The point of rotation is marked.

a.

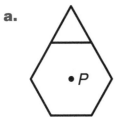

                   90° clockwise   180° clockwise   270° clockwise

b.

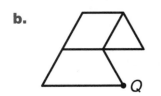

                   90° clockwise   180° clockwise   270° clockwise

c.

                   90° clockwise   180° clockwise   270° clockwise

                   Use with Lesson 107.

Math Boxes 107

1. Evaluate each expression. Use the rules for order of operations.

   a. $8 + 5 * 7 = $ _____

   b. $9 - 6/3 = $ _____

   c. $6 * 4/2 = $ _____

   d. $5 * 8 - (4 + 3) = $ _____

   e. $4 - 10 + 7 * 2 = $ _____

   161

2. Add or subtract.

   a. $14 + (-72) = $ _____

   b. _____ $= 27 - (-28)$

   c. _____ $= -63 + (-87)$

   d. _____ $= -58 + 105$

   e. $-33 - (-89) = $ _____

   57 58

3. Draw a tree diagram for the following problem. Then answer the question.

   A bag contains one red counter, two blue counters, and one white counter. You take out one counter. Then you take out a second counter without replacing the first counter. What is the probability of taking out one red

   counter and one white counter (in either order)? _____

   178 179

4. Multiply. Write each answer in simplest form.

   a. $7\frac{1}{5} * \frac{3}{8} = $ _____

   b. $2\frac{4}{9} * 1\frac{1}{5} = $ _____

   c. $1\frac{1}{6} * \frac{7}{6} = $ _____

   d. $5\frac{2}{3} * 4\frac{1}{4} = $ _____

   e. $9 * \frac{8}{7} = $ _____

   37

5. Complete.

   a. $33\frac{1}{3}\%$ of $222 = $ _____

   b. 25% of $648 = $ _____

   c. _____ $= 40\%$ of 525

   d. _____ $= 12.5\%$ of 72

   e. _____ $= 70\%$ of 110

   135

Use with Lesson 107.

395

Math Boxes 108

1. Norice can read 45 pages an hour. At that rate, about how long will it take her to finish a 380-page book?

_____

140

2. Multiply.

a. $5.25 * 2.003 =$ _____

b. $4.29 * 67.1 =$ _____

c. _____ $= 0.08 * 0.017$

d. _____ $= 52.31 * 19.9$

e. _____ $= 380 * 6.55$

52

3. Write each number in number-and-word notation.

a. 68,000 _____

b. 2,500,000 _____

c. 345,000,000 _____

d. 89,000,000,000 _____

e. 7,400,000,000,000 _____

5

4. Write the following in standard notation.

a. $5.38 * 10^7 =$ _____

b. _____ $= 6.91 * 10^{-5}$

c. _____ $= 3.04 * 10^9$

d. _____ $= 9.9011 * 10^5$

e. $7.2 * 10^{-6} =$ _____

7 8

5. Fill in the blanks in each sentence.

a. $3 * (90 + 3) =$ 164

$(3 *$ _____$) + (3 *$ _____$)$

b. $8 * (40 + 5) =$

$($_____$ * 40) + (8 *$ _____$)$

c. $(10 - 3) * 6 =$

$(10 *$ _____$) - (3 *$ _____$)$

d. $(9 * 50) + (9 *$ _____$)$

$= 9 * ($_____$ + 4)$

e. $(7 * 20) - (7 * 3)$

$=$ _____$ * ($_____$ -$ _____$)$

6. Answer each question with an algebraic expression.

a. Tommy is $1\frac{1}{2}$ inches taller than he was last year. Last year he was x inches tall. How tall is Tommy this year?

_____

b. Jane is twice as old as her brother Lyle was 3 years ago. Lyle is y years old now. How old is Jane?

_____

156

Rotation Symmetry

Cut out the figures on Activity Sheet 4. Cut only along the dashed lines. Using the procedure demonstrated by your teacher, determine the number of different ways each figure can be rotated (but not flipped) so that the image exactly matches the preimage. Record the order of rotation symmetry for each figure.

83

1.

Order of rotation symmetry _____

2.

Order of rotation symmetry _____

3.

Order of rotation symmetry _____

4.

Order of rotation symmetry _____

Challenge

5. The 10 of hearts has point symmetry. When the card is rotated 180°, it looks the same as the original card.

original   180°
position   rotation

The 9 of spades does not have point symmetry. When the card is rotated 180°, it does not look the same as the original card.

original   180°
position   rotation

Which of the cards in an ordinary deck of playing cards (not including face cards) have point symmetry? _____

_____

_____

If you are interested in learning a magic trick that uses point symmetry with playing cards, see page 258 in your *Student Reference Book*.

Math Boxes 109

1. Divide.

a. $\frac{3}{5}\Big/\frac{4}{9}$ = _____

b. $\frac{5}{7}\Big/\frac{9}{8}$ = _____

c. $\frac{1}{8}\Big/\frac{6}{7}$ = _____

d. $\frac{10}{3}\Big/\frac{1}{5}$ = _____

e. $\frac{9}{1}\Big/\frac{6}{7}$ = _____

2. Use the distributive property. Show your work.

a. $7 * (30 - 3)$ =

_____

_____

b. $12 * (10 + 5)$ =

_____

_____

3. Tell what additional information you need to solve the following problem.

In 1912, Fanny Durack of Australia won the first women's 100-meter freestyle swimming event in the Olympic Games in 1 minute 22.2 seconds. Dawn Fraser, the next Australian to win this event, set Olympic records in 1956, 1960, and 1964. In 1964, her time was 59.5 seconds. How much faster was Fraser in 1964 than in 1956?

_____

_____

Source: *1997 World Almanac.*

4. Without using a protractor, find the measure of each numbered angle. Write each measure on the drawing.

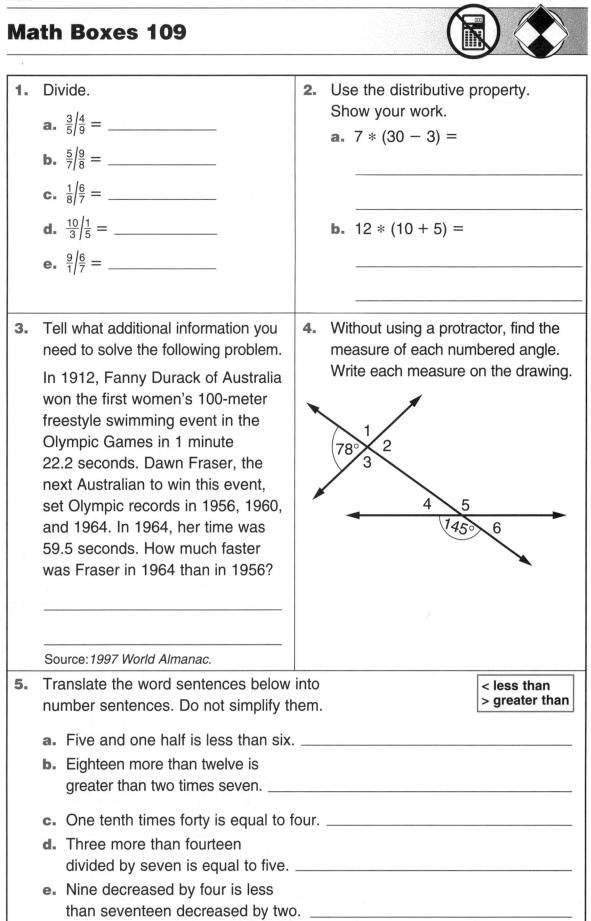

5. Translate the word sentences below into number sentences. Do not simplify them.

| < less than |
| > greater than |

a. Five and one half is less than six. _____

b. Eighteen more than twelve is greater than two times seven. _____

c. One tenth times forty is equal to four. _____

d. Three more than fourteen divided by seven is equal to five. _____

e. Nine decreased by four is less than seventeen decreased by two. _____

398

Cross Sections of a Clay Cube

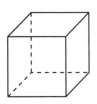 Form a clay cube. Draw your prediction of the shape of the cross section that will be formed by the first cut shown below. After making the cut, draw the actual shape and describe (name) the shape. Re-form the cube and repeat these steps for the other cuts.

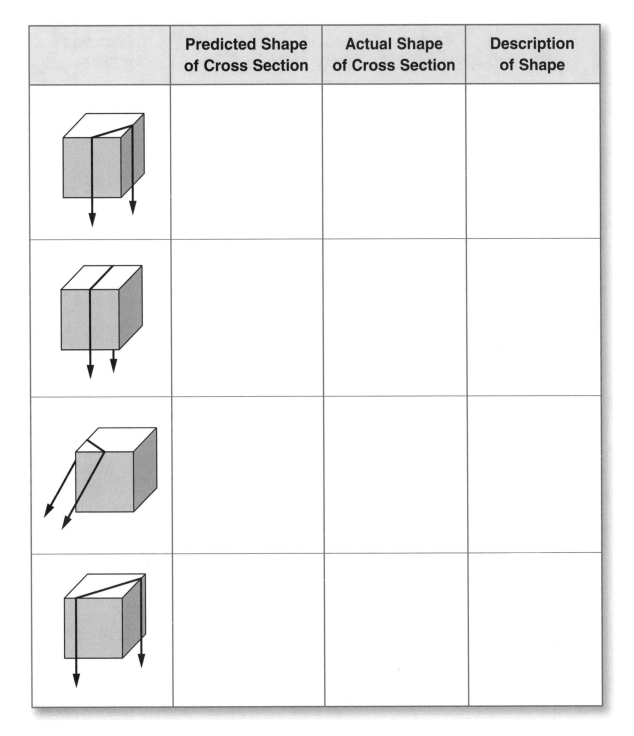

	Predicted Shape of Cross Section	Actual Shape of Cross Section	Description of Shape

Cross Sections of a Clay Cylinder

 Form a clay cylinder. Draw your prediction of the shape of the cross section that will be formed by the first cut shown below. After making the cut, draw the actual shape and describe (name) the shape. Re-form the cylinder and repeat these steps for the other cuts.

	Predicted Shape of Cross Section	Actual Shape of Cross Section	Description of Shape

Cross Sections of a Clay Cone

Form a clay cone. Draw your prediction of the shape of the cross section that will be formed by the first cut shown below. After making the cut, draw the actual shape and describe (name) the shape. Re-form the cone and repeat these steps for the other cuts.

	Predicted Shape of Cross Section	Actual Shape of Cross Section	Description of Shape
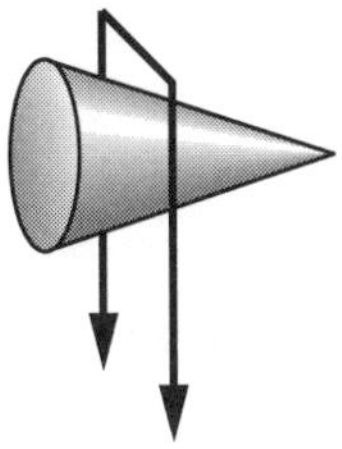			
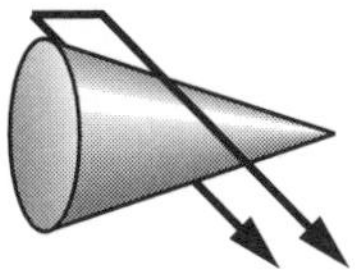			
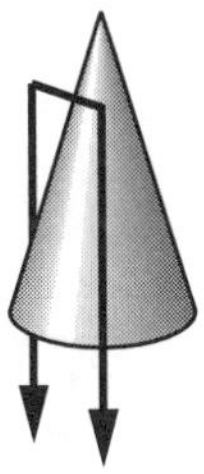			
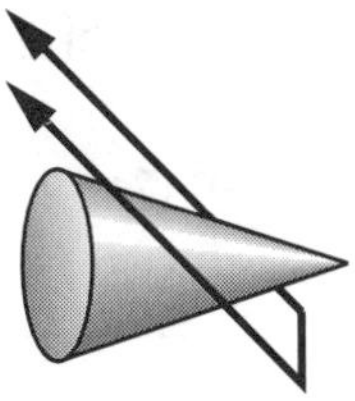			

Use with Lesson 110.

Math Boxes 110

---

1. Evaluate each expression. Use the rules for order of operations.

   a. $9 - 3 * 2 =$ _____

   b. $5 * 6/7 =$ _____

   c. $3 + 2^2 * 8 =$ _____

   d. $11 - 2 * 4 + 7 =$ _____

   e. $8 + 1/6 - 2 =$ _____

2. Add or subtract.

   a. $235 + (-150) =$ _____

   b. $-76 - 24 =$ _____

   c. _____ $= 143 - 258$

   d. $-99 + 167 =$ _____

   e. _____ $= 380 - (-59)$

---

3. Draw a tree diagram for the following problem. Then answer the two questions.

The cafeteria is serving spaghetti, hamburgers, and hot dogs for lunch. The drinks are milk, soda, and juice. If you choose your meal and drink

at random, what is the probability of having a hot dog? _____

What is the probability of having a hot dog and juice? _____

---

4. Multiply. Write each answer in simplest form.

   a. $4\frac{3}{7} * \frac{8}{5} =$ _____

   b. $\frac{16}{11} * 4\frac{2}{3} =$ _____

   c. $\frac{25}{4} * \frac{10}{6} =$ _____

   d. $3\frac{1}{7} * 5\frac{8}{9} =$ _____

   e. $7 * \frac{6}{15} =$ _____

5. Complete.

   a. _____ $= 80\%$ of 80

   b. _____ $= 75\%$ of 128

   c. _____ $= 66\frac{2}{3}\%$ of 189

   d. 60% of $255 =$ _____

   e. 37.5% of $480 =$ _____

Math Message: Venn Diagram

In what ways are a doughnut and a coffee mug similar? In what ways are they different? Record your thoughts in the Venn diagram below.

153

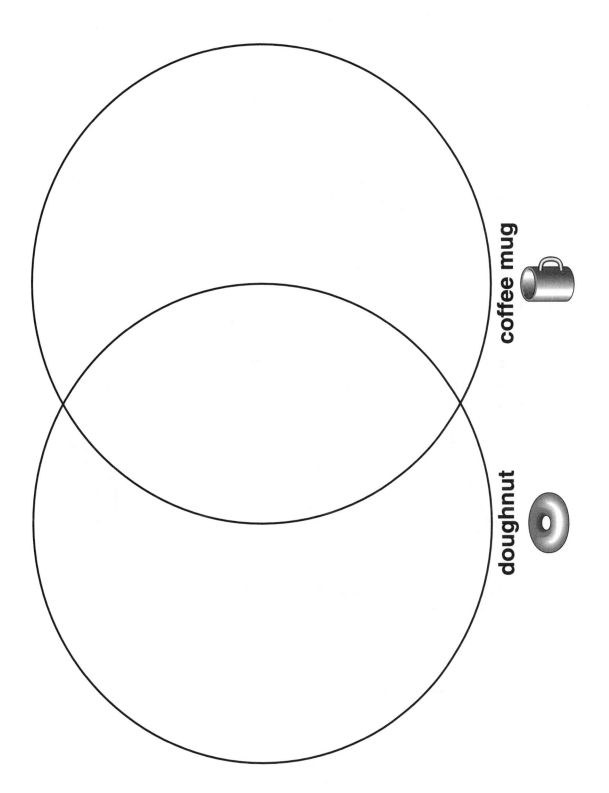

coffee mug

doughnut

Rubber-Sheet Geometry

You and your partner will need the following materials: 3 latex gloves, a straightedge, one pair of scissors, and a permanent marker.

Step 1: Cut the fingers and thumb off each glove.

Step 2: Make a vertical cut through each of the three "cylinders" that remain. This creates three rubber sheets.

Step 3: Use a permanent marker and a straightedge to draw the following figures on the rubber sheets. Draw the figures large enough to fill most of the sheet.

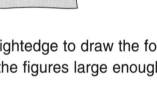

Step 4: Work with your partner to stretch the rubber sheets to see what other figures you can make.

Step 5: Complete journal page 405.

Rubber-Sheet Geometry (cont.)

1. Experiment with the figures on your rubber sheets. Circle any of the figures in the right-hand column that are topologically equivalent to the corresponding original figure in the left-hand column.

Original Figure	Transformed Figures
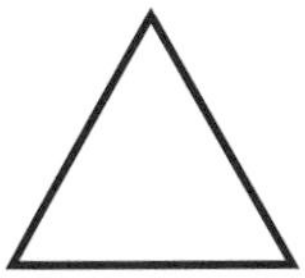	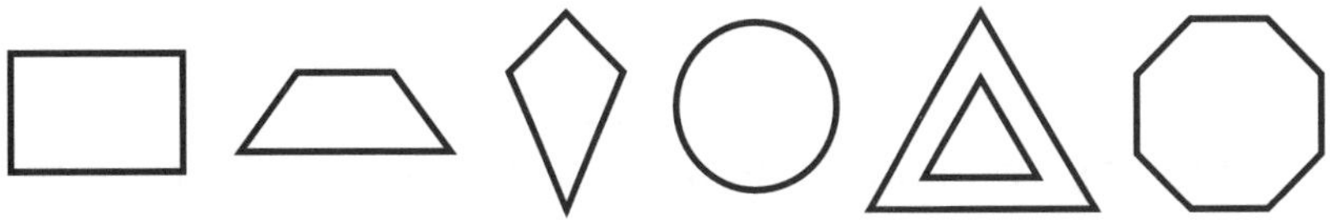
	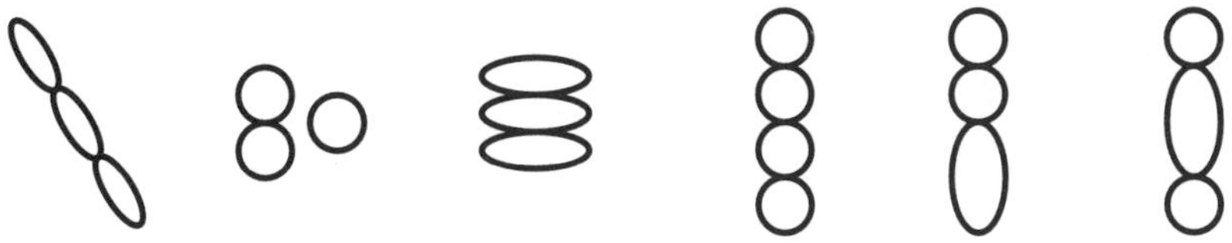
	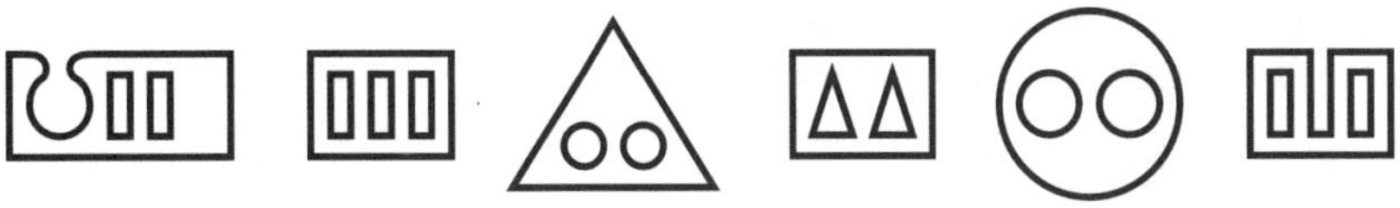

2. Choose one of the above figures that you did not circle and explain why it is not topologically equivalent to its original figure.

_____

_____

_____

_____

Math Boxes 111

---

1. Grant collects marbles. His favorite store sells marbles for 69 cents per marble. How many marbles can he buy if he has $15.00?

_____

2. Multiply.

a. $44.2 * 35 =$ _____

b. $708 * 0.52 =$ _____

c. $4.14 * 3.09 =$ _____

d. _____ $= 625.7 * 8.3$

e. _____ $= 99.4 * 3.7$

---

3. Write each number in number-and-word notation.

a. 52,000 _____

b. 6,500,000 _____

c. 945,000,000 _____

d. 77,000,000,000

_____

e. 12,500,000,000,000

_____

4. Convert from scientific notation to standard notation.

a. $2.73 * 10^5 =$ _____

b. $1.03 * 10^{-4} =$ _____

c. $4.226 * 10^8 =$

_____

d. _____ $= 8.001 * 10^{-2}$

e. _____

$= 5.435 * 10^9$

---

5. Fill in the blanks in each sentence.

a. $8 * (30 + 4) =$

$(8 * $ _____ $) + (8 * $ _____ $)$

b. $9 * (20 + 7) =$

$($ _____ $* 20) + (9 * $ _____ $)$

c. $(50 - 3) * 6 =$

$(50 * $ _____ $) - (3 * $ _____ $)$

d. $(8 * 40) + (8 * $ _____ $) =$

$8 * ($ _____ $+ 7)$

e. $(6 * 70) - (6 * 9) =$

_____ $* ($ _____ $-$ _____ $)$

6. Answer each question with an algebraic expression.

a. Rudolph now has three times as many customers for baby-sitting as he had one year ago. Then he had *x* customers. How many customers does he have now?

_____

b. Alicia earns $2.00 each time she helps mow the lawn. In June, she helped *y* times. In July, she helped 2 more times than in June. How much did she earn in July? _____

Use with Lesson 111.

Construct a Möbius Strip

Step 1: Gather the following materials: a sheet of newspaper or adding machine tape; a pair of scissors; tape; and a bright color crayon, marker, or pencil.

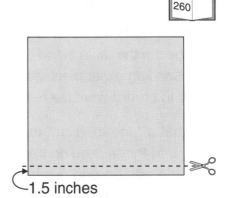

260

Step 2: Cut a strip of newspaper about $1\frac{1}{2}$ inches wide and as long as possible, or cut a strip of adding machine tape about 2 feet long. Save the remaining newspaper or tape for the activities on pages 408 and 409.

1.5 inches

Step 3: Turn over one end of the strip (give one end a half-twist), and tape the two ends together to form a loop.

Step 4: Label the strip with the letter B.

Step 5: Draw a line along the center of the strip until you reach your starting point.

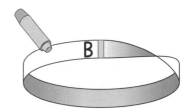

Step 6: Poke your scissors through the paper somewhere on the line that you just drew. Then cut the strip along that line. Record your results in the table on page 408, in the row for Experiment B.

Experiment with Möbius Strips

Möbius strips can be twisted and cut in different ways to produce a variety of results.

Using a $1\frac{1}{2}$-inch wide strip of newspaper, try each of the twist-and-cut combinations described in the table below. Record your results. Be sure to label the strips with the corresponding experiment letter so that you can refer to them later. Before making a cut, try to predict what the results of the cut will be.

Note that a "one-third cut" means that the strip should be cut into thirds. You do this with one continuous cut for a strip with an odd number of half-twists and with two continuous cuts for a strip with an even number of half-twists. For the one-third cut, it is helpful to draw lines on the strip before cutting. The lines should start and end at the same point. With an even number of half-twists, you will need to draw two lines.

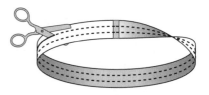

Experiment	Number of Half-Twists	Kind of Cut	Results of Cut
A	0	center	• *2 separate strips* • *same lengths as original* • *$\frac{1}{2}$ the width of original* • *no half-twists in either strip*
B	1	center	
C	1	one-third (1 cut)	

Experiment with Möbius Strips (cont.)

Experiment	Number of Half-Twists	Kind of Cut	Results of Cut
D	2	center	
E	2	one-third (2 cuts)	
F	3	center	
G	3	one-third (1 cut)	

Inside Out!

Imagine a bottle with no inside. Felix Klein was a German mathematician in the late 1800s. He designed a bottle with no inside. If you poured water into the bottle, it would flow right back out. Interestingly, if you cut the Klein bottle in half, you get two Möbius strips. (Actually, a real Klein bottle cannot be constructed, since the neck of the bottle can't pass back through without making a hole.)

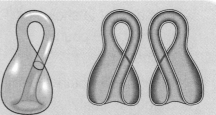

Math Boxes 112

1. I am a regular polygon with all obtuse angles. I have the smallest number of sides of any polygon with obtuse angles. How many sides do I have? _____

Draw me below.

73

2. Marty had a candle sale. He began with 4 red candles for every 3 white candles. He sold the red candles for $0.35 and the white candles for $0.39. He sold 75 white candles and had 7 times that many white candles left. How many red candles did he start with? _____

Explain how you found your answer.

_____

_____

141

3. Complete.

a. 5 ft = _____ yd

b. 3 ft 9 in = _____ in

c. 19 ft = _____ yd

d. 200 in = _____ ft

e. 204 in = _____ yd

4. Subtract. Write your answer in simplest form.

a. $8\frac{1}{3} - \frac{4}{7} =$ _____

b. _____ $= 5\frac{1}{6} - \frac{7}{5}$

c. _____ $= 12 - 4\frac{8}{9}$

d. _____ $= 6\frac{10}{4} - \frac{6}{8}$

e. $14\frac{1}{2} - 3\frac{6}{4} =$ _____

34 | 35

5. Jim's favorite cheese costs $2.50 per pound.

Rule: Cost = $2.50 per pound $*$ weight in pounds

Formula: $c = 2.50 * w$

a. Plot a point to show the cost of 6 pounds of cheese.

b. How much would 6 pounds cost?

_____

c. Complete the table and the graph.

Weight (lb) w	Cost ($) 2.5 $* w$
$\frac{1}{2}$	
1	
$3\frac{1}{2}$	
	$12.50
7	

138

Use with Lesson 112.

Math Message: Time to Reflect

1. During the past year, you studied many topics in mathematics—positive and negative numbers, rates and ratios, scientific notation, probability, algebraic expressions and equations, transformations of geometric figures, and so on. You used a variety of tools, including the calculator, Geometry Template, ruler, meter stick, compass, and pan balance. You worked on the Solar System project and other activities involving mathematics outside the classroom.

   a. What mathematics did you learn this year that was new and interesting?

   Why did you find it interesting? _____

   _____

   b. What topics would you like to know more about?

   _____

2. Some mathematical skills are listed below. How would you rate yourself on each? Check the appropriate box. Add another mathematical skill to the list and rate yourself on it.

Skill	I know this well.	I am doing okay.	I need to do more work.
Knowing the multiplication and division facts			
Working with percents			
Estimating answers			
Using formulas			
Using a calculator			
Solving equations			
Reading and writing numbers in scientific notation			
Calculating with positive and negative numbers			

Sources

Unit 6

Ash, Russell. *The Top 10 of Everything.* New York: Dorling Kindersley, 1994.

Donley, Richard E. *Everything Has Its Price.* New York: Simon and Schuster, 1995.

Louis, David. *2201 Fascinating Facts.* New York: Greenwich House, 1983.

Science and Technology Department of the Carnegie Library of Pittsburgh. *The Handy Science Answer Book.* Detroit: Visible Ink, 1994.

Sutcliffe, Andrea. *Numbers.* New York: Harper Perennial, 1996.

The World Almanac for Kids, 1996.

Unit 7

Strauss, Stephen. *The Sizesaurus.* New York: Kadansha International, 1995.

Sutcliffe, Andrea. *Numbers.* New York: Harper Perennial, 1996.

Unit 9

Huff, Daniele. *How to Figure It.* New York: W.W. Norton, 1996.

Pappas, Theoni. "Mathematics." From *Math Talk: Mathematical Ideas in Poems for Two Voices.* San Carlos, California: Wide World Publishing/Tetra, 1991.

Solution Search Cards

$x > 9$	$y^2 < 5$	$m < 3.5$	$q * 2 > 20$
$(9 * z) + 2 > 65$	$100 / k > 25$	$5 \neq s$	$b < 6$
$-2 + a \geq 5$	$w - 3 < 2$	$r / 2 \geq 5$	$49 \leq p^2$
$81 > f^2$	$c * 7 \leq 14$	$10 < 50/d$	$\sqrt{25} \leq t$

Use with Lesson 91.   **Activity Sheet 3**

Rotation Symmetry

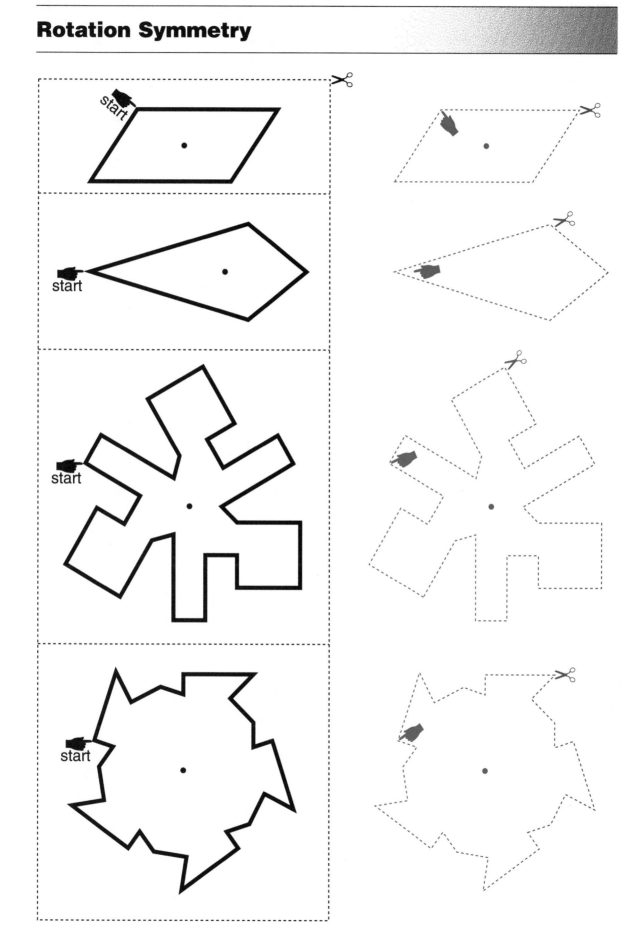

References

Multiplication/Division Facts Table

*,/	1	2	3	4	5	6	7	8	9	10	11	12
1	1	2	3	4	5	6	7	8	9	10	11	12
2	2	4	6	8	10	12	14	16	18	20	22	24
3	3	6	9	12	15	18	21	24	27	30	33	36
4	4	8	12	16	20	24	28	32	36	40	44	48
5	5	10	15	20	25	30	35	40	45	50	55	60
6	6	12	18	24	30	36	42	48	54	60	66	72
7	7	14	21	28	35	42	49	56	63	70	77	84
8	8	16	24	32	40	48	56	64	72	80	88	96
9	9	18	27	36	45	54	63	72	81	90	99	108
10	10	20	30	40	50	60	70	80	90	100	110	120
11	11	22	33	44	55	66	77	88	99	110	121	132
12	12	24	36	48	60	72	84	96	108	120	132	144

"Easy" Fractions

"Easy" Fractions	Decimals	Percents
$\frac{1}{2}$	0.50	50%
$\frac{1}{3}$	$0.\overline{3}$	$33\frac{1}{3}\%$
$\frac{2}{3}$	$0.\overline{6}$	$66\frac{2}{3}\%$
$\frac{1}{4}$	0.25	25%
$\frac{3}{4}$	0.75	75%
$\frac{1}{5}$	0.20	20%
$\frac{2}{5}$	0.40	40%
$\frac{3}{5}$	0.60	60%
$\frac{4}{5}$	0.80	80%
$\frac{1}{6}$	$0.1\overline{6}$	$16\frac{2}{3}\%$
$\frac{1}{8}$	0.125	$12\frac{1}{2}\%$
$\frac{3}{8}$	0.375	$37\frac{1}{2}\%$
$\frac{5}{8}$	0.625	$62\frac{1}{2}\%$
$\frac{7}{8}$	0.875	$87\frac{1}{2}\%$
$\frac{1}{10}$	0.10	10%
$\frac{3}{10}$	0.30	30%
$\frac{7}{10}$	0.70	70%
$\frac{9}{10}$	0.90	90%

Prefixes

uni-	one	tera-	trillion (10^{12})
bi-	two	giga-	billion (10^9)
tri-	three	mega-	million (10^6)
quad-	four	kilo-	thousand (10^3)
penta-	five	hecto-	hundred (10^2)
hexa-	six	deca-	ten (10^1)
hepta-	seven	uni-	one (10^0)
octa-	eight	deci-	tenth (10^{-1})
nona-	nine	centi-	hundredth (10^{-2})
deca-	ten	milli-	thousandth (10^{-3})
dodeca-	twelve	micro-	millionth (10^{-6})
icosa-	twenty	nano-	billionth (10^{-9})

Symbols

+	plus or positive	x^n	nth power of x	⌐	right angle
−	minus or negative	$\sqrt{x}$	square root of x	⊥	is perpendicular to
*, ×	multiplied by	%	percent	‖	is parallel to
÷, /	divided by	$\frac{a}{b}$, a:b, a/b	ratio of a to b	$\triangle ABC$	triangle ABC
=	is equal to		or a divided by b	$\angle ABC$	angle ABC
≠	is not equal to		or the fraction $\frac{a}{b}$	$\angle B$	angle B
<	is less than	°	degree		
>	is greater than	(a,b)	ordered pair		
≤	is less than or equal to	$\overleftrightarrow{AS}$	line AS		
≥	is greater than or equal to	$\overline{AS}$	line segment AS		
		$\overrightarrow{AS}$	ray AS		

Probability Meter

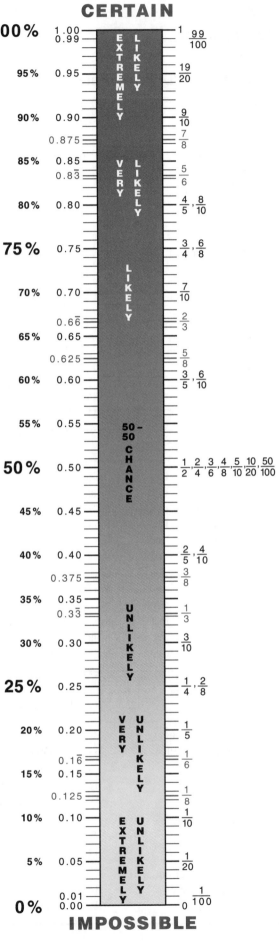

CERTAIN

100%	1.00		1	99/100
	0.99	EXTREMELY LIKELY		
95%	0.95			19/20
90%	0.90			9/10
	0.875			7/8
85%	0.85	VERY LIKELY		5/6
	0.83̄			
80%	0.80			4/5, 8/10
75%	0.75			3/4, 6/8
70%	0.70	LIKELY		7/10
	0.66̄			2/3
65%	0.65			
	0.625			5/8
60%	0.60			3/5, 6/10
55%	0.55	50–50 CHANCE		
50%	0.50			1/2, 2/4, 3/6, 4/8, 5/10, 10/20, 50/100
45%	0.45			
40%	0.40			2/5, 4/10
	0.375			3/8
35%	0.35	UNLIKELY		1/3
	0.33̄			
30%	0.30			3/10
25%	0.25			1/4, 2/8
20%	0.20	VERY UNLIKELY		1/5
	0.16̄			1/6
15%	0.15			
	0.125			1/8
10%	0.10	EXTREMELY UNLIKELY		1/10
5%	0.05			1/20
	0.01			1/100
0%	0.00		0	

IMPOSSIBLE

Exponents

Rule	Example
$n^a = n * n * n * \ldots * n$	$10^3 = 10 * 10 * 10 = 1000$
$10^a * 10^b = 10^{a+b}$	$10^2 * 10^3 = 10^5$
$\dfrac{10^a}{10^b} = 10^a/10^b = 10^{a-b}$	$\dfrac{10^5}{10^2} = 10^{5-2} = 10^3$
$10^{-a} = \dfrac{1}{10^a}$	$10^{-4} = \dfrac{1}{10^4}$

Rational Numbers

Rule	Example
$\dfrac{a}{b} = \dfrac{n*a}{n*b}$	$\dfrac{2}{3} = \dfrac{4*2}{4*3} = \dfrac{8}{12}$
$\dfrac{a}{b} = \dfrac{a/n}{b/n}$	$\dfrac{8}{12} = \dfrac{8/4}{12/4} = \dfrac{2}{3}$
$\dfrac{a}{a} = a * \dfrac{1}{a} = 1$	$\dfrac{4}{4} = 4 * \dfrac{1}{4} = 1$
$\dfrac{a}{b} + \dfrac{c}{b} = \dfrac{a+c}{b}$	$\dfrac{3}{5} + \dfrac{1}{5} = \dfrac{3+1}{5} = \dfrac{4}{5}$
$\dfrac{a}{b} - \dfrac{c}{b} = \dfrac{a-c}{b}$	$\dfrac{3}{5} - \dfrac{1}{5} = \dfrac{3-1}{5} = \dfrac{2}{5}$
$\dfrac{a}{b} * \dfrac{c}{d} = \dfrac{a*c}{b*d}$	$\dfrac{1}{4} * \dfrac{2}{3} = \dfrac{1*2}{4*3} = \dfrac{2}{12}$

To compare, add, or subtract fractions:

1. Find a common denominator.

2. Rewrite fractions as equivalent fractions with common denominator.

3. Compare, add, or subtract these fractions.

Place-Value Chart

trillions	100B	10B	billions	100M	10M	millions	hundred-thousands	ten-thousands	thousands	hundreds	tens	ones	.	tenths	hundredths	thousandths
1000 billions			1000 millions			1,000,000s	100,000s	10,000s	1000s	100s	10s	1s	.	0.1s	0.01s	0.001s
10^{12}	10^{11}	10^{10}	10^9	10^8	10^7	10^6	10^5	10^4	10^3	10^2	10^1	10^0	.	10^{-1}	10^{-2}	10^{-3}

Metric System

Units of Length

1 kilometer (km)	=	1000 meters (m)
1 meter	=	10 decimeters (dm)
	=	100 centimeters (cm)
	=	1000 millimeters (mm)
1 decimeter	=	10 centimeters
1 centimeter	=	10 millimeters

Units of Area

1 square meter (m^2)	=	100 square decimeters (dm^2)
	=	10,000 square centimeters (cm^2)
1 square decimeter	=	100 square centimeters
1 are (a)	=	100 square meters
1 hectare (ha)	=	100 ares
1 square kilometer (km^2)	=	100 hectares

Units of Volume

1 cubic meter (m^3)	=	1000 cubic decimeters (dm^3)
	=	1,000,000 cubic centimeters (cm^3)
1 cubic decimeter	=	1000 cubic centimeters

Units of Capacity

1 kiloliter (kL)	=	1000 liters (L)
1 liter	=	1000 milliliters (mL)

Units of Mass

1 metric ton (t)	=	1000 kilograms (kg)
1 kilogram	=	1000 grams (g)
1 gram	=	1000 milligrams (mg)

U.S. Customary System

Units of Length

1 mile (mi)	=	1760 yards (yd)
	=	5280 feet (ft)
1 yard	=	3 feet
	=	36 inches (in)
1 foot	=	12 inches

Units of Area

1 square yard (yd^2)	=	9 square feet (ft^2)
	=	1296 square inches (in^2)
1 square foot	=	144 square inches
1 acre	=	43,560 square feet
1 square mile (mi^2)	=	640 acres

Units of Volume

1 cubic yard (yd^3)	=	27 cubic feet (ft^3)
1 cubic foot	=	1728 cubic inches (in^3)

Units of Capacity

1 gallon (gal)	=	4 quarts (qt)
1 quart	=	2 pints (pt)
1 pint	=	2 cups (c)
1 cup	=	8 fluid ounces (fl oz)
1 fluid ounce	=	2 tablespoons (tbs)
1 tablespoon	=	3 teaspoons (tsp)

Units of Weight

1 ton (T)	=	2000 pounds (lb)
1 pound	=	16 ounces (oz)

Units of Time

1 century	=	100 years
1 decade	=	10 years
1 year (yr)	=	12 months
	=	52 weeks (plus one or two days)
	=	365 days (366 days in a leap year)
1 month (mo)	=	28, 29, 30, or 31 days
1 week (wk)	=	7 days
1 day (d)	=	24 hours
1 hour (hr)	=	60 minutes
1 minute (min)	=	60 seconds (sec)

System Equivalents

1 inch is about 2.5 cm (2.54)
1 kilometer is about 0.6 mile (0.621)
1 mile is about 1.6 kilometers (1.609)
1 meter is about 39 inches (39.37)
1 liter is about 1.1 quarts (1.057)
1 ounce is about 28 grams (28.350)
1 kilogram is about 2.2 pounds (2.205)
1 acre is about 2.5 hectares (2.47)

Rules for Order of Operations

1. Do operations within parentheses or other grouping symbols before doing anything else.
2. Calculate all powers.
3. Do multiplications or divisions in order, from left to right.
4. Then do additions or subtractions in order, from left to right.

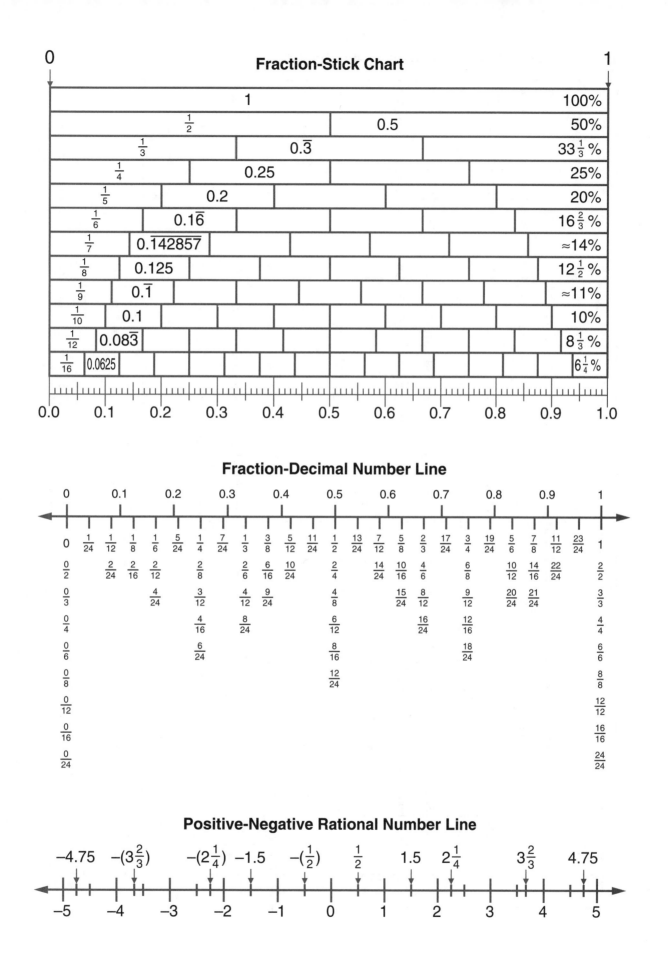

Fraction-Stick Chart

1		100%
$\frac{1}{2}$	0.5	50%
$\frac{1}{3}$	$0.\overline{3}$	$33\frac{1}{3}\%$
$\frac{1}{4}$	0.25	25%
$\frac{1}{5}$	0.2	20%
$\frac{1}{6}$	$0.1\overline{6}$	$16\frac{2}{3}\%$
$\frac{1}{7}$	$0.\overline{142857}$	$\approx 14\%$
$\frac{1}{8}$	0.125	$12\frac{1}{2}\%$
$\frac{1}{9}$	$0.\overline{1}$	$\approx 11\%$
$\frac{1}{10}$	0.1	10%
$\frac{1}{12}$	$0.08\overline{3}$	$8\frac{1}{3}\%$
$\frac{1}{16}$	0.0625	$6\frac{1}{4}\%$

0 1

0.0 0.1 0.2 0.3 0.4 0.5 0.6 0.7 0.8 0.9 1.0

Fraction-Decimal Number Line

0   0.1   0.2   0.3   0.4   0.5   0.6   0.7   0.8   0.9   1

0	$\frac{1}{24}$	$\frac{1}{12}$	$\frac{1}{8}$	$\frac{1}{6}$	$\frac{5}{24}$	$\frac{1}{4}$	$\frac{7}{24}$	$\frac{1}{3}$	$\frac{3}{8}$	$\frac{5}{12}$	$\frac{11}{24}$	$\frac{1}{2}$	$\frac{13}{24}$	$\frac{7}{12}$	$\frac{5}{8}$	$\frac{2}{3}$	$\frac{17}{24}$	$\frac{3}{4}$	$\frac{19}{24}$	$\frac{5}{6}$	$\frac{7}{8}$	$\frac{11}{12}$	$\frac{23}{24}$	1
$\frac{0}{2}$		$\frac{2}{24}$	$\frac{2}{16}$	$\frac{2}{12}$		$\frac{2}{8}$		$\frac{2}{6}$	$\frac{6}{16}$	$\frac{10}{24}$		$\frac{2}{4}$		$\frac{14}{24}$	$\frac{10}{16}$	$\frac{4}{6}$		$\frac{6}{8}$		$\frac{10}{12}$	$\frac{14}{16}$	$\frac{22}{24}$		$\frac{2}{2}$
$\frac{0}{3}$			$\frac{4}{24}$			$\frac{3}{12}$		$\frac{4}{12}$	$\frac{9}{24}$			$\frac{4}{8}$			$\frac{15}{24}$	$\frac{8}{12}$		$\frac{9}{12}$		$\frac{20}{24}$	$\frac{21}{24}$		$\frac{3}{3}$
$\frac{0}{4}$						$\frac{4}{16}$		$\frac{8}{24}$				$\frac{6}{12}$				$\frac{16}{24}$		$\frac{12}{16}$					$\frac{4}{4}$
$\frac{0}{6}$						$\frac{6}{24}$						$\frac{8}{16}$						$\frac{18}{24}$					$\frac{6}{6}$
$\frac{0}{8}$												$\frac{12}{24}$											$\frac{8}{8}$
$\frac{0}{12}$																							$\frac{12}{12}$
$\frac{0}{16}$																							$\frac{16}{16}$
$\frac{0}{24}$																							$\frac{24}{24}$

Positive-Negative Rational Number Line

−4.75 −$(3\frac{2}{3})$ −$(2\frac{1}{4})$ −1.5 −$(\frac{1}{2})$ $\frac{1}{2}$ 1.5 $2\frac{1}{4}$ $3\frac{2}{3}$ 4.75

−5 −4 −3 −2 −1 0 1 2 3 4 5

Equivalent Fractions, Decimals, and Percents

															Decimal	Percent
$\frac{1}{2}$	$\frac{2}{4}$	$\frac{3}{6}$	$\frac{4}{8}$	$\frac{5}{10}$	$\frac{6}{12}$	$\frac{7}{14}$	$\frac{8}{16}$	$\frac{9}{18}$	$\frac{10}{20}$	$\frac{11}{22}$	$\frac{12}{24}$	$\frac{13}{26}$	$\frac{14}{28}$	$\frac{15}{30}$	0.5	50%
$\frac{1}{3}$	$\frac{2}{6}$	$\frac{3}{9}$	$\frac{4}{12}$	$\frac{5}{15}$	$\frac{6}{18}$	$\frac{7}{21}$	$\frac{8}{24}$	$\frac{9}{27}$	$\frac{10}{30}$	$\frac{11}{33}$	$\frac{12}{36}$	$\frac{13}{39}$	$\frac{14}{42}$	$\frac{15}{45}$	$0.\overline{3}$	$33\frac{1}{3}\%$
$\frac{2}{3}$	$\frac{4}{6}$	$\frac{6}{9}$	$\frac{8}{12}$	$\frac{10}{15}$	$\frac{12}{18}$	$\frac{14}{21}$	$\frac{16}{24}$	$\frac{18}{27}$	$\frac{20}{30}$	$\frac{22}{33}$	$\frac{24}{36}$	$\frac{26}{39}$	$\frac{28}{42}$	$\frac{30}{45}$	$0.\overline{6}$	$66\frac{2}{3}\%$
$\frac{1}{4}$	$\frac{2}{8}$	$\frac{3}{12}$	$\frac{4}{16}$	$\frac{5}{20}$	$\frac{6}{24}$	$\frac{7}{28}$	$\frac{8}{32}$	$\frac{9}{36}$	$\frac{10}{40}$	$\frac{11}{44}$	$\frac{12}{48}$	$\frac{13}{52}$	$\frac{14}{56}$	$\frac{15}{60}$	0.25	25%
$\frac{3}{4}$	$\frac{6}{8}$	$\frac{9}{12}$	$\frac{12}{16}$	$\frac{15}{20}$	$\frac{18}{24}$	$\frac{21}{28}$	$\frac{24}{32}$	$\frac{27}{36}$	$\frac{30}{40}$	$\frac{33}{44}$	$\frac{36}{48}$	$\frac{39}{52}$	$\frac{42}{56}$	$\frac{45}{60}$	0.75	75%
$\frac{1}{5}$	$\frac{2}{10}$	$\frac{3}{15}$	$\frac{4}{20}$	$\frac{5}{25}$	$\frac{6}{30}$	$\frac{7}{35}$	$\frac{8}{40}$	$\frac{9}{45}$	$\frac{10}{50}$	$\frac{11}{55}$	$\frac{12}{60}$	$\frac{13}{65}$	$\frac{14}{70}$	$\frac{15}{75}$	0.2	20%
$\frac{2}{5}$	$\frac{4}{10}$	$\frac{6}{15}$	$\frac{8}{20}$	$\frac{10}{25}$	$\frac{12}{30}$	$\frac{14}{35}$	$\frac{16}{40}$	$\frac{18}{45}$	$\frac{20}{50}$	$\frac{22}{55}$	$\frac{24}{60}$	$\frac{26}{65}$	$\frac{28}{70}$	$\frac{30}{75}$	0.4	40%
$\frac{3}{5}$	$\frac{6}{10}$	$\frac{9}{15}$	$\frac{12}{20}$	$\frac{15}{25}$	$\frac{18}{30}$	$\frac{21}{35}$	$\frac{24}{40}$	$\frac{27}{45}$	$\frac{30}{50}$	$\frac{33}{55}$	$\frac{36}{60}$	$\frac{39}{65}$	$\frac{42}{70}$	$\frac{45}{75}$	0.6	60%
$\frac{4}{5}$	$\frac{8}{10}$	$\frac{12}{15}$	$\frac{16}{20}$	$\frac{20}{25}$	$\frac{24}{30}$	$\frac{28}{35}$	$\frac{32}{40}$	$\frac{36}{45}$	$\frac{40}{50}$	$\frac{44}{55}$	$\frac{48}{60}$	$\frac{52}{65}$	$\frac{56}{70}$	$\frac{60}{75}$	0.8	80%
$\frac{1}{6}$	$\frac{2}{12}$	$\frac{3}{18}$	$\frac{4}{24}$	$\frac{5}{30}$	$\frac{6}{36}$	$\frac{7}{42}$	$\frac{8}{48}$	$\frac{9}{54}$	$\frac{10}{60}$	$\frac{11}{66}$	$\frac{12}{72}$	$\frac{13}{78}$	$\frac{14}{84}$	$\frac{15}{90}$	$0.1\overline{6}$	$16\frac{2}{3}\%$
$\frac{5}{6}$	$\frac{10}{12}$	$\frac{15}{18}$	$\frac{20}{24}$	$\frac{25}{30}$	$\frac{30}{36}$	$\frac{35}{42}$	$\frac{40}{48}$	$\frac{45}{54}$	$\frac{50}{60}$	$\frac{55}{66}$	$\frac{60}{72}$	$\frac{65}{78}$	$\frac{70}{84}$	$\frac{75}{90}$	$0.8\overline{3}$	$83\frac{1}{3}\%$
$\frac{1}{7}$	$\frac{2}{14}$	$\frac{3}{21}$	$\frac{4}{28}$	$\frac{5}{35}$	$\frac{6}{42}$	$\frac{7}{49}$	$\frac{8}{56}$	$\frac{9}{63}$	$\frac{10}{70}$	$\frac{11}{77}$	$\frac{12}{84}$	$\frac{13}{91}$	$\frac{14}{98}$	$\frac{15}{105}$	0.143	14.3%
$\frac{2}{7}$	$\frac{4}{14}$	$\frac{6}{21}$	$\frac{8}{28}$	$\frac{10}{35}$	$\frac{12}{42}$	$\frac{14}{49}$	$\frac{16}{56}$	$\frac{18}{63}$	$\frac{20}{70}$	$\frac{22}{77}$	$\frac{24}{84}$	$\frac{26}{91}$	$\frac{28}{98}$	$\frac{30}{105}$	0.286	28.6%
$\frac{3}{7}$	$\frac{6}{14}$	$\frac{9}{21}$	$\frac{12}{28}$	$\frac{15}{35}$	$\frac{18}{42}$	$\frac{21}{49}$	$\frac{24}{56}$	$\frac{27}{63}$	$\frac{30}{70}$	$\frac{33}{77}$	$\frac{36}{84}$	$\frac{39}{91}$	$\frac{42}{98}$	$\frac{45}{105}$	0.429	42.9%
$\frac{4}{7}$	$\frac{8}{14}$	$\frac{12}{21}$	$\frac{16}{28}$	$\frac{20}{35}$	$\frac{24}{42}$	$\frac{28}{49}$	$\frac{32}{56}$	$\frac{36}{63}$	$\frac{40}{70}$	$\frac{44}{77}$	$\frac{48}{84}$	$\frac{52}{91}$	$\frac{56}{98}$	$\frac{60}{105}$	0.571	57.1%
$\frac{5}{7}$	$\frac{10}{14}$	$\frac{15}{21}$	$\frac{20}{28}$	$\frac{25}{35}$	$\frac{30}{42}$	$\frac{35}{49}$	$\frac{40}{56}$	$\frac{45}{63}$	$\frac{50}{70}$	$\frac{55}{77}$	$\frac{60}{84}$	$\frac{65}{91}$	$\frac{70}{98}$	$\frac{75}{105}$	0.714	71.4%
$\frac{6}{7}$	$\frac{12}{14}$	$\frac{18}{21}$	$\frac{24}{28}$	$\frac{30}{35}$	$\frac{36}{42}$	$\frac{42}{49}$	$\frac{48}{56}$	$\frac{54}{63}$	$\frac{60}{70}$	$\frac{66}{77}$	$\frac{72}{84}$	$\frac{78}{91}$	$\frac{84}{98}$	$\frac{90}{105}$	0.857	85.7%
$\frac{1}{8}$	$\frac{2}{16}$	$\frac{3}{24}$	$\frac{4}{32}$	$\frac{5}{40}$	$\frac{6}{48}$	$\frac{7}{56}$	$\frac{8}{64}$	$\frac{9}{72}$	$\frac{10}{80}$	$\frac{11}{88}$	$\frac{12}{96}$	$\frac{13}{104}$	$\frac{14}{112}$	$\frac{15}{120}$	0.125	$12\frac{1}{2}\%$
$\frac{3}{8}$	$\frac{6}{16}$	$\frac{9}{24}$	$\frac{12}{32}$	$\frac{15}{40}$	$\frac{18}{48}$	$\frac{21}{56}$	$\frac{24}{64}$	$\frac{27}{72}$	$\frac{30}{80}$	$\frac{33}{88}$	$\frac{36}{96}$	$\frac{39}{104}$	$\frac{42}{112}$	$\frac{45}{120}$	0.375	$37\frac{1}{2}\%$
$\frac{5}{8}$	$\frac{10}{16}$	$\frac{15}{24}$	$\frac{20}{32}$	$\frac{25}{40}$	$\frac{30}{48}$	$\frac{35}{56}$	$\frac{40}{64}$	$\frac{45}{72}$	$\frac{50}{80}$	$\frac{55}{88}$	$\frac{60}{96}$	$\frac{65}{104}$	$\frac{70}{112}$	$\frac{75}{120}$	0.625	$62\frac{1}{2}\%$
$\frac{7}{8}$	$\frac{14}{16}$	$\frac{21}{24}$	$\frac{28}{32}$	$\frac{35}{40}$	$\frac{42}{48}$	$\frac{49}{56}$	$\frac{56}{64}$	$\frac{63}{72}$	$\frac{70}{80}$	$\frac{77}{88}$	$\frac{84}{96}$	$\frac{91}{104}$	$\frac{98}{112}$	$\frac{105}{120}$	0.875	$87\frac{1}{2}\%$
$\frac{1}{9}$	$\frac{2}{18}$	$\frac{3}{27}$	$\frac{4}{36}$	$\frac{5}{45}$	$\frac{6}{54}$	$\frac{7}{63}$	$\frac{8}{72}$	$\frac{9}{81}$	$\frac{10}{90}$	$\frac{11}{99}$	$\frac{12}{108}$	$\frac{13}{117}$	$\frac{14}{126}$	$\frac{15}{135}$	$0.\overline{1}$	$11\frac{1}{9}\%$
$\frac{2}{9}$	$\frac{4}{18}$	$\frac{6}{27}$	$\frac{8}{36}$	$\frac{10}{45}$	$\frac{12}{54}$	$\frac{14}{63}$	$\frac{16}{72}$	$\frac{18}{81}$	$\frac{20}{90}$	$\frac{22}{99}$	$\frac{24}{108}$	$\frac{26}{117}$	$\frac{28}{126}$	$\frac{30}{135}$	$0.\overline{2}$	$22\frac{2}{9}\%$
$\frac{4}{9}$	$\frac{8}{18}$	$\frac{12}{27}$	$\frac{16}{36}$	$\frac{20}{45}$	$\frac{24}{54}$	$\frac{28}{63}$	$\frac{32}{72}$	$\frac{36}{81}$	$\frac{40}{90}$	$\frac{44}{99}$	$\frac{48}{108}$	$\frac{52}{117}$	$\frac{56}{126}$	$\frac{60}{135}$	$0.\overline{4}$	$44\frac{4}{9}\%$
$\frac{5}{9}$	$\frac{10}{18}$	$\frac{15}{27}$	$\frac{20}{36}$	$\frac{25}{45}$	$\frac{30}{54}$	$\frac{35}{63}$	$\frac{40}{72}$	$\frac{45}{81}$	$\frac{50}{90}$	$\frac{55}{99}$	$\frac{60}{108}$	$\frac{65}{117}$	$\frac{70}{126}$	$\frac{75}{135}$	$0.\overline{5}$	$55\frac{5}{9}\%$
$\frac{7}{9}$	$\frac{14}{18}$	$\frac{21}{27}$	$\frac{28}{36}$	$\frac{35}{45}$	$\frac{42}{54}$	$\frac{49}{63}$	$\frac{56}{72}$	$\frac{63}{81}$	$\frac{70}{90}$	$\frac{77}{99}$	$\frac{84}{108}$	$\frac{91}{117}$	$\frac{98}{126}$	$\frac{105}{135}$	$0.\overline{7}$	$77\frac{7}{9}\%$
$\frac{8}{9}$	$\frac{16}{18}$	$\frac{24}{27}$	$\frac{32}{36}$	$\frac{40}{45}$	$\frac{48}{54}$	$\frac{56}{63}$	$\frac{64}{72}$	$\frac{72}{81}$	$\frac{80}{90}$	$\frac{88}{99}$	$\frac{96}{108}$	$\frac{104}{117}$	$\frac{112}{126}$	$\frac{120}{135}$	$0.\overline{8}$	$88\frac{8}{9}\%$

Note: The decimals for sevenths have been rounded to the nearest thousandth.